Everyday Law
for Children

The Everyday Law Series

Edited by Richard Delgado and Jean Stefancic,
University of Pittsburgh Law School

Available

Everyday Law for Individuals with Disabilities
Ruth Colker and Adam A. Milani (2006)

Everyday Law for Children
David Herring (2006)

Forthcoming

Everyday Law for the Elderly
Lawrence Frolik

Everyday Law for African Americans
Harold A. McDougall III

Everyday Law for Gays and Lesbians
Anthony Infanti

Everyday Law for Latino/as
Steve Bender, Joaquin Avila, and Raquel Aldana-Pindell

Everyday Law for Consumers
Michael L. Rustad

Everyday Law for Immigrants and Foreign Nationals
Victor Romero

Everyday Law for Patients
Alan Scheflin and A. Steven Frankel

Everyday Law for the Homeless
Linda Tashbook and Susanna Leers

*Everyday Law for Women: Sexuality,
Reproductive Freedom, and the Family*
April Cherry

Everyday Law for Children

David J. Herring

Paradigm Publishers
Boulder • London

Copyright © 2006 Paradigm Publishers

Published in the United States by Paradigm Publishers, 3360 Mitchell Lane Suite E, Boulder, CO 80301 USA.

Paradigm Publishers is the trade name of Birkenkamp & Company, LLC, Dean Birkenkamp, President and Publisher.

Library of Congress Cataloging-in-Publication Data
Herring, David J.
    Everyday law for children / David J. Herring.
      p.   cm — (The everyday law series)
    Includes bibliographical references and index.
    ISBN-13: 978-1-59451-251-3 (hardcover : acid-free paper)
    ISBN-10: 1-59451-251-5 (hardcover : acid-free paper)
    1. Children—Legal status, laws, etc.—United States—Popular works.   I. Title.
II. Series.
    KF3735.Z9H47   2006
    344.7303'27—dc22

                                                                        2006003609

Printed and bound in the United States of America on acid free paper that meets the standards of the American National Standard for Permanence of Paper for Printed Library Materials.

Designed and Typeset by Mulberry Tree Enterprises.

10   09   08   07   06   1   2   3   4   5

Contents

1
Introduction

Legal Theories and Approaches Affecting Children

One cannot acquire a full, clear understanding of the law and how it affects children and their families. This is so because the fundamental social values surrounding children and families often conflict and are incoherent when viewed together. The conflict is deep and, worse, deeply disguised. The rhetoric of one value often mirrors that of the other, but the intended meanings and actual implications differ significantly.

This situation of disguised conflict allows participants in public discussions of children and families to manipulate others in order to achieve the specific results they desire. They can make statements seemingly in accordance with shared values while undermining the well-being of children and families. Because public discussions of children and families contribute significantly to the construction of the law affecting these constituencies, it is important to recognize and understand the conflict in fundamental social values that permeates public discussions of children and families. Only in this way can one reach a somewhat accurate understanding of the relevant law.

The goal of this chapter is to identify and discuss the primary conflict in values at play in discussions of children and families. The discussion will allow us to recognize rhetoric that leads to the manipulation of public discussions in order to serve factious goals. Interestingly, it will reveal a powerful conflict among groups of adults rather than a conflict between adults and children.

Understanding the primary conflict allows us to understand not only the construction of law but also the operation of laws and policies that affect children and their families. This understanding is vital for gaining insight into how the law and public systems affect children in their everyday lives. Recognizing the primary conflict and the manipulation of rhetoric within public discussions of children and families allows us to make more sense of the law and to come to a deeper understanding of how to use and even change the law as we confront it in everyday life. This point will become apparent in subsequent chapters as we address specific situations affecting children and their families.

The vehicle for our discussion of the primary conflict is the development of two strains of rights doctrine and rhetoric: parental rights and children's rights.

Parental Rights

Coming first in time, the formal development of parental rights doctrine grew out of fear of a state-imposed vision of the good life and the appropriate methods for raising children. The United States Supreme Court embraced and addressed this fear in two significant decisions handed down in the 1920s.[1] The first case concerned a Nebraska law that prohibited all public and private primary schools from conducting instruction in a foreign language. Striking down the law, Justice McReynolds based the Court's decision, in part, on the constitutional right of parents to control their children's upbringing, a right that included having them receive instruction in languages other than English.

In explaining the Court's decision, Justice McReynolds harkened back to Plato's vision of communal ownership of children, which would entail taking children from their parents and placing them in the hands of the state.[2] No parent would know his or her own children, and children would not know their parents. Biologically unrelated nurses would raise the children of the leadership class, developing them into ideal citizens for the state.

Justice McReynolds rejected Plato's vision in the strongest terms, finding that it was in fundamental and direct conflict with American values. American institutions protect individual liberty and insulate the individual from state control. One important aspect of individual liberty is a parent's possession and control of his or her children. In an era when the Court frequently found an individual's control of his or her property and labor to constitute a fundamental right protected by the Fourteenth Amendment, the Court had little difficulty in finding that parents' possession and control of their children constituted such a right. The Nebraska law that denied parents the right to control their children's education unreasonably infringed on this fundamental right and thus was unconstitutional.

The Court, in calling forth and attacking the straw man of Plato's vision of communal, state-directed child care in order to address a state statute that only barred education in a foreign language, might seem engaged in overkill. However, when Justice McReynolds wrote the opinion in the Nebraska case, he may have viewed the case against the background of an Oregon statute that more fundamentally threatened parental control. At that time, Oregon required every child to attend a public school.[3] This requirement effectively precluded parents from sending their children to private schools. They could not have their children attend religious schools or other private schools that provided instruction different from that provided by public schools. In effect, they could not send their children to a school where instruction would occur outside the direct view and control of state actors—public school teachers and administrators. This Oregon statute may have struck the Court as verging on Plato's vision or as taking a significant step toward realizing it.

Some parents affected by the statute challenged it in court, arguing that it violated their constitutional rights. The United States Supreme Court accepted the case. Justice McReynolds again authored the Court's opinion. The Court decided that the Oregon statute was unconstitutional because it violated the parents' Fourteenth Amendment due process rights. Justice McReynolds constructed the Court's opinion on the foundation articulated in his earlier opinion in the Nebraska case. He wrote for a unanimous Court, "The fundamental theory of liberty upon which all governments in the Union repose excludes any general power of the State to standardize its children by forcing them to accept instruction from the public teachers only. The child is not the mere creature of the State; those who nurture him and direct his destiny have the right, coupled with the high duty, to recognize and prepare him for additional obligations."[4]

With this decision, the Court completed the initial construction of a constitutional right of parental control of children. The Court not only tolerated and fiercely protected parents' right to control their children but also expressly encouraged parents to make important life decisions for them. Parents possess an extremely large degree of control in this area, and the state must exercise a great deal of restraint.

The Court's expansion of economic rights through the due process clause of the Fourteenth Amendment lost momentum and was largely reversed during the 1930s.[5] However, the Court's construction of parental rights seemingly remained intact, as several subsequent decisions made plain.

In 1972, the Court addressed a case dealing with a Wisconsin statute that required parents to enroll their children in a formal educational program beyond the eighth grade.[6] Amish parents challenged the statute because the Amish community opposed formal schooling beyond the eighth grade. They asserted that the Wisconsin compulsory education law violated both their right to religious freedom and their right to control the upbringing of their children.

The Supreme Court found that the Wisconsin law was unconstitutional as applied to Amish children, basing its decision on concepts of both religious freedom and parental control. The Court's opinion reaffirmed both parents' right to control their children and its earlier decisions in the Nebraska and Oregon cases. As a result of this decision, parents within the Amish community may dictate the religious practices of their children even if that means denying them a formal education. This authority emanates from the United States Constitution, and the majoritarian state cannot diminish or override it.

The dissenting opinion of Justice Douglas is important because it raised the issue of children's input into decisions that profoundly affect their lives, such as the extent of formal education they receive.[7] Justice Douglas argued forcefully that the Court should consider the views of the affected high school–age Amish children. A majority of the justices rejected this argument, viewing the case as one that presented only two sets of interests—those of the Amish parents and those of the state. Implicitly, parents' authority to control their children restrains the authority not only of the state but also that of children themselves. By ignoring the children's preferences and desires, the Court established parents as the decisive authority over children's lives in a very wide area of operation.

The Court reemphasized this latter point in a 1982 decision in which it examined the interests of children, parents, and the state in termination of parental rights cases.[8] In these cases, the state seeks to end the parent-child relationship. Once a court orders termination of parental rights, the affected child and parent stand as completely un-related individuals in the eyes of the law.

Prior to the Court's decision, the New York statute authorizing the termination of parental rights required the state to prove by a preponderance of the evidence that the particular parent is unfit. This burden of proof is relatively low, requiring the state to prove only that the allegations of parental unfitness are somewhat more likely true than not. In contrast, a burden of proof that demands clear and convincing evidence requires the state to prove that the allegations are almost certainly true. The Court faced the question of whether the New York statute's low standard of proof violated parents' constitutional rights.

In contrast to the Court in the Wisconsin case, the Court in this case did not ignore the children's interests in the New York termination procedures. However, it effectively silenced children by equating their interests with those of their parents. The Court expressly found that children share an interest with their parents in family reunification and in the avoidance of the termination of their relationship.

The Court made this finding in the face of the realities surrounding many children in involuntary termination of parental rights proceedings. These children are likely not to have lived with either of their biological parents for the two to five years prior to the termination proceedings. Most often, they have lived in a foster care home, interacting with their biological parents infrequently. Their interactions have primarily been with foster parents who have likely woken them every morning, made meals for them every day, entertained them regularly, transported them to various activities, and otherwise been available to meet their daily needs.[9]

Despite this common situation of estrangement between affected parents and their children at the time of termination proceedings, the Court refused to acknowledge that children have interests that may diverge from those of their biological parents. The Court effectively subsumed the children's interests within their parents' rights. Once the Court allied the children's interests with those of their parents, it became easy to find that they overpowered the state's interests in the relatively low standard of proof. Although the Court could have plausibly allied the children's interests with those of the state, the Court implicitly rejected this approach, making the case for a constitutionally required heightened standard of proof in termination of parental rights proceedings strong, if not compelling. The Court viewed parental rights as dominant, with a foundation in the due process requirements of the Constitution and with the capacity to subsume children's interests and overwhelm the states' interests.

Parental Rights and Flawed Adoption Procedures

The strength of parental rights emerges even more vividly in two high-profile state court adoption cases in the 1990s. In the case of "Baby Jessica," Jessica's mother gave her daughter up for adoption at birth.[10] While voluntarily releasing her own parental rights, Jessica's mother identified the wrong man as Jessica's father. This man released his rights to Jessica, but Jessica's actual father did not. Subsequently, Jessica's father learned of her existence and his relationship to her. He then sought to gain custody of his daughter and to void the adoption.

Because of an extended court battle that involved judges in two states, Jessica lived and thrived in the custody of her adoptive parents for the first three years of her life. However, both the Iowa Supreme Court and the Michigan Supreme Court decided that the biological father's parental rights had never been terminated and were in full force.[11] The state could not displace or disregard the father's rights simply because third-party adoptive parents could arguably provide a better home. The doctrine of parental rights dictated that the biological father have custody of Jessica no matter what separate interests Jessica or the state may have in a different outcome.

As a result, Jessica's father had absolute authority to decide whether Jessica would live with her adoptive parents or with him. He decided that she would live with him. In a tearful scene shown on national news programs, Jessica's attorney took Jessica out of the home of her adoptive parents and handed her over to the father's representatives. Jessica's father was now in full control of her life.

In the "Baby Richard" case, Richard's mother gave her son up for adoption shortly after he was born.[12] Richard's biological father was traveling outside the United States when the mother gave Richard up for adoption and was not aware of the mother's pregnancy or of Richard's birth.

Upon the father's return to the United States, he immediately sought custody of Richard in the Illinois courts. The lower courts awarded custody to the adoptive parents, viewing them as more financially secure and emotionally stable.[13] The Illinois Supreme Court reversed, holding that the father's parental rights dictated that he have custody of Richard.[14] Even if Richard would be better off financially and emotionally with his adoptive parents, his father's rights could deny him that outcome. After four years with his adoptive parents, Richard went to live with his biological father.

These cases show that parental rights are strong enough to prevail even if it means inflicting harm on a child and destroying family associations that have functioned effectively for years. Parental rights appear to be virtually limitless.

Third Party Visitation and Parental Rights

However, several United States Supreme Court justices have recently expressed divergent views on the strength of parental rights.[15] The case turned on a Washington third-party visitation statute that permitted "any person" to petition for visitation with a child.[16] A judge hearing such a petition could order visitation whenever he or she found that the visits may serve the affected child's best interests.

A Washington State trial judge had applied the statute and granted the visitation petition of the grandparents of two young girls. Specifically, the judge ordered visits between the grandparents and the girls to occur one weekend per month, one week during the summer, and four hours on each of the grandparent's birthdays. The girls' mother objected to visits occurring more than once a month, but the trial judge overrode the parent's wishes because he found that more frequent visits with the grandparents would be best for the girls.

The Washington appellate courts reversed the trial judge's decision and found the broad state statute to be unconstitutional, and the United States Supreme Court affirmed.[17] However, the justices failed to reach a consensus on the reasoning for their decision, authoring six separate opinions—one plurality opinion, two concurring opinions, and three dissenting opinions. On one end of the spectrum is Justice Thomas's concurring opinion. Justice Thomas clearly and concisely found that parents have a fundamental right to direct the upbringing of their children. Because this right is fundamental, the state must have a compelling reason for any infringement. In this case, Thomas asserted that the State of Washington "lacks even a legitimate governmental interest—to say nothing of a compelling one—in second-guessing a fit parent's decision regarding visitation with third parties."[18]

In his separate concurring opinion, Justice Souter largely agreed with Justice Thomas, finding that striking down the Washington statute on its face is consistent with the "Court's prior cases addressing the substantive interests at stake." However, he was much more equivocal on whether parents have a fundamental right to decide with whom their children will associate. He simply stated that "we have long recognized that a parent's interests in the nurture, upbringing, companionship, care, and custody of children are generally protected by the Due Process Clause of the Fourteenth Amendment."[19] In this way, he affirmed the decision of the Washington Supreme Court to strike down the statute without having to define with any specificity the overall nature and strength of parental rights. It is unclear whether he viewed parents' rights as fundamental.

In the plurality opinion, Justice O'Connor found that the Washington statute was not unconstitutional on its face but only as applied in the specific case. For the justices who joined in her opinion, the basic problem was that the trial judge did not give any special weight at all to the mother's determination of her daughter's best interests. However, the justices failed to define the "special weight" to be accorded to a parent's decision about his or her children's visitation with a third party, simply stating that "if a fit parent's decision of the kind at issue here becomes subject to judicial review, the court must accord at least some special weight to the parents' own determination."[20]

With these words and with the refusal to strike down the statute on its face, it hardly seems that Justice O'Connor was articulating or protecting a fundamental right. She perceived no problem with court intervention as long as the court applied an appropriate presumption in favor of the parent, a presumption that is rather weak—one that the state cannot "normally" overcome as to fit parents and one that a court must accord "at least some special weight."[21] In the end, Justice O'Connor's opinion leaves a great deal of room for state legislatures to draft statutes that allow for judicial review of a parent's third-party visitation decision and for state judges, on a case-by-case basis, to overcome a presumption in favor of a parent's decision.

Justices Stevens and Kennedy wrote separate dissenting opinions. They both refused to find that the Washington statute was invalid on its face because it sweeps in many permissible results. For example, they believed it would be constitutionally permissible to order visitation between a child and a previous caregiver who is not a parent of the child. Thus, the Washington statute did not necessarily run afoul of the Fourteenth Amendment.

Both justices asserted that the Washington Supreme Court erred in holding that the federal Constitution requires a showing of actual or likely harm to the child before a court may order visitation over a parent's objections. They each expressly recognized that parents have a fundamental liberty interest in caring for and guiding their children without undue interference by the state. But following this recognition, Justice Stevens asserted, "We have never held that the parent's liberty interest in this relationship is so inflexible as to establish a constitutional shield, protecting every arbitrary parental decision from any challenge absent a threshold finding of harm."[22] In both Justice Steven's and Justice Kennedy's views, a parent's right to decide with whom his or her child will associate is not absolute, even in situations in which a denial of visitation will not threaten harm to the child. In fact, Justice Kennedy expressly asserted that the best interests of the child standard may be an appropriate decision-making rule in some third-party visitation cases, thus allowing a judge to displace the decision of a parent in many circumstances.

Justice Scalia wrote a separate, three-paragraph dissent that places him at the other end of the spectrum from Justice Thomas. He refused to speak in terms of parents' constitutional rights, asserting that the Washington statute does not touch on any fundamental liberty interest for purposes of the due process clause. In making this assertion, Justice Scalia discounted the applicability of the Court's prior decisions finding a substantive constitutional right of parents to direct the upbringing of their children. He noted that the Court decided the core cases in this line during an "era rich in substantive due process holdings that have since been repudiated."[23] He acknowledged the fractured opinions of the other justices in this case and concluded that the theory of unenumerated parental rights has small claim to *stare decisis* protection. In the end, Justice Scalia balked at overruling the earlier cases, but he expressly refused to extend them to the third-party visitation context.

Interestingly, Justice Scalia spoke strongly about parental rights. He stated, "In my view, a right of parents to direct the upbringing of their children is among the 'unalienable Rights' with which the Declaration of Independence proclaims 'all men . . . are endowed by their Creator.' And in my view that right is also among the 'other [rights] retained by the people' which the Ninth Amendment says the Constitution's enumeration of rights 'shall not be construed to deny or disparage.'"[24]

However, Justice Scalia refused to utilize the Declaration of Independence or his conception of unenumerated rights "to deny legal effect to laws that (in my view) infringe upon what is (in my view) that unenumerated right."[25] In his view, the Constitution does not confer such power on judges. Rather, the Constitution leaves the articulation and application of the unenumerated right of parents to control their children to the legislative and public policy arenas. It appears that in these settings, legislator or citizen Scalia would argue strongly that "the state has *no power* to interfere with parents' authority over the rearing of their children."[26] But as a Supreme Court justice, despite his strong personal feelings, Justice Scalia refused to find that the Washington statute touched on any fundamental liberty interest for purposes of the Constitution.

The decision on the Washington third-party visitation statute stands as the Supreme Court's last word addressing parental rights. The various opinions, when viewed together, leave the status and strength of parental rights in serious doubt. A majority of the justices authored or joined opinions that implicitly, if not expressly, call into question the fundamental nature of parental rights for purposes of constitutional analysis.

Ironically, the separate dissenting opinions of Justices Stevens and Kennedy may shed the most light on Justice O'Connor's plurality opinion and Justice Souter's concurring opinion. More specifically, the dissenters' identification of the interests of other individuals (e.g., the child, a former caretaker, a grandparent) may help explain Justice Souter's failure to apply strict scrutiny and the plurality's narrow, "only as applied" review of the Washington statute. Cases applying a third-party visitation statute do not present an ordinary two-party rights case that pits an individual against the state and in which one may view strict scrutiny or broader review as more appropriate. Instead, these cases involve at least four entities: the custodial parent, the child, the third party seeking visitation, and the state.

Justice Stevens expounds on the interests of children, concluding that parental interests cannot dictate the result in every instance—they must be limited. He expressly recognizes that the Court has not addressed the nature of children's liberty interests in preserving established familial or family-like bonds with nonparents, but he states,

"It seems to me extremely likely that, to the extent parents and families have fundamental liberty interests in preserving such intimate relationships, so, too, do children have these interests, and so, too, must their interests be balanced in the equation."[27] In the end, parental rights must, in many conceivable situations, yield to the interests of other individuals.

Children's Rights

The legal protection of parental rights, then, has been weakening, just as a countervailing force—children's interests—has gained strength.[28] Children's interests have a long history of operating as a limit on parental rights. These interests have given rise to a rhetoric of children's rights, a powerful and growing political force in American society. The rhetoric of children's rights exists in tension with the rhetoric of parental rights. Despite the Supreme Court's equating children's interests and parents' interests in situations in which the state seeks to terminate parental rights, children's interests often depart from those of their parents. Because of this parent-child conflict and children's inability, often, to protect their own interests, the question of who can appropriately protect children's interests arises. Primarily, government actors have taken on this role, creating such measures as child labor laws, antipoverty and health care programs aimed at children, the best interests of the child decision-making standard, compulsory education laws, and comprehensive child welfare laws. In essence, society has used the rhetoric of children's rights to justify government programs designed to protect children and to ensure that children experience an appropriate childhood. Government actors monitor and regulate specific families, frequently stepping in to protect children from their parents' abuse, neglect, or unwise decisions.[29]

Because children's rights rhetoric often results in government actors actively providing care and protection for children, many view these rights as primarily positive rather than negative. Positive rights require the state to take affirmative action rather than to simply leave individuals alone by avoiding intrusion in their lives.

The positive nature of children's rights helps explain why, in contrast to parental rights, the courts have largely declined to constitutionalize children's rights. The Supreme Court has consistently refused to recognize rights that require the state to actively provide care, protection, or services to individuals, leaving decisions to provide such affirmative care to the legislative and public policy arenas.[30]

With children's rights, the Supreme Court made rejection of the concept of positive rights vividly clear in a case involving a four-year-old boy.[31] Joshua DeShaney was repeatedly physically abused by his father. Despite receiving several reports of Joshua's abuse, the county child welfare agency did not investigate fully or act to protect the boy. Subsequently, Joshua's father beat him severely. Joshua sustained permanent, severe, and debilitating brain injuries.

Acting on behalf of Joshua, Joshua's mother brought suit against the child welfare agency. Joshua claimed that the county agency had violated his constitutional rights by not protecting him from his father's abuse.

In considering Joshua's constitutional claim, the United States Supreme Court held that Joshua did not possess a right to affirmative, active state protection from his father's abuse. Because the public agency had not taken formal responsibility for Joshua's protection, it did not have a duty to protect him from his father. As long as public actors do not actively intervene in children's lives, the state does not have to do anything to secure their safety and well-being. Through legislation and administrative policies, a state may decide to impose a duty on itself to protect children, but the United States Constitution does not require this.

Similarly, the Court has denied children positive rights in other, less dramatic ways. For example, although the Court had previously held that children have a right to an attorney in delinquency proceedings, the Court largely denied them that right in civil child protection proceedings.[32] When primarily older children (i.e., children over age ten) are caught up in a system that appears adultlike and metes out punishment (i.e., the criminal justice system), the Court accords them adultlike constitutional rights. However, when children of all ages, especially those ten years old or younger, are caught up in the civil child protection system, the Court denies them basic legal representation, effectively silencing them within a system that often, from the affected child's perspective, seems to mete out punishment (e.g., removal from parental custody, extended stays in foster care placements, adoption). Although the federal government and individual state governments may decide to provide legal representation for children,[33] the Constitution does not compel them to do so.

The Court has also failed to require state actors to respect and preserve children's relationship interests. In a case in which foster parents challenged New York officials' power to remove foster children from their homes without sufficient notice and justification, the Court decided that foster parents do not have a constitutional right to maintain an established long-term relationship with their foster children.[34] Although the Court focused on the foster parents' interests, it implicitly addressed those of the children as well. The Court effectively held that, like foster parents, children do not have a constitutional right to maintain a long-standing foster family relationship. The family association that consists of foster parents and foster children is one created by contract with the state, and it lacks any constitutional status. The state may, consequently, disrupt or destroy this association as it sees fit. In the end, a state may decide to recognize children's relationship interests, but the Constitution does not require a state to affirmatively protect them.

Adult Interest in Child Well-being

The result of the Supreme Court decisions is the express recognition of a relatively strong, constitutionally based right of parents (especially biological parents) to control children's lives standing alongside, and in tension with, constitutionally weak or unrecognized rights of children (especially younger children) to control their own lives. The Court leaves the vindication of children's interests to the legislature or to administrative policymakers. Within these spheres, the Constitution does not mandate public action to protect specific interests held by children. Thus, legislators and policymakers are largely free to define and protect children's interests as they see fit.

Two important points emerge from this discussion. First, the fundamental conflict in this area is not between children and adults but between two groups of adults. On one side stand parents who do not agree with widely accepted views of what measures are necessary or desirable to secure child well-being. On the other side stand citizens and public officials who are dedicated to securing their desired view of child well-being for all children even if it conflicts with the decisions and values of children's parents. Both groups of adults engaged in this fundamental conflict want to control children's upbringing and lives. Neither group wants to cede control to children, especially young children. Thus, children are not direct participants in conflicts over control of their lives.[35]

Second, in the absence of constitutional mandates pertaining to children's interests, lawmakers and policymakers have pursued a diverse array of measures aimed at securing children's interests and well-being. This has resulted in a hodgepodge of laws across jurisdictions. More fundamentally, it has resulted in collections of laws within specific jurisdictions that do not constitute a coherent whole. Which children's issues and interests lawmakers and policymakers address depends on the political and social forces of the moment.[36]

Of course, political and social forces have led to important legislation that defines and protects children's interests. The passage of child labor laws provides an illustration. Prior to enactment, parents had an almost absolute right to control their children's activities and labor. Barbara Bennett Woodhouse has described the conditions of childhood that resulted from this degree of parental control within industrial society:

> In 1900, one of every six children between the ages of ten and fifteen worked for wages. One-third of the workforce in southern textile mills was children aged ten to thirteen. Stories of sixty-hour workweeks in the deafening roar of the mill, the perpetual gloom of the coal mine, or the blazing sun of industrialized farms supplanted cultural images of children learning a skill in apprenticeship to a local craftsman or tending farm animals at mother's or father's side.[37]

Children were simply a component of their parents' human capital.

Many adults disagreed with parents' decisions to require or allow their children to work, believing strongly that it harmed children by robbing them of an appropriate childhood. These citizens pressed state and federal legislators to enact laws that limited the amount of time children could work, in some instances denying parents' authority to engage their children in paid employment altogether. Although the laws faced constitutional roadblocks and popular opposition, especially in the southern states, child labor legislation eventually prevailed.

The adults who worked to enact the child labor laws came to be known as the "child savers." They worked to prevent young children from becoming uneducated indentured laborers in the mechanized world of the Industrial Revolution. One aspect of their efforts was to take away from parents the authority to decide whether children would work for wages. As with many children's rights issues, this reform effort set off a battle between adult constituencies over the authority to control children's lives. One group of adults attempted to enlist state actors to wrest control of children from their parents. Following a lengthy public discussion and political battle, this group won majority support for eliminating parents' control over their children in the area of paid work.

The compulsory education laws provide another example of adults becoming interested in a specific aspect of child well-being. At the time those laws came into being, many urged that children have a right to education. They asserted that the state has a corresponding duty to compel parents to enroll their children in a program of formal education. State legislatures responded by enacting laws that required children to attend school, usually until age sixteen.[38]

Enactment of compulsory education laws was a logical reaction to the enactment of child labor laws. When the state prohibited parents from sending their children to work, children had a significant amount of time that they could devote to educational activities, and the state had a ripe opportunity to mandate that children attend school. As a result, parents not only lost the authority to send their children to work but also lost control over their children's education. Their children now had to attend school and receive a state-approved education. One group of adults became interested in a specific area of child well-being, namely, education, and worked to overcome the control of another group of adults—parents who did not want to provide their children with the desired educational experiences.

A third and final example of selective adult interest in a matter of child well-being is provided by laws enacted to secure legal representation for children in cases of parental abuse and neglect. The federal government requires states to provide legal representation for children in these cases. States that refuse to comply stand to lose federal funding for their child welfare systems. Consequently, all states provide dependent children with some form of representation.[39]

This example of adult interest in child well-being presents an especially powerful illustration of a conflict between groups of adults. Not only did a group of adults battle parents' interests in order to enact the law, but the resulting law ensures active, ongoing interference in parental control over children in the context of dependency cases.

Once appointed, a children's attorney becomes closely engaged with his or her client and with other members of the client's family. The attorney will investigate the family situation, gaining access to the intimate details of a child's life and those of the child's parents. Once the attorney completes the investigation, the attorney must argue for what he or she believes is in the child client's best interests. Although the child's wishes are a factor in determining what course of action is in her or his best interests, these wishes are not decisive. The attorney is free to disagree and to advocate a different position. The attorney's discretion is especially broad when representing younger children who may be unable to articulate their wishes or who may not possess the capacity to adequately consider and make important life decisions.

This situation reveals how children's rights rhetoric often masks multiple levels of conflict among adults for the control of children's lives. A motivated group of adults works to have the state give an attorney authority to investigate a family's situation, reach independent decisions concerning the child client's interests, and enforce those decisions through the judicial process. The state effectively empowers adult attorneys to make decisions for children over the objections of both the affected children and their parents. This situation is characterized as a vindication of children's rights—specifically, the right to legal representation.

The examples of adults pursuing specific children's interests indicate how we have arrived at a scattered collection of laws, devoid of any core constitutional foundation or theory, that protect children's interests. This congeries of mostly statutory law reflects majoritarian adult interests that shift over time and geographic territory. This is the nature of children's rights and explains why children occupy a legally subordinate position compared to adults.

The Growing Power of Children's Rights Rhetoric

Despite its subordinate legal position, children's rights rhetoric operates as a potent force within current American and international society. Although it has not been formally accepted by the United States government, the United Nations Convention on the Rights of the Child reflects the strong trend to create, formalize, and protect concepts of children's rights.[40] Many adults speak of children as a society's most valuable resource—a resource all adults should actively protect and nurture. Thus, if we look beyond legal formalities and doctrine, we see the growing strength of children's interests or rights.

In contrast, we see the diminishment of parental rights rhetoric. Many reject the idea that parents have the authority to control and dictate the conditions of their children's lives. In rejecting this idea, they assert that strong parental rights place children in the position of parent-owned property. They paint a picture of children as owned objects that lack interests and rights.[41]

This trend to diminish parental rights finds vivid expression in the increasingly popular assertion that "it takes a village to raise a child."[42] Powerfully anti–parents' rights in tone and in practical implications, this phrase sends a strong message that parents cannot adequately provide for their children on their own. Parents have no exclusive property-like claim on their children, who instead look to broad community support for nurturance and proper development. Because the entire community has a strong claim on children, parental claims and possibly parental responsibilities must sometimes take a subordinate position.

The trend of popular rhetoric appears to be in one direction. It holds that as a society, we must dedicate ourselves to securing our children's best interests. This is our duty, our highest obligation and ambition. If we construct and respect some form of parental rights, it is only in the service of children's interests. If parents need to have a sense of ownership of their children in order to fully live up to their duty of securing child well-being, then we will structure our society to provide such a sense, but only to the extent that the benefits to children exceed the costs. In other words, a limited scheme of parental rights is simply an acceptable and necessary means to fulfilling society's duty to secure child well-being.[43]

But this strong trend in the area of public rhetoric obscures the core emotions that have led to the strong legal doctrine constructing and protecting parental rights. The new rhetoric coexists with a deep desire and drive to care for and control one's children. The genetic tie is strong—a basic component of human nature that tends to give rise to powerful parent-child relationships and may account for the sensed broader social obligation to secure child well-being.[44]

Thus, while the rhetoric of children's interests dominates current public discourse, the rhetoric of parents' rights lurks as a powerful force that exists in tension with concepts of children's rights. This tension identifies the essential conflict between groups of adults related to child well-being.

To summarize: One group consists of parents. This group includes all parents, but it is usually mobilized through the actions of a subgroup of parents who, in specific situations, want to control their children's lives in ways that depart from those accepted by most adults. In the past, these parents may have resisted child labor laws, holding fast to the view that children and families benefit when children engage in paid labor. They may have resisted mandatory education laws, feeling that children can be educated through informal arrangements. The home schooling movement reflects this view. Other current examples are parents who insist on the appropriateness of harsh corporal punishment or refuse medical treatment for their children based on religious principles.

The other group of adults consists of individuals who would pursue their own vision of child well-being by imposing it on parents and society. In the past, they provided the social and political force behind the child labor law movement, working to deny parents the authority to engage their children in paid labor. They also drove the compulsory education law initiatives. Their vision for child well-being required children to be in school, not in the factory. Parents who saw things differently were simply regarded as mistaken. More recently, this group works to secure adequate food, shelter, education, and health care for children, to ensure freedom from abuse and neglect, and to provide legal representation for children involved in custody disputes.

This second group of adults often deploys the rhetoric of children's rights to drive their positions forward. Children have a "right" to avoidance of paid employment, to an adequate education, to health services, and to legal representation, among other social benefits. This group will define just what is included in the concept of children's rights as they expand their vision of child well-being.[45] Although children often cannot effectively assert their own rights, these adults identify, define, and implement children's rights by working to impose their vision of children's needs and well-being on parents and society.

Two Metanarratives

The fundamental conflict between the two adult groups reflects two divergent metanarratives surrounding the family and children.

The Private Family

Martha Fineman has identified the metanarrative of the "private family."[46] Interestingly, scholars indicate American society's embrace of the private family ideal is a relatively recent development.[47] Many view the family in colonial times as a corporate entity serving many public functions. For example, the family was a center for commercial activity. The typical, even ideal, family association produced items for its own consumption and for the market. It included children who parents and other family members educated and trained to serve the community within their long-term family associations.[48]

This view of the family changed throughout the nineteenth century and the early twentieth century.[49] Society's transformation by the Industrial Revolution affected perceptions of the family. The family's direct contribution to the market diminished. Commercial activity increasingly took place outside the family association. Many perceived the family as retreating from the public spheres of market and political activity. The family was increasingly seen as occupying a separate, private sphere that served as a sanctuary from other areas of activity.[50]

This perceived separation from public spheres combined with American society's growing value of self-reliance. This value arose, at least in part, from the American vision of the frontier family.[51] Many viewed these families as autonomous, providing for their needs through their own efforts and decisions. The ideal family was self-reliant, functioning well on its own and deserving protection from public intrusion.

Although this conception of the ideal family was not based on social reality during the nineteenth and early twentieth centuries, American society largely embraced it. Specifically, society sought to create and support the nuclear family by separating it from extended kinship and other associations.[52]

The law reflected and reinforced this ideal by privileging the nuclear family form. For example, the law removed restrictions on marriage, promoting individual choice and the formation of nuclear families that acted with a great deal of autonomy from kinship groups and other intermediate associations.[53] The law constricted opportunities for women, placing them as much as possible within the private family sphere and denying them full access to the market and political arenas.[54] The courts refused to intervene and alter decisions made within nuclear family associations, even when the decisions led to harsh treatment of the less powerful members of those associations.[55]

Social forces and rhetoric, reinforced through the development of the law, created and provided support for a specific conception of the private family. Namely, the public ideal consisted of female domesticity and economic privatism.[56] The law protected and actively supported the product of this ideal—the autonomous, self-reliant family. In public rhetoric, this private family came to reflect enterprise, Americanism, and patriotism.[57] This family is All-American and all good, albeit not prevalent in American society.

The private family ideal provides one of the core metanarratives for the American family. This metanarrative captures society's perceptions of, and hopes for, the family as an associational unit entitled to protection from the state.

As an autonomous association, the family enjoys freedom from state intervention because this freedom allows it to serve important functions within society. For Fineman, the family's most important function is to provide care and support for dependent individuals (e.g., children, the elderly, the disabled). The family relieves the broad society and governmental officials from the burden of caring for dependent persons. In order to encourage and reward families for taking on this inevitable, chronic, and heavy burden, the state allows families a great deal of freedom from public regulation and control. Accordingly, this approach provides support for parental rights and holds the state at a distance.

One can see the current operative effects of this metanarrative in assessing child welfare approaches and practices. Policymakers have formulated and promoted the idea that state actors can save the family as a unit, rather than the child as an individual, in situations of child abuse and neglect. Congress, state legislators, and child welfare officials have actively provided support for family preservation and reunification services when confronting the problem of child maltreatment.[58] Through the development and support of aggressive service programs, the public provides intensive, short-term support services to parents in order to prevent the removal of a child from parental custody or to achieve reunification of a child and parent as soon as possible following removal. Policymakers intend public assistance to be intensive but limited in time. The goal is to have the family quickly regain its autonomous status and to care for its dependent members, usually by having parents provide adequate care for their children.

The idea of the private family also exerts influence in the context of adoption. Traditionally, state laws have not allowed courts to create open adoption arrangements that provide for continued contact between the adopted child and the birth parents or other biologically related individuals.[59] The standard approach has been to allow only closed adoptions within which the adoptive parents exercise virtually complete control over the adopted child's associations and relationships. The state takes this approach in order to provide the adopted child with a fresh start within the new family.

This approach persists despite substantial evidence that children have the capacity to maintain contact and form attachments with multiple adults and that doing so may benefit children developmentally.[60] Rather than allowing and encouraging the adopted child to establish and/or maintain a relationship with his or her biological family, the state assigns the child to a new autonomous family association. Public actors construct the adoptive family in the image of the ideal family form.

Child Well-being

The powerful metanarrative of the private family does not occupy the entire field, it stands in tension with a second powerful metanarrative—that of child well-being.[61] This narrative construct arose in the context of early child protection initiatives by social progressives labeled "child savers." During the first half of the nineteenth century, this progressive movement focused on removing children from situations of neglect or poverty.[62] The child savers used social concern for children to gain public authority to remove children from parental custody and place them in institutions or apprenticeships.[63]

The sudden explosion of concern for children's living conditions appeared to have two primary sources. First, many began to embrace humanitarian goals that included children's well-being.[64] Second, the wealthy elite became increasingly fearful of the social disorder and lawlessness presented by immigrant and poor families. These fears led to a hope that the public could reform deviant families and wayward children.[65]

This hope rested on the public ideal of the nuclear family model. This model set new norms for proper family relations that had women's domesticity and nurturing childhood conditions at their base.[66] The social progressives were successful in legalizing these new norms. The public gained authority to act *in loco parentis*, displacing parents. Legislatures and courts authorized public actors to remove children from families that did not meet the ideal of the private, sanctified domestic family.[67]

The social progressives continued their efforts throughout the last half of the nineteenth century and the first part of the twentieth century. During this period, they focused more on child cruelty and mistreatment and less on child neglect and family poverty. The highly publicized case of abuse and neglect of a child named Mary Ellen in New York City in 1874 helped draw attention to child maltreatment.[68] Child savers became involved in an effort to prevent abuse and to make children's homes safe even if the children remained in poverty. Rather than remove children from poor families, the public increasingly attempted to preserve their original families and make their homes safe. In fact, poor families increasingly looked to child-saving organizations for assistance and support.[69]

This preventive approach demanded intervention in families that did not meet the autonomous, nuclear family ideal. If a subject family failed to respond adequately, public actors would remove children and place them in better homes. Thus, the child savers worked to provide foster homes and adoptive homes for affected children. Although the level of care varied significantly, the public appeared to view these placements as providing superior homes.[70]

Through this process of intervention, the moral reformers imposed a new family model characterized by female domesticity and extended childhood. Because numerous working-class and poor families could not fit this model, they became the primary targets for intervention. As Stephanie Coontz explains, social activists, legislators and judges implemented a system of professional elitism and judicial discretion:

> New "experts" tried to invest middle-class childrearing values with scientific weight. Profamily activists enthusiastically eliminated legal and administrative restrictions on court officials and social workers, empowering them to make arbitrary judgments as to whether a youth was "predelinquent," a family was "decent," or a widow was "morally fit" to receive a pension that enabled her to keep her children at home. Indeterminate sentences in reformatories further augmented the power of "rule writers" to discipline individuals whose ideas about family life and gender roles departed from Protestant middle-class norms.[71]

A concrete example of this effort was the increased prevalence of judicial assessment of adoptive homes and other placements during the last part of the nineteenth century and the first part of the twentieth century.[72] This precursor to American society's embrace of the best interests of the child standard introduced a high degree of judicial discretion in child placement decisions. The courts became primary agents in securing child well-being.

Two Metanarratives at Odds

In summary, during the same period that American society developed the metanarrative of the private family, the child saver movement emphasized the public concern with and involvement in child rearing,[73] constructing the metanarrative of child well-being. Through this construct the family becomes the essential association because it provides the associational setting for the most precious being—the developing child. Childhood is sacred. It is a period of life that is to be very special.[74] Parents are supposed to spend most of their time serving and supporting the child's development within the family association, entering the market and political arenas primarily to support the family.

Society's strong focus on child well-being leads to effects that extend beyond relationships within the family association itself, providing the state with justification and authority to monitor and regulate children's environments generally. For example, Christopher Lasch in his classic work on the family, *Haven in a Heartless World*, describes how modern society's consuming focus on the well-being of children has led the public to structure, regulate, and control children's environments.[75] Under the banner of promoting child health and development, the public, often through the use of state power, has effectively imposed public standards on parents.

Child labor laws and compulsory education laws stand as strong legislative examples of the impact of the metanarrative of child well-being. But the development of the best interests of the child standard in child custody and visitation disputes provides an even more direct and powerful example. In deciding custody disputes between two fit, minimally adequate parents, judges compare the particular parents on various factors thought to be relevant to child well-being.[76] In this way, courts supposedly base custody decisions on considerations of child well-being rather than considerations of parental interests and power. In making custody decisions, judges do not formally and independently consider the possibly devastating effect on a parent that results from losing custody. The only way this factor would gain a court's consideration would be if it affected the child in a significant way. This disregard of parents is even more pronounced in third-party visitation proceedings in which a third-party such as a grandparent can obtain a visitation order over the objections of a child's parents because a judge finds that such visitation would promote the subject child's well-being.[77] The metanarrative of child well-being is powerful and seems to only be gaining power as it increasingly permeates society and becomes incorporated in laws affecting children and families.

The laws affecting children often reflect the tension between the powerful metanarrative of the private family and the strengthening metanarrative of child well-being. Because these powerful concepts can justify divergent and contradictory goals and policies, they lend themselves to manipulation by politicians, legislators, judges, and policymakers interested in promoting particular ideological goals and result-oriented policies. In broad terms, conservatives can tap into the narrative of the private family in order to justify a low level of public intrusion in and support for families and children. In contrast, liberals can enlist the idea of child well-being in order to justify a broad array of social programs that benefit families and children.

The metanarratives do not necessarily lead to specific goals and policies, but they do color and affect the public discussion of children and families within the context of policy debates such as those surrounding welfare reform. Parents in the traditional nuclear family are to independently ensure adequate financial and child care resources so that they do not burden the public with requests or demands for support. Although the public does provide significant support to these "autonomous" families, it is largely hidden from view.[78] The widely held perception is that these families take care of their own members and everyone flourishes.

In exchange for sustaining themselves without overt public support, the public allows families to largely manage their own affairs. Parents in these families enjoy a great deal of freedom in deciding where they live, where they work, where and how their children are educated, what values they convey to their children, and with whom their children will associate. The public does not closely monitor, regulate, control, or second-guess parental decisions made within these "autonomous" families.[79]

With the private, autonomous family as the desirable vision, many consider any family that falls short to be deviant, if not inadequate. Once a parent has to call on the public for support, he or she becomes suspect. This parent fails to meet society's expectations as constructed through the narrative of the private family.[80]

For these deviant families, the metanarrative of child well-being becomes dominant. Because the parents cannot sustain the family on their own, the public raises questions about their adequacy to raise their children. These questions justify the public in monitoring and regulating these families—ones that cannot fully realize the vision of autonomy.

The impact of this vision of the family on the discussion and application of welfare law and policy is telling. The public will provide support to parents so that they can sustain themselves and their families. But the public provides this support grudgingly—only at a minimal level and for a limited period. In addition, while the parents receive public support, government actors will subject them and their children to public monitoring, regulation and control. Government actors will watch them much more than members of associations that live up to the vision of the private, autonomous family because the public must actively assure child well-being within their deviant families.[81]

This discussion demonstrates how powerful narratives related to families and children can be manipulated and played against each other for ideological reasons. Those who cling to the belief that individuals and families should be autonomous and able to support themselves without public assistance can use both metanarratives in pursuit of their vision. For families that can live up to the desired autonomous ideal, the narrative of the private family is controlling. It overwhelms concerns about child well-being, with the public vesting considerable authority and power in parents. However, for families that fail to meet the ideal, a second narrative, that of child well-being, becomes dominant. It overwhelms the principles of family and parental autonomy, providing justification for fairly extensive public monitoring, regulation and control. Thus, depending on a particular family's situation, the controlling narrative varies, often in order to serve an ideology or vision of family economic autonomy. And although the law does not create the overarching narratives or ideologies, it reflects them and, most important, reinforces and validates them.

A similar shift in the use of the two powerful metanarratives appears in the discussion of foster care and adoption. Many discuss the condition of lengthy foster care placements primarily in terms of child well-being. Public officials perceive foster children as being in need of a broad array of services, ranging from mental health services to special education services to basic economic support.[82] The public seemingly has a duty to secure child well-being for these state wards.

One important goal for long-term foster children is finding them a permanent placement, with the first priority being an adoptive placement.[83] Child welfare laws and policies are largely structured to achieve this goal—for example, by encouraging a child's foster parents to adopt the child.[84] Once adoption is achieved, the narrative of the private family takes over. The child is now a member of a private family, a family that has a duty to be self-supporting and autonomous.[85] As a result, the same family that received extensive public support and services as a foster family now receives a much lower level of public support. The public retreats from the foster family's life and simply hopes that the new private adoptive family can, largely on its own, secure child well-being. The family is now in the desired state—private, autonomous, and without need of significant public support or intervention. Once again, the law comes to reflect and reinforce the overarching narratives surrounding the family in American society.

The tension between the twin tales—the private family and child well-being—shows up in laws and policies affecting children in their daily lives. Acknowledging and considering this basic tension helps explain which laws and policies are adopted and how they are applied in pragmatic terms. In the subsequent chapters, we will examine six types of situations that illustrate how decisions regarding children take place against a background of two antagonistic metanarratives.

The first three situations illustrate areas of law and policy in which the narrative of child well-being is foremost. In these types of situations, the public appears to have actively accepted its responsibility to provide support for children and their families. However, the narrative of the private family becomes powerful in these types of situations when public resources fall short of meeting the needs of affected children.

The next three situations are areas in which the public appears to actively reject the metanarrative of child well-being. Public actors seem to realize that the costs of embracing a goal of child well-being in these situations are politically and economically unsustainable from the outset. In these areas, the narrative of the private family, along with additional rhetoric of individual autonomy and responsibility, silences children's claims.

The goal is to examine each of these situations and to gain a fuller understanding of the political and social forces at play in designing relevant laws and policies. It is also to understand the actual pragmatic implementation of the applicable laws and policies in each situation. The hope is that this deeper understanding of laws and policies affecting children will direct us in securing children the assistance and support they need. Although public systems affecting children are deeply flawed, these systems can work if we understand them and force them to deal with specific children's needs and problems. The key is to recognize and break away from the adult battle over the control of children's lives and the manipulation of metanarratives in the service of adult ideologies and, instead, have public actors focus on and address children's basic needs and opportunities.

Notes

1. *Meyer v. Nebraska*, 262 U.S. 390 (1923); *Pierce v. Society of Sisters*, 268 U.S. 510 (1925).

2. See Plato, *The Republic of Plato*, trans. Allan Bloom (New York: Basic Books, 1991), 458e–65c.

3. *Pierce*, 268 U.S. 510; Barbara Bennett Woodhouse, "'Who Owns the Child': *Meyer* and *Pierce* and the Child as Property," *William & Mary Law Review* 33 (1992): 995.

4. *Pierce*, 268 U.S., 535.

5. See *West Coast Hotel Co. v. Parrish*, 300 U.S. 379 (1937).

6. *Wisconsin v. Yoder*, 406 U.S. 205 (1972).

7. *Wisconsin v. Yoder*.

8. *Santosky v. Kramer*, 455 U.S. 745 (1982).

9. See David J. Herring, *The Public Family: Exploring Its Role in Democratic Society* (Pittsburgh: University of Pittsburgh Press, 2003), 145–46.

10. For a description of this case and its aftermath, see Herring, *The Public Family*,147–49; Michele Ingrassi and Karen Springen, "She's Not Baby Jessica Anymore," *Newsweek*, March 21, 1994, 60.

11. See *In the Interest of BGC*, 496 N.W.2d 239 (1992); *In re Baby Girl Clausen*, 502 N.W.2d 649 (Mich. 1993).

12. See *In re Petition of Doe*, 638 N.E.2d 181 (Ill. 1994); *In re Petition of Kirchner*, 649 N.E.2d 324 (Ill. 1995).

13. *In re Petition of Kirchner*.

14. *In re Petition of Kirchner*.

15. See *Troxel v. Granville*, 120 S. Ct. 2054 (2000).

16. Washington Revised Code § 26.10.160(3) (1994).

17. *Troxel*, 2054; *In re Custody of Smith*, 969 P.2d 21 (Wash. 1998).

18. *Troxel*, 2068.

19. *Troxel*, 2066.

20. *Troxel*, 2062.

21. *Troxel*, 2061–62.

22. *Troxel*, 2071.

23. *Troxel*, 2074.

24. *Troxel*, 2074.

25. *Troxel*, 2074.

26. *Troxel*, 2074.

27. *Troxel*, 2072.

28. See Herring, *The Public Family*,159; Woodhouse, "'Who Owns the Child'"; Bruce C. Hafen, "Children's Liberation and the New Egalitarianism: Some Reservations about Abandoning Youth to Their Rights," *Brigham Young University Law Review* (1976): 605; Lee E. Teitelbaum, "Children's Rights and the Problem of Equal Respect," *Hofstra Law Review* 27 (Summer 1999): 799.

29. Herring, *The Public Family*, 159–79.

30. See, for example, *DeShaney v. Winnebago County Department of Social Service*, 489 U.S. 189 (1989); *Harris v. McRae*, 448 U.S. 297 (1980).

31. DeShaney, 489 U.S. 189.

32. *Lassiter v. Department of Social Services of Durham County, North Carolina*, 452 U.S. 18 (1981). See also Martin Guggenheim, "The Right to Be Represented but Not Heard: Reflections on Legal Representation for Children," *N.Y.U. Law Review* 59 (1984): 76, 89–93.

33. See, for example, 42 U.S.C.A. § 5106a (1996); 42 Pa. Cons. Stat. Ann. § 6311 (Supp. 2000).

34. *Smith v. Organization of Foster Families for Equality and Reform*, 431 U.S. 816 (1977).

35. See, generally, Herring, *The Public Family*, 159–79.

36. Herring, *The Public Family*.

37. Woodhouse, "'Who Owns the Child,'" 1059–60.

38. See Woodhouse, "'Who Owns the Child,'" 1016–17.

39. See 42 U.S.C.A. § 5106a (1996); Colo. Rev. Stat. Ann. § 14 10 116 (West 2000); Wash. Rev. Code Ann. § 26.10.070 (West 1997).

40. United Nations Convention on the Rights of the Child, http://www.unicef.org/crc/crc.htm.

41. See Woodhouse, "'Who Owns the Child'"; Herring, *The Public Family*, 144–50.

42. See Hillary Rodham Clinton, *It Takes a Village: And Other Lessons Children Teach Us* (New York: Simon & Schuster, 1996).

43. See Elizabeth S. Scott and Robert E. Scott, "Parents as Fiduciaries," *Virginia Law Review* 81 (1995): 240; Barbara Bennett Woodhouse, "Of Babies, Bonding, and Burning Buildings: Discerning Parenthood in Irrational Action," *Virginia Law Review* 81 (1995): 2493.

44. Robert Trivers, *Social Evolution* (Menlo Park, CA: Benjamin/ Cummings, 1985); Herring, *The Public Family*, 1–33.

45. See, for example, United Nations Convention on the Rights of the Child.

46. Martha L. A. Fineman, "Masking Dependency: The Political Role of Family Rhetoric," *Virginia Law Review* 81 (1995): 2181, 2205. A *metanarrative* or *public narrative* is a story that is familiar or recognizable, and by assuming a hierarchy of cultural representations and values, it aids groups of people in forming collective identities (2204 n. 56).

47. See Stephanie Coontz, *The Way We Never Were: American Families and the Nostalgia Trap* (New York: Basic Books, 1992); Lee E. Teitelbaum, "Family History and Family Law," *Wisconsin Law Review* (1985): 1135.

48. See Teitelbaum, "Family History and Family Law," 1138–40; Coontz, *The Way We Never Were*, 126.

49. See Coontz, *The Way We Never Were*; Teitelbaum, "Family History and Family Law," 1141–44.

50. See Teitelbaum, "Family History and Family Law."

51. See Coontz, *The Way We Never Were*, 73 (also explaining how the value of self-reliance was subsequently reinforced by the American vision of the suburban family).

52. See Coontz, *The Way We Never Were*, 128–30.

53. See Coontz, *The Way We Never Were*.

54. See Coontz, *The Way We Never Were*; Teitelbaum, "Family History and Family Law," 1141–43, 1174–75.

55. See Teitelbaum, "Family History and Family Law," 1145–46; 1174–75 (quoting and discussing the Nebraska Supreme Court's statement in the well-known and notorious case of *McGuire v. McGuire*, "the living standards of a family are a matter of concern to the household, and not for the courts to determine. . . . As long as the home is maintained and the parties are living as husband and wife it may be said that the husband is legally supporting his wife and the marriage relationship is being carried out." *McGuire v. McGuire*, 157 Neb. 226, 238, 59 N.W.2d 336, 342 [1953]).

56. See Coontz, *The Way We Never Were*, 135–36.

57. See Coontz, *The Way We Never Were*, 138–39.

58. See, for example, Family Preservation and Support Act, 42 U.S.C. § 629a (2002); Pennsylvania Juvenile Act, 42 Pa. Cons. Stat. §§ 6301(b)(1) and (3) (2002); 55 Pa. Code § 3130.61(b)(3) (1999); Theodore J. Stein, *Child Welfare and the Law*, rev. ed. (Washington, DC: CWLA Press, 1998), 59–61.

59. See, for example, *McNamara v. Thomas*, 741 A.2d 778 (Pa. Super. Ct. 1999); Marsha Garrison, "Parent's Rights v. Children's Interests: The Case of the Foster Child," *N.Y.U. Review of Law & Social Change* 22 (1996): 371, 377–78. This standard approach is changing, with several states now expressly authorizing open adoption arrangements. See, generally, Donald N. Duquette et al., *Guidelines for Public Policy and State Legislation Governing Permanence for Children*, vi i 31 (Washington, DC: Department of Health and Human Services, Administration for Children and Families, Administration on Children, Youth, and Families, Children's Bureau, 1999).

60. See Duquette et al., *Guidelines*.

61. See Herring, *The Public Family*, 70–72; 159–79.

62. See Naomi Cahn, "Perfect Substitutes or the Real Thing?" *Duke Law Journal* 52 (2003): 1077, 1088–97.

63. See Cahn, "Perfect Substitutes or the Real Thing?"; Coontz, *The Way We Never Were*, 129–30.

64. See Cahn, "Perfect Substitutes or the Real Thing?" 62, citing Elizabeth Pleck, *Domestic Tyranny: The Making of Social Policy against Family Violence from Colonial Times to the Present* (New York: Oxford University Press, 1987).

65. See Cahn, "Perfect Substitutes or the Real Thing?"

66. See Coontz, *The Way We Never Were*, 129–30.

67. See Coontz, *The Way We Never Were*, 129–30.

68. See Cahn, "Perfect Substitutes or the Real Thing?" 1091.

69. See Cahn, "Perfect Substitutes or the Real Thing?" 1092–95.

70. See Cahn, "Perfect Substitutes or the Real Thing?" 1097–99.

71. Coontz, *The Way We Never Were*, 139.

72. See Cahn, "Perfect Substitutes or the Real Thing?"1112–15.

73. See Teitelbaum, "Family History and Family Law," 1146–47.

74. See Teitelbaum, "Family History and Family Law," 1143–44.

75. Christopher Lasch, *Haven in a Heartless World: The Family Besieged* (New York: Basic Books, 1977).

76. See David J. Herring, "Rearranging the Family: Diversity, Pluralism, Social Tolerance and Child Custody Disputes," *Southern California Interdisciplinary Law Journal* 5 (1997): 205, 222–25.

77. See David J. Herring, "*Troxel* and the Rhetoric of Associational Respect," *University of Pittsburgh Law Review* 62 (2001): 649.

78. See Coontz, *The Way We Never Were*, 68–91; Fineman, "Masking Dependency," 2205–6.

79. See Herring, *The Public Family*, 150–52.

80. See Fineman, "Masking Dependency," 2182, 2192–94; Martha Fineman, *The Neutered Mother, The Sexual Family, and Other Twentieth Century Tragedies* (New York: Routledge, 1995), 177–98.

81. Fineman, *The Neutered Mother*.

82. See Peter J. Pecora et al., *The Child Welfare Challenge: Policy, Practice, and Research*, 2d ed. (New York: Aldine de Gruyter, 2000).

83. See Anthony N. Maluccio et al., *Permanency Planning for Children: Concepts and Methods* (New York: Tavistock, 1986), 5; David J. Herring, "The Adoption and Safe Families Act—Hope and Its Subversion," *Family Law Quarterly* 34 (2000): 329, 330–33.

84. See Herring, "The Adoption and Safe Families Act," 336–40.

85. See Herring, *The Public Family*, 41–44.

Part I

Active Public Support for Child Well-Being

In certain situations, the public's inclination is to intervene in children's lives in order to secure their well-being. Unfortunately, this inclination does not guarantee that the public will devote the resources necessary for the effective pursuit of child well-being. As a result, children must interact with public systems that, and government actors who, lack adequate resources to achieve the goals that arise from the public's inclination to intervene in their lives. These impoverished interactions affect children in their everyday lives and can be understood and addressed only through an examination of specific situations.

The three chapters in this part describe such specific scenarios. Each begins with a story drawn from actual case experiences. The story provides a platform for the description of a specific public system, allowing for an exploration of the system's design and goals. The story also reflects and reveals the tensions arising from insufficient public resources and the dominant metanarratives of the private family and child well-being. Each chapter will suggest pragmatic strategies and contacts designed to help children experiencing the type of situation addressed in that chapter.

2

The Public Child
Welfare System

Consider the case of Katherine and Natalie Miller during the summer of 2003. It is lengthy and complex,[1] but not atypical. It reflects the common twists and turns of children's experiences within urban public child welfare systems.

Katherine was born on September 12, 1992, and Natalie on February 2, 1994. In September 1997, when the girls were four and three, the New York City child protective authorities removed them from their mother, Kim Moore. Natalie had called the police to report that her mother had left them unattended. Kim admitted that she had a substance abuse problem. The authorities placed the girls in foster care with their maternal aunt. They stayed with her until December 1997 when the authorities returned them to their mother's custody, under agency supervision.

Kim began using cocaine again in 1999. The public authorities discovered Kim's substance abuse and removed Katherine and Natalie in May of that year. The authorities initially placed the girls in a nonkinship foster home, but one month later, they returned the girls to their maternal aunt's home, where they have remained ever since.

After four years in their aunt's home, the girls wanted their aunt to adopt them, and she wished to do so as well. The aunt, a store manager, lived on Long Island, where the girls attended public school. The girls appeared to be deeply attached to their aunt and to have thrived in her custody. The girls said that they did not want to return to their mother's custody. Although they had no problem visiting with her regularly, they were angry at her for her substance abuse problems and the instability it has caused in their lives. They feared being returned to her. Their mother and their aunt were on good terms.

During the four years that the girls lived with their aunt, their mother's life was eventful and somewhat chaotic. In September 2001, she gave birth to a son, Ronald Heath. On discovering that Ronald had been born with cocaine in his system, public authorities immediately placed him in foster care with one of Kim's sisters, a different sister than the one caring for Katherine and Natalie.

In June 2002, New York City police arrested Kim, charging her with felony drug possession. She pled guilty, and the Brooklyn Treatment Court ordered Kim into the Veritas residential drug treatment program instead of sentencing her to a prison term. While in the treatment program, Kim gave birth to her fourth child, Charles, on December 6, 2002. Kim completed her required treatment, and the court dismissed all charges on June 26, 2003. She continued to reside within the Veritas program and to have custody of Charles. She had not used cocaine in more than a year.

At the beginning of summer 2003, Kim is 34 years old. She has previously participated in substance abuse programs, having abused cocaine intermittently since 1990. She graduated from her first drug treatment program in 1992, receiving a high school equivalent degree at that time. Following the second placement of her daughters in foster care in 1999, Kim spent a week in a detoxification program at Yonkers General Hospital. She then entered an in-patient rehabilitation program in upstate New York with a referral to an outpatient program upon completion. Kim failed to attend the outpatient program and began to use cocaine again in March 2000.

During 2000, Kim met Ronald's father, Randy Heath. Randy is employed as a linen sorter at a hotel, a job he has held since 1996. He has an apartment in Brooklyn. He is a recovering crack cocaine addict, having graduated from a residential drug treatment program in 1993. Randy is also Charles's father. He provides financial support for Charles, visits with him regularly, and remains in an intimate relationship with Kim.

A month after Ronald's birth in September 2001, Kim entered Pride Site, a residential drug treatment program. Pride Site developed a plan to reunify Kim with Randy and with her children. Kim visited her two daughters every week and had Ronald with her twice a week at Pride Site.

In January 2002, before completing the Pride Site plan, Kim decided to leave the program against clinical advice. From January through May 2002, Kim did not contact her children or any child services workers. Despite her participation in treatment programs, Kim had continued to abuse drugs from May 1999 until her arrest in June 2002. She asserted that she had not been ready to commit to her recovery until the Brooklyn Treatment Court ordered her to enter the Veritas residential treatment program.

In summer 2003, Kim is entering level 3 of the residential program, the last phase before she will move out. She regularly attends individual and group drug treatment therapy sessions and receives independent therapy to address her issues of anger and guilt. Kim is primarily angry at her past mistakes of relapsing into substance abuse and losing custody of her children. She is determined not to relapse again.

Kim realizes that her daughters are angry with her for her drug use. She thinks this is why they want to live with her sister and be adopted. She also believes that the public agency caseworker has been encouraging her daughters to desire adoption by consistently discussing it with them. Kim does recognize that her sister has provided the girls with excellent care, wants to adopt them, and would allow her to take part in the girls' lives. However, Kim feels that the girls know she is their mother and that she cared for them for the first five and six years of their lives. Therefore, although recognizing the girls are afraid because they suspect she may relapse in the future, Kim believes very strongly that the girls should eventually be returned to her custody.

Specifically, Kim proposes family counseling between her and the girls in order to allay their anxiety. They could discuss and acknowledge Kim's progress in addressing her substance abuse problem and they could confront and explore the damage Kim has caused the girls. Kim also proposes that her sister or her mother keep the girls while she completes her treatment program.

In order to leave the Veritas program, Kim must save $2,500 and obtain adequate housing. She has a pending application for a public housing certificate. (Kim cannot live with Randy in his Brooklyn apartment because the surrounding neighborhood is one in which she has used drugs in the past and would likely trigger a relapse.)

Kim has saved $388. She has also been trained as a home health aide and has been employed since May 2003. Kim's ultimate plan is for the court to return her daughters to her custody once she leaves Veritas.

Kim's counselor at Veritas recommends that the public authority return Katherine and Natalie to Kim's custody. Although she has never met or observed Kim's daughters, the counselor makes her recommendation primarily based on Kim's progress in the drug treatment program and her interactions with her baby, Charles. The program's nursery staff have noted that Kim is very loving toward Charles. The counselor also relies on the support services Kim will receive once she moves out of the residential program. Kim will move into an apartment, attend weekly groups for preventive aftercare, submit to periodic urine testing, continue in psychotherapy, and keep her job. She will also receive public assistance payments and child care support for Charles. Kim will graduate from the program only after six months of successful engagement with the support services.

The counselor relates that Kim has had verbal conflicts with other residents and program staff. The program referred her to psychotherapy, but Kim still has unresolved anger that sometimes gets in the way of her treatment. In the last three months, Kim has had no conflicts with staff, has been helpful to them, and appears to trust them.

The counselor also referred Kim and Randy to joint counseling after noting problems in their relationship related to Kim's inability to control her temper. The counselor does not know Randy and has only observed him when he comes to visit Kim and Charles. However, because Kim's long-term plan is to have herself, Randy, and all four children live together as a family, the counselor felt joint counseling would be appropriate and helpful.

The counselor notes Kim's success in the Veritas program. Only half of their clinic population meet the criteria for successful completion, and Kim is in the successful group. Because of her success in treatment and the fact that she is the girls' biological mother, the counselor believes the public authority should reunify Kim and her daughters. Although the counselor has never seen Kim's children or their foster mother, she always advocates for family reunification when a parent successfully completes the drug treatment program.

In contrast to the counselor, the attorney appointed to represent Katherine and Natalie argues for the girls' adoption by their aunt. He has spoken with the girls. Because they express a desire to be adopted by their aunt and an unwillingness to return to their mother, the attorney has adopted this position.

The court responsible for supervising the girls' placement in foster care has conducted a contested dispositional hearing throughout the summer of 2003. Kim did not contest the public authority's allegation that her conduct over the years meets the legal definition of "permanent neglect." In terms of New York state law, Kim has permanently neglected her daughters.[2] However, she objects to the public authority's proposed disposition of the case—termination of her parental rights and commitment of Katherine and Natalie to the public child welfare agency so that they could be adopted. Instead, Kim requests that the court suspend final judgment for up to one year.

In making her decision, the family court judge explains that a suspended judgment would provide a grace period of up to one year during which a parent is given an opportunity to demonstrate the ability to be a fit parent. The issue in this case is whether the court should suspend judgment in order to allow the mother to complete the transition from the treatment program to the community, to obtain a residence for her and her four children, and to undergo a course of counseling with her two girls. The mother asserts by completing a year at Veritas, she has earned the right to a suspended judgment.

The judge also acknowledges that it would be inappropriate to simply compare the mother's financial and parenting resources with those of the foster mother. But just as the foster mother is not entitled to continued custody of the children only because she possesses superior resources or parenting skill, the mother is not entitled to return of the children only because she has completed treatment. Once a parent's permanent neglect is established, due process no longer requires the court to regard the interests of the parent and the children to be one and the same.[3] The court must determine the outcome solely from the perspective of the children's interests, with the children's interest in permanent security being paramount to the parent's interest to raise his or her own children.

The extent of the parent's rehabilitation is only one factor that the court must consider in determining whether the parent is the best resource for the children. The court must also consider whether the parent can meet the children's needs within a reasonable time—one year.[4] In addition, the court must consider the length of time the children have already spent in the foster home, the relative strength of the children's attachment to the biological parent and the foster parent, the probable effect of reunification with the biological parent on the children's emotional, social, and physical development, and whether reunification would adequately ensure the children's safety.

The judge, while acknowledging the value of preserving biological relationships, notes that Katherine and Natalie have suffered a history of instability due to repeated placement in foster care. The judge acknowledges the girls' express desire not to be returned to their mother as a compelling factor in considering whether to suspend judgment. The court also notes that Kim, by blaming the public agency and caseworker for the girls' desire to be adopted, fails to acknowledge the legitimacy of the girls' need for stability and security.

Although Kim's failure could be addressed through individual and family therapy, the judge feels that this type of intervention would only further the girls' interests if it offered a high probability of reunification. Because of Kim's long history of drug use and instability, the judge does not consider that probability high. The judge commends Kim for refraining from cocaine use during the past year. However, she concludes that Kim's present sobriety is not sufficient to warrant a suspended judgment. In balancing the aunt's demonstrated ability to provide the girls with a stable home that the girls enjoy against the likelihood of the girls achieving stability in their mother's home within the one-year period of suspended judgment, the judge determines that a suspended judgment would not be in order. Therefore, the judge terminates Kim's parental rights and frees Katherine and Natalie for adoption by their aunt.[5] Charles remains in Kim's custody, and Kim continues to work for reunification with Ronald.

The story of Kim and her children is not unusual. Many cases centering on families in public child welfare systems are just as chaotic and complex. In fact, despite the current emphasis on timely permanent resolution, many cases remain in the system for years, taking sharp twists and turns as the public agency and the courts provide services, make decisions, and address the constant occurrence of unanticipated events.

The Family Metanarratives at Odds

Although not atypical, Kim's story provides a vehicle for insights into public systems that have a significant impact on particular children's lives. Her family's story both reflects and reveals the basic tension between the metanarrative of the private family and the metanarrative of child well-being. The public's initial hope lies squarely with the private family. Parents are supposed to take care of their children without public aid or intrusion.[6]

This was Katherine and Natalie's situation for the first years of their lives. They lived with their mother. The public allowed her to take care of the girls as she saw fit, with the hope that there would be no problems. Kim had a duty to provide adequate care for her children, and as long as she fulfilled that duty, the public would allow her to make important decisions for the girls without significant interference.

The absence of public interference extends to the area of monitoring the girls' experience in Kim's care. Public officials do not actively and closely watch parents fulfilling their duty to provide adequate care to their children. However, state legislatures have expressly authorized many individuals to monitor parental care. Spurred by federal law, every state has enacted statutes that allow individuals to report incidents of improper parental care.[7] In fact, these laws require individuals serving in particular roles such as physician or schoolteacher to report inadequate or improper parenting. States have set up extensive child abuse registries to receive these reports.

This public system structure characterized by restraint in direct monitoring of families and by deputization of individuals to report incidents of child abuse and neglect is a *residual* system. This type of system only comes into play after an incident of child maltreatment occurs, is observed, and is reported to state actors.[8] It contrasts sharply with a *preventive* system that actively provides support to parents and is in a position to directly monitor parental behavior. Although the design and implementation of a preventive system might significantly reduce incidents of child maltreatment, the American public has rejected such an approach.[9] The metanarrative of the private family prevails in this area, dictating public systems that only react to incidents of parental failure after the fact.

This explains why Kim had custody of Katherine for the first four years of her life and Natalie for the first three despite Kim's recognized substance abuse problems. As far as the public was concerned, no one had observed Kim's problems to result in inadequate care for the girls. The public had sent the girls home with Kim at birth, basically saying, "Call us if there is a problem." The public did not assign state actors to monitor the situation.

Nonetheless, state actors entered the scene in September 1997 when three-year-old Natalie contacted the police because her mother had left her and Katherine unattended and unsupervised. Natalie's call mobilized the residual public child welfare system and trumped the narrative of the private family. It signaled that the public could no longer trust this particular private family to fulfill its duties.

Because Kim could not sustain the presumption of autonomy initially granted to her family, her family lost its private quality. The public had to rescue Katherine and Natalie. Consequently, the narrative of child well-being took over, overwhelming the concept of the private family. The public's initial hope for family autonomy faded and the public's reaction became one of child rescue, family intervention, and service provision.

This public reaction of child rescue is tempered for several reasons. First, although the hope and power of the private family concept may diminish because of a parent's failures, this concept never disappears entirely.[10] The public wishes to revive its initial hope through rehabilitation of the original private family. The family that experiences child rescue operations and significant public intrusion and support is viewed as deviant—one that must be fixed, but in most cases not one that must be abandoned or destroyed.

Second, many feel strongly that children benefit significantly from maintaining a close relationship with their biological parents.[11] The biological relationship makes it likely that the parent will be more concerned about a child's well-being than other unrelated individuals. In addition, a child is likely to have a strong desire to know his or her biological parents and genetic background.

These factors support the initial assignment of children to the custody of their biological parents. Once this initial assignment occurs, a parent and a child usually begin to interact and to form strong attachments and bonds. Children such as Katherine and Natalie who live the first years of life with a biological parent usually form very strong bonds with that parent. Disruption of this bond will be painful and probably harmful to healthy development. Thus, attempts to preserve and rehabilitate a child's relationship with a biological parent are likely to serve child well-being. All of these considerations related to biological ties and nurturing bonds temper the child rescue reaction that would immediately and completely free a child from a relationship with a biological parent who has mistreated them in some way.

Third, the lack of resources available within public child welfare systems limits the child rescue reaction in response to incidents of child maltreatment. The public has not devoted the resources necessary to allow state actors to effectively displace parents for extended periods. Many recognize that foster care placements often do not provide children with adequate care in the long term.[12] Children in foster care often experience multiple moves and other disruptions that do not allow them and their foster parents to make strong commitments to each other. This instability and uncertainty may result in significant developmental harm. This risk of harm exists even if state actors seek the more permanent resolution of termination of parental rights and adoption. Even if such an effort is successful, it often takes years to achieve, exposing children to a lengthy period of instability. Also, this type of effort often will not succeed because of a substantial shortage of adoptive homes, especially for older children and those with special needs.[13] As a result, state actors may only succeed in creating a legal orphan who remains trapped in an unstable and uncertain living situation. The bottom line is that the state makes a bad parent and the pursuit of long-term child rescue operations does not serve child well-being. Consideration of these realities justifies efforts to rehabilitate the original private family and tempers the child rescue response.

Fourth, considerations of race and culture place limits on child rescue operations. Many view the removal of children from their parents' custody and their neighborhoods as a significant threat to minority families and culture.[14] Although these children may be safer physically after removal, they lose their racial and cultural roots. In addition, the community loses its children and its future.

The perception of this racial and cultural threat grows when one considers the way public child welfare systems and the child rescue response disproportionately affect minority children, families, and communities.[15] In order to preserve minority families and culture, many commentators emphasize family rehabilitation. This emphasis tempers the child rescue mentality and response.

Consideration of the resiliency of the private family ideal, the importance of the biological parent-child relationship, the lack of public resources to enable state actors to secure adequate parental substitutes, and the factors of race and culture preclude an all-out, long-term child rescue approach to incidents of child maltreatment. Although the metanarrative of child well-being is highly salient in these situations, it is not completely controlling. It cannot simply overpower all over considerations surrounding families in crisis.

Federal Child Welfare Law

Consider how the development of federal child welfare law demonstrates this same tension. Concerned about children being trapped in temporary foster care placements for years at a time, Congress responded by enacting the Adoption Assistance and Child Welfare Act (AACWA) of 1980.[16] Many of the AACWA's provisions drew their justification from permanency planning considerations. Social work scholars and professionals had developed these concepts with the overall goal of achieving timely permanent placements for children caught up in public child welfare systems. The first priority is to return children to their original homes as soon as possible. If this action is not possible, the priority is to place children in adoptive homes. Formal long-term foster placements are a poor third choice, but acceptable.

Permanency concerns gave rise to important provisions included in the AACWA, one being the "reasonable efforts" requirement.[17] The law mandated public child welfare agencies to make reasonable efforts to prevent the removal of children from their parents' custody. It also directed agencies to make reasonable efforts to reunify children with their parents if removal had been necessary in order to protect children from a serious threat of harm. Although Congress and the courts failed to define "reasonable efforts" in any specific way, child welfare policymakers and administrators realized an obligation to provide children and families with services designed to prevent removal or achieve reunification.

More problematic than, and likely the root cause of, the failure to define the reasonable efforts requirement was the failure to establish an effective enforcement mechanism. Congress relied on state judges to review public agency efforts in each case and determine if they met the requirement. This reliance proved misguided. The consequence of a rigorous review of and negative finding concerning the reasonable efforts requirement is a loss of federal foster care funds.[18] State judges, especially those elected by citizens in the particular area that would lose federal funds, have little incentive to enforce the federal law. In fact, these judges have a strong incentive to subvert this provision of the AACWA—which is what occurred.[19] Many attorneys, taking their cues from judges, did not litigate the issue of reasonable efforts with any vigor. Judges drafted court orders that almost always included a statement that the public agency had made reasonable efforts, with court order forms in many jurisdictions eventually including preprinted statements to this effect.[20]

Interestingly, the public child welfare agencies do not challenge this judicial practice by unilaterally and actively defining and implementing the reasonable efforts requirement. This is primarily because of a lack of resources. With current funding levels, these agencies cannot adequately design, create, and staff the service programs they need in order to effectively prevent removals or achieve reunification while also securing child safety.[21] Under these conditions, public agencies must decide whether to pursue family integrity while putting children at immediate risk or to pursue child rescue while putting families and long-term child well-being at risk. Often, agencies pursue both strategies, with the chosen strategy in any particular case depending primarily on the philosophy and values of the caseworker. This variance in approach leads agencies to leave some children within their original families at significant risk of maltreatment and to place other children in foster homes at significant risk of lengthy stays in temporary placements.

These divergent approaches and results provided the foundation for two valid, yet seemingly contradictory, arguments for the reform of the AACWA. On one hand, proponents of child safety marshaled evidence to show that the reasonable efforts requirement, as public agencies understood it, placed children at significant risk of serious harm. Agencies were simply leaving children with, or quickly returning children to, their original parents who had abused or neglected them. Unfortunately, because of a lack of resources, agencies were not able to adequately support these preserved or reunified families and to protect affected children. Drawing attention to several high-profile cases of severe child abuse, proponents of this argument characterized the reasonable efforts requirement as requiring "unreasonable efforts," suggesting that government actors were implementing the requirement too zealously, unreasonably exposing children to risk of harm.[22]

On the other hand, proponents of permanency planning had evidence to argue that public agencies were not vigorously implementing the reasonable efforts requirement. The foster care population had increased steadily from the mid-1980s through the mid-1990s. Public child welfare agencies were removing children from the custody of their parents at a relatively high rate, and once removed, children frequently remained in temporary foster care placements for extended periods—an average of two to six years, depending on the jurisdiction.[23] Thus, the AACWA's reasonable efforts requirement did not appear to have the intended effect of reducing foster care drift or achieving timely permanent placements for children. Whether because of a lack of will or lack of resources, public child welfare agencies had failed to make the efforts necessary to prevent foster care placements or to achieve timely permanent placements.

In 1997, Congress reacted to both of the powerful arguments for reform by approving the Adoption and Safe Families Act (ASFA),[24] which revised the reasonable efforts requirement in two important ways. The ASFA also introduced seemingly strict time lines, along with financial incentives for adoption outcomes, in order to achieve timely permanent placements.

Congress revised the reasonable efforts requirement by designating a set of cases for which public agencies did not have to make any efforts to prevent removal or achieve reunification. These "aggravated circumstances" cases included extreme parental maltreatment of the subject child or another child in the parent's care. In these cases, the law requires public agencies and state courts to pursue aggressively a permanent placement other than reunification (usually adoption) at the very beginning of the process.[25]

Congress also expressly stated that the paramount consideration in making reasonable efforts is the child's health and safety. The provision sends a clear signal to public child welfare agencies. In striving to prevent removal or to achieve reunification, agencies cannot expose children to a high degree of risk of harm. In other words, reasonable efforts cannot become "unreasonable efforts." The original family may be important, but efforts to preserve it cannot unreasonably endanger children's health and safety.[26]

In pursuing the actual implementation of permanency planning concepts, Congress established aggressive time lines to achieve permanent placements.[27] For aggravated circumstances cases, the ASFA requires public agencies to seek the termination of parental rights within thirty days. For cases in which public agencies must make reunification efforts, the ASFA requires agencies to seek the termination of parental rights when children have spent fifteen of the last twenty-two months in foster care placements. Although the ASFA includes three large exceptions to the latter requirement, Congress sent a strong message that a primary goal of federal law is to achieve timely permanent placements for children.

Congress also appeared to alter the original placement priorities of permanency planning. Whereas return of children to their original homes had been the strongly preferred outcome, the ASFA shifts the emphasis to adoption as equally acceptable. Congress made this clear with the financial incentives surrounding adoption. The ASFA provides states with $4,000 per child adopted in excess of a benchmark figure determined by the particular state's adoption numbers in past years. (The amount is $6,000 per child if the adopted child is a "special needs" child, a definition met by many children in foster care.[28]) By significantly increasing the number of adoption outcomes, several states have been able to secure millions of additional dollars from the federal government. Congress sought such increases through the passage of the ASFA, and the law appears to be quite effective. In addition to the financial incentives, the law also requires public agencies to make reasonable efforts to secure timely adoption outcomes whenever adoption becomes the permanent placement goal in a case. This new provision signals the desirability of adoption in comparison to lengthy stays in foster care and even in comparison to reunification following what looks to be a lengthy parental rehabilitation. In enacting these provisions, Congress appears to view adoption outcomes, if not superior to family reunification, as equally desirable and certainly not troubling.[29]

The ASFA's adjustments to the reasonable efforts requirement and construction of adoption incentives indicate Congress's embrace of child well-being as the primary goal of public child welfare systems. Child rescue is the driving force. The rescue mentality allows public agencies to completely abandon efforts at family reunification in the most serious cases. In other cases, the agencies make efforts only to the extent these efforts do not place children at any significant risk. In addition, aggressively using adoption to make the rescue permanent is not troubling. In fact, such a permanent resolution is desirable if rehabilitation of the original parent is going to take more than twelve to eighteen months.

But the victory of the metanarrative of child well-being, as reflected in current federal law, is not absolute. The tension with the narrative of the private family remains. This is most apparent in the ASFA's three broad exceptions to the requirement that public agencies seek termination of parental rights whenever children have spent fifteen of the last twenty-two months in foster care, a provision intended to secure child well-being through timely permanent placements. Public agencies are not required to seek termination if they can present compelling evidence that such a course of action would not serve the best interests of the affected child, if the agency has failed to make adequate efforts to rehabilitate the particular parents and reunify the family, or if the agency has placed the affected child with relatives or kin.[30] The first exception could potentially apply to a large number of cases, especially those of older children who have formed a strong bond with their original parents. However, because of the ambiguous nature of the best interests of the child standard, the last two exceptions are most consistently operational within current public child welfare systems. Public child welfare agencies are often resource poor and unable to make serious efforts to reunify families. As a result, parents can frequently establish that agencies have failed to provide them with adequate services, delay termination of their rights, and gain another opportunity at reunification even if this disserves affected children.[31]

An even larger loophole to the ASFA's requirement is provided by the kinship placement exception. Many public agencies, especially in urban areas, place a large percentage of foster children with kin. This is a placement priority in current practice, and under the ASFA, such placements have the effect of suspending the time requirements for seeking the termination of parental rights and leaving children in harmful legal limbo.[32] Through the placement of children with their extended families and the delay of termination proceedings, the metanarrative of the private family prevails to a significant degree, even in a system reformed around the goal of securing child well-being. One could argue that Congress effectively pulled its punches and displayed a lack of conviction in drafting the ASFA in a way that hedged on child rescue.[33]

Another Look at Kim's Story

The tension between the two primary metanarratives is reflected in the case of Kim and her daughters. The immediate reaction of public officials upon receiving information that Kim had left her four- and three-year-old daughters unattended was one of child rescue. Kim admitted a substance abuse problem that apparently diminished her parenting abilities. Public officials viewed this situation as calling for removal of the children from their mother's custody in the name of child well-being.

However, the public agency tempered its rescue effort from the very beginning. Almost immediately, they placed girls with a relative—Kim's sister. The agency was not going to completely protect the girls from their original family. Although a more complete rescue and escape may have served child well-being more vigorously, the agency seemingly made an automatic, unthinking decision to jeopardize some degree of child well-being in order to maintain the girl's original family, albeit in extended form.

The agency's tempered rescue response is even more apparent in its decision to return the girls to their mother's custody within three months. At the time of removal, Kim had used cocaine for approximately seven years and had completed a drug treatment program that proved ineffective. Yet agency officials acted as though Kim had addressed her substance abuse problem within three months, at least to a degree that allowed her to be an adequate parent. Even with the intermittent supervision provided by the agency, this decision appears unwarranted, driven by unrealistic hope that the original private family could be quickly restored. This hope placed the girls at risk and set Kim up for failure as a parent. Kim likely still had a substance abuse problem that would affect her parenting.

Sure enough, the agency rescued the girls again within eighteen months of their return to Kim. Following a half-hearted attempt at family reunification, the pendulum swung back to a child rescue approach. This time agency officials were more serious, placing the girls in temporary foster care for a period that would extend over four years. However, the agency placed them with their maternal aunt, holding back from providing the girls with a full rescue and a clean break from their biological family. The narrative of the private family, albeit in extended form, remained as a significant force despite rescue efforts carried out in the name of child well-being.

In addition, the public agency did not close the door to family reunification. Apparently, the agency made services available to Kim. Although she continued to use cocaine, Kim participated sporadically in treatment services until her arrest three years after the agency had removed her daughters from her custody. The arrest and prospect of a jail term appear to be the events that truly motivated Kim to follow through with treatment. Following three years of erratic services and treatment failures, the criminal justice system provided Kim with an opportunity for rehabilitation and a strong, although belated claim for family reunification. In a pragmatic sense, the public agency had failed to rescue the girls, placing them at significant risk by simply presuming that kin placements are desirable and by leaving them in a legally temporary placement for several years.

As Kim began to make serious progress in treatment and appeared on a course to possible reunification with her daughters, the public agency became serious about protecting the girls. The agency actively sought a legally permanent placement for them—adoption by their maternal aunt who had proven able to provide adequate care. If achieved, the adoption, in the eyes of the law, would transform Kim into the role of the girls' aunt rather than their mother. The threat she posed by being able to rehabilitate herself and claim custody would effectively disappear.

This is the legal course of action the judge had to consider: Should she provide Kim with another year for rehabilitation, or should she end Kim's parental relationship with the girls so the aunt could adopt them? In the judge's reasoning, we again see the ever-present power of the private family ideal tempering the child rescue approach. She expressly refused to compare Kim's financial resources and parenting capabilities with those of her sister. In fact, the judge asserted that the foster mother is not entitled to custody simply because she possesses superior financial or parenting resources. The legal scheme the judge described is not one designed only to rescue the girls or to secure their well-being. If it was, the public system would not shy away from a direct comparison of homes and parents. It would also not accord such favor to original, usually biological, parents.

The judge did resist the force of the original family ideal that grows out of the private family concept. In the end, she did compare homes, finding that the stability of the aunt's home and care contrasted sharply with Kim's unstable history. This stability served the girls' interests, whereas Kim's situation left too much to doubt. The tipping point for the judge appears to have been the girls' desire to remain with their aunt permanently. It was not that Kim was completely without hope and incapable as a parent. The agency allowed Kim to have custody of her infant son Charles and the judge expressed hope for her continued rehabilitation. But placing the girls in Kim's custody would not serve their particular interests.

Reaching this permanent placement outcome for Katherine and Natalie took a long time. They essentially lived in temporary placements for over five years, bouncing from the custody of their mother to their aunt, back to their mother and finally to their aunt. For the last four years, they lived in the legal limbo of temporary foster care, never sure whether they would remain with their aunt or return to their mother at the whim of some public official. Because they were living with a relative, the law did not require the public agency to seek termination of parental rights and adoption. The law tolerated foster care drift that posed a risk of harm to the girls' healthy development.

The Result: Resource Poor Child Welfare Systems

The tension between the metanarrative of the private family and that of child well-being as represented by public rescue of maltreated children has led to the underresourced, schizophrenic public child welfare system currently in operation. On one hand, we are not sure if we want to preserve families that pose risks to particular children. This unsure commitment results in a shortage of family support services and the restrained, if not reluctant, provision of those services that do exist. On the other hand, we are uncertain if we want to rescue children from risky situations in order to secure their well-being. This uncertainty sometimes leads to a failure to remove children from dangerous situations and long delays in finding permanent placements for children who are unlikely to return to their original parents. It also may result in a possible overreliance on placement with kin who may not be able to provide adequate care. The overall result is children being buffeted within public child welfare systems, often becoming trapped for extended periods in temporary placements with parental figures who will not or cannot make a full, permanent commitment to them.[34]

The public child welfare system is a dysfunctional one that calls for escape. The irony is that the federal law is well designed and stands firmly on well-conceived principles of permanency planning. If fully implemented, the ASFA would provide children with a significant degree of safety, a good opportunity for reunification with their original parents, and the timely permanent resolution of their placement status, whether through reunification, adoption, guardianship, or formal long-term foster care.

Unfortunately, despite this conceptually sound design, the law fails in the trenches and in the everyday lives of children. Some children are left with parents who pose a significant risk to their health and safety. Others are removed from their parents' custody unnecessarily in situations where the provision of support services would make the original home safe and at least nominally adequate. Once removed, many children experience extended stays in temporary foster care placements, often going through multiple moves among foster homes and their original families. As the use of kinship foster care becomes prevalent, many children are left in temporary placement limbo for years, never certain what the next court hearing will bring.

The reason for this failure of public child welfare systems is the widespread and pervasive lack of resources.[35] Family support services and other preventive programs are in short supply and underfunded, often only being provided as part of a limited demonstration project. Substance abuse programs and other reunification services are also in short supply. Public child welfare agencies themselves are often understaffed, resulting in caseworkers carrying caseloads well in excess of those recommended for effective responses to situations that pose significant risks for children and effective long-term casework. The courts are also understaffed, with judges handling daily dockets that allow only ten to twenty minutes per case and with lawyers representing hundreds of clients.[36]

In this straitened environment, the service and adversarial systems are stretched to the limit and beyond. Effective case planning, practice, and supervision become impossible. To make matters worse, the families in poverty that are primarily affected by these resource-starved systems have no real political power. It is thus unlikely that the resource situation will change.

The Role of Child Advocates

Within this reality, the most effective device for escape is a knowledgeable, vigorous, yet tactful advocate. No other actor can be as helpful to children in their everyday lives within public child welfare systems. Child advocates can guide children through a dysfunctional system, securing the resources for their individual child clients that will allow them to leave the system permanently in a timely manner.[37]

This strategy boils down to providing children with a squeaky wheel who will speak up until public actors pay attention to a particular child and address his or her needs and interests. Of course, this strategy is not a prescription for systemic change. That is largely a hopeless endeavor in the short term—the period in which children must find solutions to their everyday problems.[38] However, it is a strategy that taps into the public's initial reaction to secure child well-being for children affected by abuse and neglect. Although the public fails to follow through on this initial reaction by funding public systems adequately, an advocate may have the opportunity to tap into the initial reaction and secure follow-through for his or her individual child clients.

Unfortunately, this approach does not provide relief to children in families that need services to provide minimally adequate care and remain intact. At this point, the concept of the private family prevails, and child advocates do not have direct access to children whom they may be able to help. And the public, despite official protestations, does not provide adequate resources to protect these children and families. But this is a long-term issue that must be addressed with care and delicacy because of the legitimate and valuable role played by the private family in a democratic society.[39]

The pressing issue with which child advocates can assist children begins once a particular private family allegedly fails to provide minimally adequate care for its child members. This is when our residual system takes action and children enter a public child protection system. This is also when child advocates come into play and can make a difference in the everyday lives of affected children.

Child Advocates in Action

Two case stories will help illustrate the power of aggressive child advocates to affect the lives of their child clients. The first concerns the zealous pursuit of termination of parental rights and adoption.[40] Jessica was an infant when she was brought to an emergency room with multiple fractures. Her fractures were not clean breaks; rather, they were caused by the intentional twisting of her limbs over a two-month period. Jessica's parents, both teenagers suffering from psychological problems, could not offer explanations for their daughter's injuries. Both parents had a history of failing to comply with mental health service programs, but they did not have substance abuse problems.

Upon assessing the case through extensive discussions with Jessica's physicians and investigation of the parents' records, Jessica's attorneys decided to immediately pursue termination of parental rights. Although the case arose years before the enactment of the ASFA, they decided to treat the matter as what now would be characterized as an "aggravated circumstances" case. In advocating for the infant's best interests, the attorneys determined that the public child welfare system need not attempt family reunification. In fact, such rehabilitation efforts would waste important public resources and would cause harm to their client. It would set their client on the typical path of foster care drift, dooming her to placement in temporary foster homes for years.

Instead, the attorneys immediately sought a stable, permanent placement in an adoptive home. They filed a petition seeking the termination of parental rights.[41] They conducted extensive discovery and witness preparation. During a three-day hearing before a juvenile court judge, they presented extensive evidence on the parents' unfitness and how termination of their rights would serve Jessica's best interests. In a written opinion that was subsequently affirmed on appeal, the judge ordered termination of the parents' rights. Within six months, Jessica's original foster family adopted her. But for her active advocates, Jessica would have experienced disruptive, likely fruitless reunification efforts and extended placement with parents who would not have been able to commit to her permanently. The advocates had a profoundly positive impact on Jessica's life.

The second case concerns six-year-old Tammy and her thirty-year-old mother, Jane. Jane has significant mental disabilities. Several psychologists have described her as functioning at the level of a six- to eight-year-old child. In contrast, Tammy is developing normally with no mental disabilities. In fact, Tammy and Jane interact more like friends or siblings close in age than they do like mother and daughter. Nonetheless, they are very close to each other, exhibiting a strong bond that seems to benefit both of them.

The public child welfare agency has removed Tammy from Jane's custody. Jane's husband Jason, Tammy's stepfather, had sexually abused Tammy. Jane has been unable to leave Jason because she depends on him both emotionally and economically. The agency's original plan was to work with Jane so that she could leave Jason and reunify with Tammy.

The attorneys appointed to represent Tammy spoke with her. She expressed a strong desire to live with her mother. Tammy missed Jane very much and did not like her current foster home because the other children teased her.

The attorneys' initial strategy was to push the child welfare agency caseworker to provide extensive services to Jane. They arranged for Jane to participate in a job training program and a parenting skills program. Both programs were designed to assist individuals with mental disabilities.

Jane participated fully in the programs, securing a job within three months. Although she was reluctant to leave her husband, she began exploring housing options that she could now afford with the agency's assistance. Unfortunately, she did not do well in the parenting classes. During visits, she continued to interact with Tammy as if they were peers and friends, not mother and daughter. She appeared incapable of providing adequate care for Tammy. The goal of reunifying Tammy and Jane so they could live on their own seemed completely unrealistic.

With this realization, Tammy's advocates began viewing Jane more as a sibling than as a mother. The agency's goal for closely bonded siblings would normally be to place them together in a foster home. The attorneys explored private foster care providers who would accept both Tammy and Jane, eventually finding one private agency that would provide such a joint placement.

Tammy and Jane were overjoyed at the prospect of this creative solution to their situation. The public child welfare agency, however, although supportive of the joint placement in concept, balked at providing financial support for Jane's placement in foster care. Because she was an adult, the agency was not obligated to provide such support.

Again, Tammy's attorneys went into action to overcome this final barrier to achieving a good result consistent with their client's desires. They brought the public mental health agency into the case, asserting that it had an obligation to support Jane's placement. The judge agreed. As a result, mother and daughter were able to live together, preserve their close bonds, and receive adequate support and care.

The public system would not have achieved this result absent the creative and vigorous advocacy of the child's attorneys. As with the earlier case of Jessica, this advocacy secured a breakthrough outcome within a resource-starved system. One answer for children caught up in current public child welfare systems is to engage skilled advocates who have the interest and time to focus on their specific cases. These advocates can be the squeaky wheel that demands the attention of system actors and service providers.

Finding an Advocate

Unfortunately, although children have legal rights to representation, this service is often provided by thinly trained attorneys who must manage huge caseloads, often approaching five hundred to one thousand child clients each.[42] Children and those interested in their well-being must become informed about the useful role an advocate can play and must find a means for securing an effective advocate.

A good starting point is to identify and contact local attorneys and legal services offices who represent children within public child welfare systems. In Pittsburgh, for example, KidsVoice provides vigorous representation for their child clients through a powerful attorney/social worker team model (see this chapter's appendix). Other areas have similar advocacy resources.

In addition, a local Court Appointed Special Advocates (CASA) program can provide effective advocacy. CASA programs train lay volunteers to advocate for children in public systems. Each advocate only handles one or two matters and thus can engage in thorough, creative advocacy. CASA programs exist in hundreds of jurisdictions throughout the United States.

If local advocacy programs are inadequate, high-quality national advocacy organizations are available to help. The American Bar Association's Center on Children and the Law, the Juvenile Law Center in Philadelphia, and the National CASA program in Seattle are examples of such organizations. Members of these organizations have played a pivotal role in the formation of good child welfare policy and legislation. They also provide useful assistance and guidance in specific cases, helping local advocates provide creative advocacy and, in some cases, providing direct advocacy themselves. Even if they cannot help directly, the members of these organizations are well connected to the leading child advocates and advocacy organizations. Thus, they can often direct others to appropriate resources.

Conclusion

In conclusion, the public's initial reaction to maltreated children is to secure their well-being. However, this initial reaction meets resistance in the form of the conflicting value of family privacy. Both the goal of child well-being and the concept of the private family are valid and beneficial, but this conflict provides an excuse not to dedicate the resources necessary to achieve either child well-being or autonomous private families in situations of child maltreatment. The public pursues neither goal or concept wholeheartedly, merely hoping that everything will work out on its own in the end.

Unfortunately, this hope does not serve children in their everyday lives within resource-starved public child welfare systems. These children need active, creative advocates who remind the public of the collective impulse to secure child well-being. If pushed, public systems can respond by providing necessary services and by securing stable, permanent homes for children who suffer abuse and neglect. Advocacy for individual children stands as a pragmatic vehicle for improving children's lives within conflicted, resource-poor public child welfare systems.

Notes

1. Although the names have been changed, this story is modeled on *In re Commitment of Kaicherise M. and Nakaya B.*, No. B 14422-3/02, 2003 N.Y. Misc. LEXIS 1193, *1 (Fam. Ct. 2003).

2. *In re Commitment of Kaicherise M. and Nakaya B.*, *9; N.Y. Soc. Serv. Law § 384-b(7) (Consol. 2005).

3. *In re Commitment of Kaicherise M. and Nakaya B.*, *9 (Fam. Ct. 2003); N.Y. Fam. Ct. Law § 611634 (Consol. 2005).

4. *In re Commitment of Kaicherise M. and Nakaya B.*, *9-10 (Fam. Ct. 2003); N.Y. Fam. Ct. Law § 611634 (Consol. 2005).

5. *In re Commitment of Kaicherise M. and Nakaya B.*, *17 (Fam. Ct. 2003).

6. David J. Herring, *The Public Family: Exploring Its Role in Democratic Society* (Pittsburgh: University of Pittsburgh Press, 2003), 7–8; David J. Herring, "Exploring the Political Roles of the Family: Justifications for Permanency Planning for Children," *Loyola University Chicago Law Journal* 26 (1995): 183; Alice C. Shotton, "Making Reasonable Efforts in Child Abuse and Neglect Cases: Ten Years Later," *California Western Law Review* 26 (1990): 223, 255.

7. See, for example, 42 U.S.C. § 5106f-1 (2003); 23 Pa. Cons. Stat. Ann. § 6311-19 (West 2001); Mass. Gen. Laws Ann., chap. 119, § 51A (West 2005).

8. See, for example, 42 U.S.C. §§ 617(a)(15), 672(a)(1) (2001); Mich. Comp. Laws § 722.638 (2005).

9. See, for example, 42 U.S.C. §§ 617(a)(15), 672(a)(1) (2001); Mich. Comp. Laws § 722.638 (2005). The United States Supreme Court has interpreted the Constitution to allow this approach. See *DeShaney v. Winnebago County Social Services Department*, 489 U.S. 189 (1989).

10. 42 U.S.C. §§ 617(a)(15), 672(a)(1) (2001); Robert M. Gordon, "Drifting through Byzantium: The Promise and Failure of the Adoption and Safe Families Act of 1997," *Minnesota Law Review* 83 (1999): 637, 677–79.

11. Marsha Garrison, "Why Terminate Parental Rights?" *Stanford Law Review* 35 (1983): 423; David Herring, "Child Placement Decisions: The Relevance of Facial Resemblance and Biological Relationships," *Jurimetrics Journal* 43 (2003): 387, 406.

12. Herring, "Child Placement Decisions," 401; Michael S. Wald, "State Intervention on Behalf of 'Neglected' Children: Standards for Removal of Children from Their Homes, Monitoring the Status of Children in Foster Care, and Termination of Parental Rights," *Stanford Law Review* 28 (1976): 623; David J. Herring, "Inclusion of the Reasonable Efforts Requirement in Termination of Parental Rights Statutes: Punishing the Child for the Failures of the State Child Welfare System," *University of Pittsburgh Law Review* 54 (1992): 139, 144; Peter J. Pecora et al., "Improving Family Foster Care: Findings from the Northwest Foster Care Alumni Study," http://www.casey.org/NR/rdonlyres/4E1E7C77-7624-4260-A253892C5A6CB9E1/300/nw_alumni_study_full_apr2005.pdf (finding that one in four foster children suffer from posttraumatic stress disorder).

13. See Sarah Ramsey, "Fixing Foster Care or Reducing Child Poverty: The Pew Commission Recommendations and the Transracial Adoption Debate," *Montana Law Review* 66 (2005): 21, 45–46.

14. Herring, "Political Roles," 197; Ramsey, "Fixing Foster Care," 42; Carol B. Stack, "Cultural Perspectives on Child Welfare," *N.Y.U. Review of Law & Social Change* 12 (1983–1984): 539, 545–47; Dorothy Roberts, *Shattered Bonds: The Color of Child Welfare* (New York: Basic Books, 2002), 228–29.

15. Herring, "Political Roles," 197; Roberts, *Shattered Bonds*, 8; "The AFCARS Report: Preliminary FY2001 Estimates as of March 2003 (8)" (U.S. Department of Health and Human Services, 2003) available at www.acf.hhs.gov/programs/cb/stats_research/afcars/tar/report8.htm.

16. Pub. L. No. 96-272, 94 Stat. 500 (1980).

17. 42 U.S.C. §§ 617(a)(15), 672(a)(1) (2001); Shotton, "Making Reasonable Efforts," 223.

18. 42 U.S.C. § 670; Shotton, "Making Reasonable Efforts," 223.

19. Herring, "Political Roles," 199; Shotton, "Making Reasonable Efforts," 237.

20. Herring, "Political Roles," 199.

21. Shotton, "Making Reasonable Efforts," 227; Herring, "Inclusion," 153–54; Dorothy E. Roberts, "Is There Justice in Children's Rights? The Critique of Federal Family Preservation Policy," *Pennsylvania Journal of Constitutional Law* 2 (1999): 112, 115.

22. David J. Herring, "The Adoption and Safe Families Act—Hope and Its Subversion," *Family Law Quarterly* 34 (2000): 329, 335–36.

23. Herring, "The Adoption and Safe Families Act," 343.

24. Pub. L. No. 105-89, 111 Stat. 2115 (1997).

25. 42 U.S.C. §§ 671(a)(15), 672(a)(1) (2001).

26. 42 U.S.C. § 671(a)(15)(a).

27. 42 U.S.C. §§ 675(5)(C), 675(5)(E), 671(a)(15)(E).

28. 42 U.S.C. § 673(b).

29. Roberts, *Shattered Bonds*, 149.

30. 42 U.S.C. §§ 675(5)(E)(i), 675(5)(E)(iii) (2001).

31. Herring, "The Adoption and Safe Families Act," 344–45.

32. See Herring, "The Adoption and Safe Families Act," 343; 42 U.S.C. § 675(5)(E)(i) (2001).

33. See Herring, "The Adoption and Safe Families Act," 343; Ira M. Schwartz and Gideon Fishman, *Kids Raised by the Government* (Westport, CT: Praeger, 1999), 124.

34. Herring, "The Adoption and Safe Families Act," 336, 347–48; Roberts, *Shattered Bonds*, 74.

35. Herring, "The Adoption and Safe Families Act," 343.

36. David J. Herring, "Legal Representation for the State Child Welfare Agency in Civil Child Protection Proceedings: A Comparative Study," *University of Toledo Law Review* 24 (1993): 603, 616–22.

37. Ann Moynihan et al., foreword to "Achieving Justice: Parents and the Child Welfare System," *Fordham Law Review* 70 (2001): 287, 313.

38. Herring, "The Adoption and Safe Families Act," 352–57.

39. Herring, "Political Roles," 203; Herring, "Public Family," 48–49.

40. Both case stories are based on the author's experience in representing children and parents in the child dependency system. The names have been changed.

41. Mich. Comp. Laws Ann. § 712A.19b (West 2005); Herring, "Inclusion," n. 89.

42. Herring, "Legal Representation," 616–22.

Appendix to Chapter 2
Illustrative Service Organizations That
Address the Public Child Welfare System

National

American Bar Association Center on Children and the Law
740 15th Street, N.W.
Washington, DC 20005
Phone: 202-662-1720
Fax: 202-662-1755
E-mail: ctrchildlaw@abanet.org
Web site: http://www.abanet.org/child/home2.html

The ABA Center on Children and the Law works as a training and advocacy resource for many areas of law affecting children. It supplies publications based on funded research, as well as collaborating with state courts on improvement of adjudication of child law issues.

Child Welfare League of America
440 First Street, N.W., 3rd Floor
Washington, DC 20001-2085
Phone: 202-638-2952
Fax: 202-638-4004
Web site: http://www.cwla.org

The Child Welfare League of America (CWLA) is a league of nonprofit and for-profit member organizations dedicated to the mission of protecting children. Its national office conducts research, publishes guides, manuals, and other works, and provides support to member organizations.

Juvenile Law Center
The Philadelphia Building, 4th Floor
1315 Walnut Street
Philadelphia, PA 19107
Phone: 215-625-0551
Fax: 215-625-2808
Web site: http://www.jlc.org/index.php

The Juvenile Law Center describes itself as a public interest law firm dedicated to protecting and advancing the rights and well-being of children in jeopardy. Its work ranges from abused and neglected children to delinquent youth and children with special education needs.

National CASA Association
100 W. Harrison
North Tower, Suite 500
Seattle, WA 98119
Phone: 800-628-3233
Fax: 206-270-0078
E-mail: inquiry@nationalcasa.org
Web site: http://www.nationalcasa.org

Court Appointed Special Advocates (also known as guardians *ad litem*) are lay volunteers who provide key support and advocacy for neglected and abused children both inside and outside the court. National CASA coordinates the efforts of local CASA organizations and provides them with training and consultation.

National Council of Juvenile and Family Court Judges
P.O. Box 8970
Reno, NV 89507
Phone: 775-784-6012
Fax: 775-784-6628
E-mail: staff@ncjfcj.org
Web site: http://www.ncjfcj.org

The National Council of Juvenile and Family Court Judges offers training for judges and other professionals intimately connected with the juvenile and family court system. Also, it has organized a list of model courts to drive reform in the juvenile courts around the country. In addition, the council's support of the Resource Center on Domestic Violence: Child Protection and Custody has provided information and resources to those working in this area.

Youth Law Center
417 Montgomery Street, Suite 900
San Francisco, CA 94104-1121
Phone: 202-637-0377
Fax: 202-379-1600
E-mail: info@ylc.org
Web site: http://www.ylc.org

The Youth Law Center is a nonprofit legal office dedicated to protecting abused and at-risk children. The center's staff investigates reports of abuse, protects the children assigned to foster care, and monitors system reform.

Examples of Law School Programs and Clinics

Michigan Child Welfare Law Resource Center
University of Michigan Law School
611 Church Street, Suite 4C
Ann Arbor, MI 48104-3000
Phone: 734-998-9191
Fax: 734-998-9190
Web site: http://www.law.umich.edu/CentersAndPrograms/childlaw/

The mission of the Michigan Child Welfare Law Resource Center is to "improve the legal system's handling of child-related cases through professional development." In addition to providing information and resources to those already in the field, the center places Michigan students interested in the field of child welfare law in agencies dedicated to that service, along with providing those students grants and training.

Children and Family Justice Center
Northwestern University School of Law
357 E. Chicago Avenue
Chicago, IL 60611-3069
Phone: 312-503-0396
Fax: 312-503-0953
E-mail: e-curtis@law.northwestern.edu
Web site: http://www.law.northwestern.edu/cfjc/

A legal clinic dedicated to serving children and families, the CFJC has a team of lawyers, social workers, and law students that engage individuals, organizations, and communities on specific and general child welfare issues and disputes.

Columbia Law School Child Advocacy Clinic
435 West 116th Street
New York, NY 10027-7297
Phone: 212-854-2640
Web site: http://www.law.columbia.edu/focusareas/clinics/
    childadvocacy

The Columbia Law School Child Advocacy Clinic serves child and family clients in need of a wide range of legal assistance, from child welfare to education and immigration. The students in the clinic work with the lawyers at the Juvenile Rights Division of the Legal Aid Society of New York City.

Examples of Local Organizations in an Urban Community (Pittsburgh)

Kidsvoice
700 Frick Building
437 Grant Street
Pittsburgh, PA 15219
Phone: 412-391-3100
Fax: 412-391-3588
E-mail: info@kidsvoice.org
Web site: http://www.kidsvoiceorg.com/

A full-service advocacy organization that provides a multidisciplinary approach to child welfare that includes legal and social services. Not only does the organization attempt to place children in appropriate homes and provide effective legal advocacy; it also uses its multidisciplinary approach to provide all the elements necessary for healthy childhood development.

Pennsylvania Community Providers Association
2400 Park Drive
Harrisburg, PA 17110
Phone: 717-657-7078
Fax: 717-657-3552
E-mail: mail@paproviders.org
Web site: http://www.paproviders.org

Pennsylvania Community Providers Association (PCPA) promotes community-based services to persons dealing with mental illness, drug abuse, or other related issues. Besides acting as an umbrella organization for community groups, it also acts as a forum for the exchange of information and as a legislative advocacy group. If someone is suffering from issues that, without assistance, could result in interaction with the public child welfare system, PCPA and organizations like it are good places to start the search for vital assistance.

Allegheny County CASA
564 Forbes Avenue, Suite 902
Pittsburgh, PA 15219
Phone: 412-594-3606
Fax: 412-594-3607
E-mail: info@pgh-casa.org
Web site: http://www.pgh-casa.org

A local chapter of the National CASA Organization (listed earlier), the Allegheny County CASA serves approximately five hundred children a year "by providing volunteer advocacy for the best interests of abused and neglected children within the child welfare system."

Allegheny County Juvenile Court Project
Allegheny Building, Suite 300
429 Forbes Avenue
Pittsburgh, PA 15219
Phone: 412-391-4467
Web site: http://www.acbfparentadvocates.org/

A project of the Allegheny County Bar Association, the Juvenile Court Project employs twelve attorneys who provide legal representation for low-income parents who are involved in dependency actions in juvenile court.

3
Welfare

We view Kate in July 1998 as she carries two large garbage bags full of clothes, papers, and various household items.[1] Kate's one young child tags along by grabbing onto the bags. Dan is four years old. Kate's other child mopes along about ten feet behind. Lisa is fourteen.

Kate and her children have just joined the ranks of the homeless in a major urban area. They had been evicted from their apartment because Kate could not pay the rent. Using six of their last $30, Kate put her family on a city bus destined for a temporary shelter that a neighbor had suggested.

Kate hustled her family into the dormitory-style shelter. They were all exhausted from the long, hot bus ride across much of the city. But they were also fortunate. The shelter had enough space to let them stay there while they began to pull their lives together.

Three months earlier, Kate's boyfriend had left her. Although he had abused her at times, he had always paid the rent. When he left, Kate tried to keep the apartment by offering to work for the landlord and pleading with him for extensions. His patience ran out quickly. Kate and her children were now without a home and in crisis.

Kate began by describing her situation to the shelter officials. She responded to questions about her extended family by stating that her mother had passed away fifteen years ago and that she did not know her father. She did have a brother, Mark, who lived in the suburbs, but she didn't speak with him regularly.

Upon learning about Kate's brother, the shelter officials informed Kate that she had to contact him. They told her that she and her children must live with him if at all possible, not in the shelter. Kate called Mark, and he agreed to have them live with him and his wife.

Lisa was extremely upset about the move to her uncle's home. She refused to leave the high school that she attended because all the friends with whom she had grown up were there. Kate arranged for Lisa to live with a friend in their old neighborhood so that she could stay in her school. She was very close to her daughter, and the separation would be extremely painful, but Kate believed it was the right thing to do.

Kate and Dan settled into Mark's house and kept in touch with Lisa through frequent phone calls. Mark disapproved of Kate's lifestyle and constantly criticized her choice of men and her impending dependency on welfare. Two months after she moved in, Mark asked her to leave. Kate was actually relieved as she packed and took Danny back to the shelter.

Kate spoke with a shelter official with the now common title of "fraud investigator." The focus of the public shelter program was to prevent people like Kate from taking advantage of public resources. The official urged Kate to return to her brother's home. Kate said that this was impossible, and the official allowed her into the shelter while he investigated her case.

Kate and Dan settled down in a rundown, dirty room with two beds. Lisa joined them. Kate and Lisa shared one bed. Dan took the other. They shared a bathroom with three other families and ate in the shelter cafeteria. While Kate was overjoyed to be reunited with Lisa, the living conditions were worse than she had imagined. Lisa suffered from headaches and depression. Dan just searched for places to play and discharge his unlimited energy.

After living in the shelter for a month, Kate contacted an advocate for the homeless. This pro bono attorney commanded respect, and within a month, the public authorities moved Kate and her children to a city housing project. The apartment building was relatively new and clean, with a children's play area and flower garden. The building was home to a health clinic, an employment office, and a day care center. As far as Lisa was concerned, the best thing about their new apartment was its location within her old school district.

The housing authority did regulate occupants, imposing an eleven o'clock curfew for adults, nine-thirty for children. Security guards manned the front door and searched residents' bags as they entered.

Ever since her boyfriend had left, Kate had tried to secure a welfare grant. She had visited the welfare center twelve times in the last four months, each time waiting several hours to meet with an official. At the first six meetings, public officials informed Kate that she needed to find a job and that she had not tried enough to find work. She needed to make this effort before she would be eligible for a welfare grant.

Kate began searching full-time for a job. Lacking any resources for day care for Dan, she left him with the person staying next to her in the housing project. Kate didn't know this young woman, but she worked nights and was available during the day until Lisa arrived home from school. She agreed to watch Dan temporarily.

Kate was at a real disadvantage in searching for employment. She had not graduated from high school, dropping out when her mother died and she became pregnant. Kate also did not have any work experience, having depended on her boyfriend's support as she cared for Dan and Lisa. As a result, she received no responses from employers after she filled out hundreds of job applications.

However, she carefully documented her job search. Eventually, it was enough to convince the welfare officials that she could not find paid employment. She finally completed the necessary application process and investigations. To her amazement, Kate began receiving welfare checks of $300 per month, plus $255 per month in food stamps. Combining all her resources, she now had public support of $6,660 per year plus her public housing grant. She would come to find that her grant was insufficient to support her family, but it seemed like a great victory and provided great relief. She dreamed of being able to care for her children, poor but surviving.

Receiving a welfare grant brought a great deal of public regulation into Kate's life. A series of city fraud investigators from the Welfare Verification Department visited her apartment and interviewed her and her children. They wanted to make sure Kate wasn't living with employable individuals who should not be receiving public support. A series of housing inspectors also visited her apartment to make sure that it satisfied all public regulations and that Kate was properly maintaining it. In addition, the public housing social worker visited regularly to check on Kate's housekeeping practices and food supplies. The social worker also examined Lisa and Dan closely in order to ascertain whether Kate was maltreating them in any way.

Kate's life had fallen under the public microscope because she received public support. The public support may have not been worth this price. It hardly provided enough to support one person, let alone a family of three. Kate's children went without a great deal. She could usually purchase or obtain from food pantries enough food to sustain her family. But there was certainly no room for costly enjoyments. Even basic expenses such as public transportation required careful budgeting.

As Kate learned to live within this tight budget, she became aware of the welfare time limits. The public fraud investigators informed her that she had a five-year lifetime limit.[2] After that period of public support, she would have to pay for everything herself. She felt pressure daily. In her mind, she had no margin for error.

Of more immediate concern was the welfare law's work requirement. As Kate's welfare worker explained, because the state had to have at least half of its recipients working for their benefits, Kate would have to find a job or work in the public works crew.[3] This latter option usually meant working on a street-cleaning crew for eight hours a day. Kate could not imagine herself in this demeaning role. She also had no idea who would care for Dan. Even if she could find an opening at an adequate day care facility, it was unlikely that she could afford it.

Facing all this pressure, Kate decided to enter a welfare-to-work program. She wanted to work. She didn't like welfare. Her plan was to find publicly supported day care for Dan, participate in the program, and find a good job.

Unfortunately, Kate could not find day care for Dan. All the day care centers in her area were full. It was virtually impossible for Kate to search for employment while caring for Dan. She had to find someplace to leave him.

It was not only her desire for work that drove Kate. She did not have a great desire to leave Dan with someone else all day as she pursued some type of employment. However, the welfare rules required her to look for paid work or else lose her benefits. The only other option was to work on a public works crew in exchange for her benefits. She would have to pursue this option within the next month, at which point caring for Dan and looking for a job would both be impossible. Kate desperately wanted to avoid this situation.

Kate began canvassing the neighborhood in order to find someone who could care for Dan on a regular basis. Laura lived in another unit of the public housing project with her husband and three children, all under the age of eight. Kate didn't know what Laura's husband did, but they never seemed to be hurting for money. Laura agreed to care for Dan while Kate looked for a job.

Freed of Dan, Kate pursued her job search with determination, filling out applications for numerous entry-level positions and even having a few interviews. But her lack of any real job skills became apparent when she filled out the application forms or spoke with a supervisor at a potential employer. Every evening brought a sense of defeat and despair.

The evenings were also filled with a despondent child. Dan became nonresponsive or agitated as Kate cared for him. She had never seen him act this way. It seemed like his energy was just escaping into the air. He was very different.

Kate initially thought the change in Dan was due to the separation from her and that he would get over it. However, after about a week with Laura, he began complaining about being there. He simply said that everyone was mean to him. Again, Kate thought Dan was just having difficulty adjusting to her absence during the day.

About three weeks into her intense job search, Kate arrived a half hour late to Laura's apartment. Dan was out in the hall, unattended. Loud noise was coming from the apartment, and Dan was crying relentlessly. Kate picked up Dan and peered into Laura's apartment. Laura was not around, but her boyfriend was there with four or five other men. They were smoking crack, partying, and paying attention to no one, certainly not Dan. Kate left determined never to leave her son there again.

At that moment, Kate knew that her effort to find a job before welfare officials required her to join a public works crew had failed. She visited the social worker from the public housing authority in tears, certain that she would be cleaning roads on a work crew until her five-year welfare period ran out and she and her children became destitute. Dan would grow up with another adult caretaker, not her. Lisa would either have to raise Dan after school or run wild without responsibilities or supervision. Either way, her progress in school would be in jeopardy. The world was crashing in on Kate. She had seen it happen to her friends, and now she had arrived at the same desperate point.

The social worker was new but showed an interest in Kate that was discernible from the minute they began talking. An active listener who quickly understood Kate's situation, she realized that Kate was intelligent, although uneducated, and wanted to improve her life and provide support for her children.

The worker snagged the phone and began calling job programs across the city, advocating strongly, even pleading for them to accept Kate. She was relentless. Within one hour she had secured a place for Kate in the New Paths program. This program had a good track record of training welfare recipients and placing them in entry-level jobs in time to meet the requirements for keeping welfare benefits.

Kate was ecstatic. She had truly found a public official who cared about her and would help her. She knew she was lucky to get into the New Paths program. She had heard about it and knew that it opened up opportunities. The program had a good day care on site, so Dan would be OK. She would put in a good day of training and be home for Lisa in the evening. She would get a job, keep her subsidized apartment, and start lifting herself off welfare.

The job training sessions at New Paths proved interesting and challenging. The instructors coached Kate endlessly on the smallest matters—her dress, makeup, manner of speech, and styles of interaction. She knew their focus was on making her a good interviewee as soon as possible. They had sixty days to place her successfully and collect their fee from the state.

While they transformed her for a successful job interview, they also monitored her parenting of Dan. The workers in the program's day care facility examined Dan and the other children closely, noting any physical marks such as bruises, cuts, and burns. They spoke endlessly to Kate about proper nutrition, the harms of corporal punishment, and the benefits of reading to small children. But the entire time, it seemed they were watching her closely, talking down to her, and passing judgment on her as a poor or inadequate parent. All of this instruction felt demeaning and intrusive, but Kate felt she had to cooperate and succeed.

However, Kate was more concerned about Lisa than Dan. No one was watching this teenage girl after school. She was running wild, exposed to all the bad characters in the neighborhood, to drugs, and to sex. Kate fretted over this situation but saw no way to avoid it. She felt that she was going to lose Lisa.

After six weeks, the New Paths program placed Kate in a temporary position as a cashier at a turnpike service plaza. Kate liked the job. She felt she was doing something productive and enjoyed interacting with the customers. The logistics worked for her, too. She could drop off Dan at the day care, catch a public car pool ride for the twenty-mile commute, work from 9:00 A.M. until 5:30 P.M., pick up Dan at 6:30, and be home by 7:00. The only member of the family who seemed to suffer was Lisa. Kate hoped that Lisa could handle the afternoons on her own, but she was extremely nervous and anxious about this situation. Lisa seemed to be doing all right, but Kate knew she was at a vulnerable age for losing her way.

Within a week of starting the temporary job, Kate's supervisor asked her to apply for a permanent position. He handed Kate a questionnaire and asked her to fill it out. He also told her to go to a health clinic for a drug test. Kate answered the questions, noting that it was pretty easy to get the "right" answer. ("True or false: getting high at work helps relieve stress and makes you a better worker"; "How much is OK to take from the cash register for personal use? $100, $50, $10, none.") She also went to the clinic, supplied a urine sample, and was found not to have drugs in her system. Her supervisor was thrilled with this result because this is the step where most of his welfare recruits failed. Kate got the job and immediately felt a sense of relief. Her welfare clock had stopped running. She and her children could gain some stability and pride.

Unfortunately, her supervisor immediately changed her to the night shift. While she could spend more time with Dan and Lisa, she did not look forward to working from 10:00 P.M. to 6:00 A.M. every day. She did not deal well with little sleep, but it was a take-it-or-leave-it proposition. Adding to the anxiety was the fact she had no assurance that her schedule would not change again.

In addition to the scheduling problems, Kate's new job had several troubling aspects. While the salary seemed pretty good at $7.50 per hour, she would not receive any health benefits. Her public health benefits were minimal, and the hassle of long lines and bureaucratic paperwork effectively eliminated preventive care. Unless she or one of her children suffered a health emergency, Kate's health policy was simply to have everyone stay healthy or at least not complain.

Kate's new job also did not appear to offer any path to career advancement. She was a service employee at the lowest level of the economic ladder in the United States. She would remain in this position indefinitely.

Still, Kate felt lucky to have the job. Unfortunately, problems arose within a few weeks that made the other difficulties fade from her mind. The night shift staff did not welcome her. They gave her the dirtiest, hardest tasks and would not talk with her except to order her around. The supervisor was unwilling to help her, and she felt like an outcast. She dreaded going to work because the other workers watched every move she made and filed a formal report for every mistake. Kate's work environment was extremely stressful.

Kate's situation at home was not helping. She was always tired and slept a great deal. Dan just wandered aimlessly in the apartment or sat in front of the television. Kate fed and bathed him, but she did not play with him, read to him, or interact with him in any sustained way. Kate simply used Lisa for parenting relief after she returned home from school. Lisa took care of Dan and made dinner, with any leftover time used for doing homework, watching television, and hanging out in the neighborhood, although most of the hanging out took place after Kate had left for work. Kate knew what Lisa was doing but did not have the energy or the will to discipline or control her.

The stress from her work environment and her family situation took its toll on Kate. Her blood pressure became very high. She went to a community health clinic and obtained a prescription for blood pressure medication. However, she could not afford to purchase the medication. Kate also began to suffer from depression. Because she could not afford appropriate medical care, she descended into a real health crisis. She missed numerous days of work. Eventually, her supervisor informed her that he had decided to fire her. She just could not perform her duties in a reliable manner.

Kate was actually quite relieved when she was fired. She could feel the stress melt away. She had new energy and new hope.

Unfortunately, this feeling did not last long. She was back to square one except she now had even less time before she reached her lifetime welfare benefits limit. It still seemed like she had a long time before she reached the limit, but her experience during the past year made her realize just how difficult it would be to support herself and her family exclusively through her employment. At times she panicked at the thought of being on her own with no more public support.

This sense of panic, combined with the disruption brought about by Kate's unemployment, adversely affected Dan and Lisa. They could sense that their mother was extremely anxious. She didn't play with Dan. She constantly embarrassed Lisa in front of her friends. Kate was checking out on them, and they sensed the neglect. Dan simply learned to entertain himself, while Lisa set her mind to escaping the family as soon as possible, even if it meant ending her formal education. In the end, Kate and her children were hanging on, but they were all seriously harmed by a public welfare system that provided little support.

The Impact of Federal Public Welfare Law

Kate's chaotic experience is fairly typical of those dependent on public welfare today. The reform of public welfare laws has exacerbated this situation for families and children in poverty. Enacted in 1996, the Personal Responsibility and Work Opportunity Reconciliation Act replaced the Aid to Families with Dependent Children (AFDC) program with the Temporary Assistance to Needy Families (TANF) program.[4] The TANF provisions and requirements drastically altered the management of public welfare systems and the lives of those in poverty.

The most fundamental change in the move from AFDC to TANF lies in the nature of federal funding. Under AFDC, qualified individuals had an entitlement to federal benefits. TANF replaced this federal entitlement program with a block grant program.[5] In pragmatic terms, this means that individuals and families in poverty do not have direct claims to federal welfare funds. Instead, federal funds flow to the states, which then implement their own welfare programs.

The Work Requirement

This new funding structure provides states with a great deal of leeway, although they do have to meet several federal requirements in order to receive their grants. For example, states must require welfare recipients to work or to participate in work-related activities as a condition to receiving benefits for a period not to exceed five years.[6] Once these requirements are met, states can design their own systems that set stricter time limits on benefits, determine eligibility criteria, define work requirements, identify the services and support to provide recipients, and impose standards of behavior on recipients.[7] The result is fifty separately designed welfare programs receiving federal funds. The core idea of the federal law is to encourage states to experiment with new approaches and programs in this area.

The federal law does provide some incentives that affect states' behavior as they experiment with new approaches. First, it allows states to keep all the welfare funds they save with their new approaches. If states can reduce welfare costs, they will reap a financial benefit because they will still receive the entire federal block grant.[8] This gives states a powerful motivation to cut the costs of their welfare programs through a reduction in either recipients or programs. In addition, states suffer penalties if they do not have enough welfare recipients engaged in qualified work activities.[9] This provision gives states a powerful incentive to require recipients to work in some form.

The federal requirements and policies also affect children in several areas. For example, one goal of the previous AFDC program was to provide support for single mothers so that they could stay home and dedicate their efforts to caring for their children.[10] In contrast, the TANF program requires parents receiving welfare to leave the home in order to engage in work. A specified proportion of welfare recipients must be engaged in paid employment, unpaid work experiences, or community service.[11] If a recipient fails to meet the work requirement, she or he will lose welfare benefits. The result for children of welfare recipients is that they will spend less time with a parent, or they will live with a parent in profound poverty without the hope of public support.

Kate and her children experienced this aspect of TANF. The state agency required Kate to work, in a paying job, in a training program, or on a public works crew. As a result, Dan and Lisa could not spend much time with Kate. Dan experienced a series of babysitters and day care providers. At a critical point in his development, he lost his mother, and she was not replaced by a quality caregiver who would develop a strong, stable attachment to Dan. Lisa largely had to care for herself, and sometimes for Dan, too. At a critical stage of her development, which called for adult supervision and attention, the public system effectively left her to fend for herself. She became fully exposed to the negative peer influences that affect young teenage girls, frequently leading to pregnancy, educational failure, and delinquency.

The Time Limit

Note, too, that AFDC did not limit the amount of time individuals could receive welfare benefits. In contrast, TANF limits each recipient to five years of benefits over his or her entire life.[12] (The states can place a stricter limit on recipients.) This requirement results in individuals who otherwise meet all eligibility requirements yet are completely denied welfare benefits, a very threatening prospect. For a group of individuals experiencing profound poverty, no minimal floor of public support awaits them.

The time limit requirement affects children in important ways. For instance, it places great stress on parents, some of whom cannot become self-supporting within the designated period, if ever. Kate may fall into this group. Despite her best efforts, she could not maintain her employment. She appears destined to bounce back and forth between periods of low-wage employment and unemployment. Eventually, she will run up against the time limit, after which she and her family will no longer be entitled to receive any public support. At that point, Dan and Lisa will suffer public abandonment within a family experiencing profound and devastating poverty.

Even if Kate succeeds in finding permanent, stable employment before reaching the applicable time limit, she will live under a great deal of stress. Bear in mind that Kate is in a better situation than many welfare recipients. She has no major physical or mental health problems. She is fairly intelligent, although lacking in formal education. She has a good attitude about finding work and does not have a substance abuse problem. However, even with all her advantages, the inadequacy of her wages and public support will make life very difficult. She will have to struggle every day just to provide basic items for herself and her children.

All of this stress caused Kate health problems and employment disruption. It certainly affected Dan and Lisa. When Kate could spend time with her children, she was uptight and short-tempered with them. Her focus was on managing the logistics of an increasingly complex life, including day care, unsupervised children, and a shifting work schedule that brought her to the brink of exhaustion. She had no time for herself, and the time she spent with her children could scarcely be characterized as quality time.

The Paternity and Child Support Requirement

The federal law also requires the states to adopt aggressive programs and measures to establish paternity and to collect child support.[13] The goal is to establish paternity for children of welfare recipients as soon as possible. Once a child's father has been identified, the state system is to work to secure child support payments, with a significant portion of any payment going to compensate the state for welfare expenditures. Only a portion of any payment supports the father's child and benefits the child's family.[14]

Public officials did not require Kate to pursue child support from Dan's or Lisa's fathers. Kate knew about this possible requirement when she applied for welfare benefits. It almost caused her not to apply. She had heard horror stories from other women about abusive partners demanding contact and visitation with their children upon being compelled to pay child support. Both fathers were abusive, physically violent men who would not be a positive influence. They could seriously disrupt Kate's and her children's lives.

Because of her worries, Kate simply filled in the father's names and indicated that she did not know where they lived. The welfare officials never asked her about the fathers, and she said nothing. This appeared to be bureaucratic failure, one that pleased and relieved Kate. However, this looming requirement did add to Kate's stress. She was always worried this failure would be noticed and that she and her children would be forced to deal with these men without receiving any real benefits or protection from them.

Support for Child Care

The federal law also reorganizes financial arrangements for supporting child care programs by consolidating separate funding streams into a single Child Care and Development Block Grant.[15] In addition, Congress has increased the funds available to support child care programs through two mechanisms. First, Congress increased the direct funding allocation for this purpose. Second, Congress authorized states to transfer TANF block grant funds to child care program support.[16]

Despite this increased support, the federal law no longer requires states to guarantee the provision of child care. Thus, it falls within the discretion of the various states whether they will provide adequate child care to low-income working parents.[17] And although the block grants increase funding for child care programs, they do not provide enough support to subsidize child care for all the families that will need it as a result of the work requirements. The result for welfare recipients is a severe shortage of child care programs and services.

Kate confronted this difficult situation in trying to arrange care for Dan and Lisa. Kate could not find adequate care for Dan, leaving him in the care of a neighbor who had significant family burdens and problems of her own. The neighbor neglected Dan and put him at significant risk of harm. If public officials had discovered Dan's situation, it is likely they would have acted to protect him, possibly by removing him from Kate's custody. Because of the lack of quality child care services, Kate's family could easily become enmeshed in a demoralizing and debilitating public child welfare system.[18]

The difficulty in finding adequate care for Dan impaired Kate's capacity to search for employment. She could not submit applications and participate in interviews with Dan accompanying her. But if she left him with marginal care providers, her mind would fill with worry and anxiety. Kate found it very hard to focus on the task at hand while worrying about Dan. This situation certainly handicapped her in presenting herself as a competent, energetic, and engaged job applicant. The high-quality child care eventually provided at her public housing facility was essential to Kate's success in participating in job training and in finding employment.

As to Lisa, Kate simply assumed that Lisa was old enough to take care of herself. She knew that young teenagers were vulnerable to peer influences that could lead them to ignore their schoolwork, abuse drugs, and engage in sexual activity. However, Kate felt that she could not afford child care for two children. In addition, Lisa would likely refuse to participate in child care because other children her age were largely left on their own. Kate wasn't up to fighting with Lisa about this point.

Kate also felt that Lisa could provide adequate care for Dan after school when Kate was working. This arrangement would save Kate from paying for a full day of child care, and it became essential when Kate's employer assigned her to the night shift. Kate relied on Lisa to care for Dan throughout the night and the early morning. She knew this situation was risky, but she felt she had no choice.

As with Dan, the arrangements for Lisa placed Kate in a situation that presented a significant risk of coming to the attention of the public child welfare agency. All it would take is for something to go wrong with Lisa's care of Dan while Kate was at work (e.g., a house fire, Lisa leaving Dan alone while she went out with friends), and public officials would likely launch an investigation. Of course, this situation added significantly to Kate's stress. More important, it placed Lisa and Dan at significant risk, possibly constituting inadequate parental care. It was not likely to foster or result in their healthy development.

Inadequate Support and Punitive Measures

An important drawback of the federal law is its failure to require states to provide an adequate level of financial support for welfare recipients or to create programs that adequately support those trying to manage the transition from welfare to self-sufficiency. One goal of Congress in enacting the Personal Responsibility Act's work requirements was to increase the financial resources parents can devote to the support of their children.[19] President Bill Clinton captured this hope in his statement that "the best antipoverty program is still a job."[20] As researchers Thomas Gais and Cathy Johnson put it, "This approach to child well-being requires not only that mothers get jobs that pay at least as much as they might receive in cash assistance and Food Stamps lost as their earnings increase, but also that they receive adequate support services, such as child care and transportation assistance, to make up for the increased costs of going to work."[21]

Unfortunately, Congress did not make provision for these services. In creating TANF programs, most states have focused on achieving a significant reduction of caseloads by getting welfare recipients into paid employment, not on ensuring that families will have either adequate financial support or a realistic course for pulling themselves above the poverty line. Gais and Johnson describe a typical state's approach:

> Wisconsin, for instance, institutionalizes caseload decline as the major and overriding goal. Mothers who apply for benefits and are deemed to be employable may not receive cash assistance. They may receive Food Stamps, child care, Medicaid, case management, and job services; but the only cash they get is what they earn, and they are not considered to be "cases" under *Wisconsin Works* counting rules.[22]

They also note how states generally discourage families in poverty from combining wages and cash assistance, with the consequence of driving these families away from welfare programs. The state bureaucracies and processes are overly complex and burdensome, with numerous requirements such as job searches, orientation programs, and complex application forms. In addition, many states are greatly pre-occupied with potential fraud. They require extensive earnings information and have even implemented highly intrusive home visit programs. In the end, the new welfare programs make "welfare a hassle, as well as a helping hand."[23] The effect is to discourage not only families seeking cash assistance but also those seeking other forms of public support such as Food Stamps and Medicaid.

Because of the significant hassle, many families in poverty decide not to seek cash assistance. This is especially true in states that provide relatively low levels of cash support.[24] Even if the particular state system in theory makes it possible to receive cash assistance and not to lose all of it as a recipient begins to earn wages, for many it is not worth the trouble and frustration. The cash assistance does not raise a family out of poverty, yet it requires a substantial investment of time and effort, and it invites a high level of public intrusion. A seemingly rational reaction to this situation is for a parent to avoid the welfare program, thus increasing the number of children in poverty.

In addition to the low levels of cash assistance provided to qualifying families in poverty and the administrative barriers to qualifying for public support, the federal program contains a scheme of sanctions for families on welfare. Welfare officials impose sanctions in order to enforce a recipient's attendance at orientation meetings, participation in job search programs, and cooperation with child support efforts and orders.[25] The amount of an initial sanction varies from state to state. Gais and Johnson note that Minnesota imposes a 10 percent initial penalty while Arizona imposes a 25 percent initial penalty, with a complete cutoff of benefits following a third sanction.[26] In addition, states must impose a lifetime ban on all TANF and food stamp benefits for any individual convicted of a felony related to controlled substances.[27]

Although the sanctions are primarily targeted at altering the individual recipient's behavior, the impact is felt by every member of the recipient's family, including children. Sarah Ramsey has vividly and effectively described the burden of avoiding sanctions:

> Caregivers who had the most complex and challenging daily lives were more likely to have experienced a partial or full loss of benefits. Being able to turn forms in on time or to follow up with doctors' offices or employers' personnel offices requires keeping up with the mail; noticing and adhering to deadlines; and reading, interpreting, and responding to

questions—all of this by mothers who may have lower skill levels and poorer health in addition to raising a family and working. Only twelve percent of the sanctions were imposed because the caregiver refused to take a job or show up for a job-related activity. One recipient, for example, missed the filing deadline for a monthly form that reported income, work hours, and household data. The recipient was not avoiding work, but rather was working full time. Her noncompliance was due to factors such as the following:

> [She] could not read well; her caseworker did not speak her native language, Spanish; and her phone had been disconnected for part of the time—all of which led to communication difficulties. She had never received pay stubs before, and she had difficulty completing the week-by-week income section. She also had other sources of stress that caused her to neglect the form: in addition to holding a job that required a daily three-hour commute, she cared for six children and one grandchild, and had a boyfriend who was threatening her with violence.[28]

It is important to note that sanctions can arise from behavior that does not violate any formal welfare program rules. Some states require welfare recipients to enter into "personal responsibility agreements" that may include provisions that are very intrusive and go well beyond formal welfare requirements. Breaches of components of the agreement, or simple failures to cooperate, can provide a basis for the imposition of sanctions.[29]

The worst sanctions may be those that target children who have children. The federal law requires that teenage mothers live at their parents' home if they want to receive TANF benefits.[30] Although it contains an exception if the teenage parent can prove that living at home would not be safe, many teenage parents will be trapped in their parents' home if they want benefits for themselves and their children. In some cases, this scenario will result in a highly negative, stressful environment for the teenage mother and her child.

Finally, the federal law allows states to impose a scheme of family caps. Such schemes deny or limit benefits to unmarried women who give birth to additional children while on welfare.[31] Numerous states have developed such schemes in an effort to control women's behavior.[32] However, when these schemes fail to alter behavior, they result in even more severe poverty for children within affected families.

Kate and her family felt some of the effects of complex, overly bureaucratic state welfare systems that fail to provide adequate support and that impose financial sanctions for failure to comply with various program requirements. First, Kate had difficulty in applying for benefits—difficulties that likely would have dissuaded many applicants from pursuing benefits. Once Kate received benefits, she barely had enough to provide housing, food, and other needs for herself and her children. She certainly had no opportunity to save for the future or to plan financially for predictable problems and crises.

In addition, Kate felt the constant pressure of program requirements. Although she would have preferred to stay home with her children, that was not an option. In addition, she had to quickly get into a job preparation program. Otherwise, the state would have forced her to work in a humiliating and dead-end community service job. Once she completed the job preparation program, Kate had to find paid employment. Haunting this entire effort was the threat and stress of possible sanctions. It would be devastating if she lost a portion of her cash assistance for failing to comply with any aspect of the welfare program. The state would effectively place Kate and her children in a deep financial hole from which they may never escape as an intact family.

The most frustrating aspect of the whole situation was Kate's job. Not only did she have to work with people she did not like, but she had no pathway for advancement. The job was truly dead-end in nature. Kate could foresee no promotions and certainly no raises that would allow her to lift her family out of poverty. She would work the night shift forever, and no matter how hard she worked, she would not realize any real improvement in her life. Dan and Lisa would grow up in poverty—that was not going to change. All that seemed to be different was that she would not be caring for her children. Discouraged with her prospects and her dead-end job, Kate lost her job and exposed her family to financial pressures and possible sanctions. She and her children seemed to be truly trapped in poverty, running on a treadmill and never getting ahead.

The Two Family Metanarratives

The system of public welfare is a product of the public's initial reaction to assist those experiencing poverty and assure that every individual receive adequate food, shelter, and educational services. This appears to be an especially strong sentiment with regard to children in poverty. At least initially, these children are viewed as part of society's future. As such, their well-being is considered important. The narrative of child well-being comes into play and elicits a strong emotional reaction supporting public assistance.[33]

However, this sentiment fades quickly. The public does not seem to perceive the adult parents who care for children in poverty as deserving of public assistance. In fact, many argue that this type of public assistance actually harms these adults because it takes away their incentive to find paid employment and to become self-sufficient.[34] Without true engagement in the economy and the pride that results from being employed, adults who depend on public support fall into a depressing pattern of laziness and lethargy. Thus, many view welfare recipients as deviant—standing outside normal, productive society.

The Dominance of the Metanarrative of the Private Family

This perception of adult welfare recipients activates the competing narrative of the private, self-sufficient family in a very powerful way. Parents should be fully responsible for supporting their own children without public support. They should be fully engaged in paid employment, thus minimizing the burden on the public.[35] Their role is to mask the dependency of their children. They are to be "personally responsible"—the concept expressed in the title of the federal welfare law.

Of course, the concept of personal responsibility does not only appear in the law's title. It pervades every important provision. Its exact meaning is not immediately apparent. However, an examination of the law's provisions taken as a whole, and their implementation by state officials, allow one to see the type of personal responsibility and type of private family that the state has in mind.

Gais and Johnson provide useful and telling insights into the federal law that allows one to describe the parental and family ideal being sought. Specifically, they identify three policy theories that relate welfare program practices to the interests of children in poverty:

(1) the *family structure theory* contends that children benefit from being born only to families who are able to care for them, specifically, *not* to unmarried couples or teens, and that teen and unmarried women should not have families; (2) the *resource theory* holds that

children benefit from increased resources, such as income obtained as caregivers enter and progress in the workforce; and (3) the *environment theory* maintains that children reap psychological and sociological benefits from being part of a family environment in which the head of the household works.[36]

The federal law includes elements of all three of these approaches. The law's embrace of these theories indicates that the desired private family is one that features two married adult parents who have the capacity to provide care to their children. An important component of providing adequate care is the provision of sufficient financial resources, which parents are responsible for providing on their own, without resort to public support. This means that at least one of the parents must enter the workforce and secure paid employment. By doing so, parents serve as appropriate role models for their children. Children witness a parent fully engaged in the economy and society. Hopefully, they will benefit from a structured, better-functioning home environment and begin charting their own course of productive social and economic activity.[37]

In reviewing the design and implementation of state programs formulated in response to the federal law, the same two scholars note that states are really not pursuing the family structure theory. Other than using family caps to discourage welfare recipients from bearing additional children and complying with the federal law's direct requirement that teenage parents live in their parents' home, the states have done little to actively promote marriage or to limit pregnancies among teens and unmarried couples.[38] While adopting family caps costs little (in fact, it may save public funds), programs designed to change marital or reproductive behavior often are costly. The states have largely refused to incur these costs.

Gais and Johnson also note that states do not appear to be seriously pursuing the resource theory. They observe that many states have not effectively connected their TANF programs with other service systems such as support entitlements and workforce development programs. This aspect of system design implies "that low income families will not be able to combine earnings with public benefits and services for very long or with much ease."[39] However, research indicates that a dynamic combination of earnings and public support is necessary to raise low-income families out of poverty.[40] The states' focus on simply reducing the number of individuals receiving cash assistance and other public benefits by requiring them to work for low wages in what are often dead-end jobs indicates an indifference to, if not rejection of, the goal to secure child well-being through an increase in family resources.

Gais and Johnson conclude that states are primarily pursuing the environment theory. Welfare programs now stress work requirements in a vigorous and serious way. As they put it, "work and work-like activities are strongly promoted and facilitated, whether or not they result in increased overall income."[41] Parents receive guidance and support in finding entry-level, low-wage jobs, and little else. The states expect parents to utilize this support to move off the welfare rolls and to raise their children so that they become productive members of the economy and society.

Bear in mind, the environment theory depends on several unsupported assumptions. It assumes that work by the head of household will make for a more structured, orderly life at home, not a chaotic or stressful one; that a working parent is a better parent, one who feels greater control over her life, greater independence, and a greater competence that carries over into her family roles; and that children will be well taken care of in reasonably safe and nurturing child care centers and other facilities.[42] Of course, the environment theory also depends on the parent being employable, psychologically healthy enough to provide adequate child care, and able to find affordable, high-quality child care programs in the local area.

These assumptions and necessary conditions place a great burden on parents in poverty and their families. In combination with the public rhetoric produced by the family structure theory and the resource theory, the environment theory brings a certain type of private family ideal into stark focus. Parents should be adults. Parents should be married or at least live together. At least one of the parents should be employed and earning a wage that allows for adequate support for their children without welfare or other public assistance. Parents should provide a home that is well organized and structured, one that is stable and predictable. Parents should serve as positive role models for their children, inspiring proper development and, eventually, full engagement in a democratic society and market economy.[43]

This public ideal makes clear the dominance of the metanarrative of the private family in the area of welfare law and policy. The federal law pushes states to reform their welfare systems around this metanarrative. It assumes, without any real empirical support, that this ideal will benefit children. It is more a comforting, familiar ideology than proven method.

With this dramatic embrace of the ideal of the private family, the public's initial reaction powered by the metanarrative of child well-being is overwhelmed. The public goal of rescuing children from harmful poverty gives way to a more limited effort merely to secure a certain type of private family for each child. If parents do not respond to an adequate degree, the state leaves children to suffer in poverty.[44]

Revival of the Metanarrative of Child Well-being

This suffering, if it becomes apparent to the public and its authorized agents, may be children's ultimate hope for gaining relief from poverty. It provides an opportunity to revive the narrative of child well-being. Children in families that do not come close to achieving the desired ideal need help. The public is inclined to help. If many see the reality of child poverty, it is possible that they can overcome their comforting ideology and act to provide support for children in poverty.

This is especially true if one can focus public actors on specific cases. The narrative of child well-being exerts real power when one views the situation of a particular family in poverty. Everyone knows of the harms of poverty in general, but they are truly compelling in situations where particular children lack adequate food, clothing, housing, or educational resources. Thus, if parents, children, and their advocates can present their specific situation to public actors, they are more likely to gain relief.

The Need for Professional Advocates.   It is important to recognize that parents and children often cannot be effective in pursuing their own interests and resources within public welfare systems. They are not trained in the bureaucratic intricacies of the system or knowledgeable about the extent of their rights, their interests, and available support services. This is why many families in poverty that qualify for cash assistance, food stamps, and other public support do not receive much of the support to which they are entitled.[45] To require parents and children to carry their own advocacy burden within a complex public system constitutes a reliance on the private family ideal in a setting where it makes little sense. It stretches concepts of parental responsibility beyond any reasonable bounds.

Current public welfare systems cross this line of reasonableness when they decentralize the provision of public benefits and effectively hide the ball from families in poverty. Within such a severe, bureaucratic public benefits environment, only professional advocates can effectively make a powerful case for support for specific families.[46] They can actively assist parents and children in overcoming bureaucratic hurdles to cash assistance and other support services. For example, advocates can assist specific individuals in locating appropriate public offices, filling out necessary forms, and making sure that cases proceed in a timely manner. Advocates can also work to ensure that families are aware of and can pursue all possible public benefits, leaving no resources on the table, simply allowing them to revert back to the public coffers. In this way, advocates in this area would serve a role similar to that served by professional tax preparers used by affluent families. These tax preparers help assure that individuals and families pay no more taxes than required. Similarly, public benefits advocates would make sure that individuals and families receive the resources to which they are entitled and that they do not contribute unnecessarily to the state.

This type of advocacy is probably the most immediate hope for families and children in poverty. It is the best means to secure rights, interests, and resources within a resource-starved system powered by the narrative of the self-sufficient private family. It is also the best way to tap into and unleash the countervailing force of the metanarrative of child well-being.

The question for parents and children in poverty is how to do this. Unfortunately, it is up to them. The public has not funded proactive public benefits advocates.[47] Thus, to a significant degree, the private family ideal dominates this course of action, too.

Still, parents and children in poverty can work to find help. They can approach local legal services offices or law school clinic programs that provide direct advocacy assistance or may be able to refer them to other advocacy organizations. They can also approach public service providers. Many individual employees in these organizations are highly skilled and care a great deal. Finding these special people may be the best thing that could happen for a family in poverty and is definitely worth the effort. In addition, if the family is at risk to enter the public child welfare system, a local CASA program may be willing to provide intensive advocacy services. The goal is to secure a zealous advocate—someone who can guide the family to public resources and push every aspect of the public welfare system to provide the resources and services necessary to secure child well-being.

The Hope for System Reform.   Of course, this advocacy strategy for the short term does not preclude a long-term strategy of system reform. All families with children, whether they fit the ideal or not, need adequate resources in order to avoid the hopelessness and harms of poverty. Working parents and their families need cash assistance that will work to supplement low wages for entry-level jobs to a degree that lifts them out of poverty. They also need access to affordable, high-quality child care programs. In addition, they need knowledge of, and effective means to obtain, entitlements such as food stamps and Medicaid. Finally, parents need jobs that allow for advancement—in terms of both wages and types of work assignments. They need a work environment that provides a path out of poverty and hope for personal success.[48]

Unfortunately, as Sarah Ramsey notes, "These are not new issues. The problem in the United States is not the lack of knowledge about these issues, but rather the lack of will to resolve them."[49] Family and child advocates must work constantly for the type of system reform that will provide families in poverty with a path out of poverty and financial instability. This requires strategic and astute lobbying that makes a compelling case for increased public investment in children and their immediate caregivers, most often their biological parents. This is the only way to truly transform the everyday lives of children trapped in poverty.

Conclusion

The system of public welfare is a bureaucratic maze that, even when properly navigated, provides severely inadequate resources to families and children in poverty. The core principle underlying this system is that families should become quickly self-sufficient and fully able to fulfill the private family ideal without public support. However, this ideal is often unobtainable without increased public support. In the short term, the most effective strategy for addressing this situation is to secure for a particular family a professional advocate who can work effectively within a reluctant, resource-starved system. Such an advocate can make a special plea for the client family, providing it with the maximum public benefits the system provides in order to assure child well-being. In the long term, the answer is effective system reform that provides families in poverty with adequate support and, most important, a pathway to increasing and sustainable financial resources.

Notes

1. This story is based on the following sources: Jason DeParle, "As Welfare Rolls Shrink, Load on Relatives Grows," *New York Times*, February 21, 1999, A1; Jason DeParle, "Symbol of Welfare Reform, Still Struggling," *New York Times*, April 20, 1999, A1; LynNell Hancock, *Hands to Work: The Stories of Three Families Racing the Welfare Clock* (New York: Morrow, 2001).

2. 42 U.S.C. § 608(a)(7) (2005).

3. 42 U.S.C. § 607 (2005).

4. Personal Responsibility and Work Opportunity Reconciliation Act of 1996, 104 P.L. 193. The reauthorization of the TANF program is currently before Congress. See H.R. 4, 109th Cong. (2005).

5. 42 U.S.C. § 603 (2005).

6. 42 U.S.C. §§ 607, 608(a)(7) (2005).

7. 42 U.S.C. § 604 (2005).

8. See Morgan B. Ward Doran and Dorothy E. Roberts, "Welfare Reform and Families in the Child Welfare System," *Maryland Law Review* 61 (2002): 386, 394.

9. 42 U.S.C. §§ 603(a)(4), 603(a)(5)(E) (2005).

10. See Thomas L. Gais and Cathy M. Johnson, "Welfare Reform, Management Systems, and Their Implications for Children," *Ohio State Law Journal* 60 (1999): 1327, 1333.

11. Gais and Johnson, "Welfare Reform," 1362; 42 U.S.C. § 607 (2005).

12. 42 U.S.C. § 608(a)(7) (2005).

13. 42 U.S.C. § 608(a)(2).

14. 42 U.S.C. § 657.

15. 42 U.S.C. § 618(c).

16. 42 U.S.C. § 618(a)(3).

17. 42 U.S.C. § 618(a)(1)(A).

18. See chapter 2 for a discussion of the public child welfare system.

19. See Sarah H. Ramsey, "Children in Poverty: Reconciling Children's Interests with Child Protective and Welfare Policies," *Maryland Law Review* 61 (2002): 437, 447.

20. "Statement on Signing the Personal Responsibility and Work Opportunity Reconciliation Act of 1996," *Public Papers* 2 (August 22, 1998): 1328, 1329.

21. Gais and Johnson, "Welfare Reform," 1334.

22. Gais and Johnson, "Welfare Reform," 1348.

23. Gais and Johnson, "Welfare Reform," 1350.

24. Gais and Johnson, "Welfare Reform," 1351, table 1.

25. Gais and Johnson, "Welfare Reform," 1344.

26. Gais and Johnson, "Welfare Reform," 1344.

27. Ward Doran and Roberts, "Welfare Reform and Families," 398.

28. Ramsey, "Children in Poverty," 451 (footnotes omitted).

29. Ward Doran and Roberts, "Welfare Reform and Families," 398.

30. 42 U.S.C. § 608(a)(5) (2005).

31. See Ward Doran and Roberts, "Welfare Reform and Families," 395–96; N.J. Stat. Ann. § 44:103.5 (West 1992) (repealed 1997).

32. See, for example, Cal. Welf. & Inst. Code § 11450.04 (2005); Va. Code Ann. § 63.2604 (2005).

33. See Ramsey, "Children in Poverty," 447.

34. See Laura M. Freidman, "Comment, Family Cap and the Unconstitutional Conditions Doctrine: Scrutinizing a Welfare Woman's Right to Bear Children," *Ohio State Law Journal* 56 (1995): 637, 657; but see Ward Doran and Roberts, "Welfare Reform and Families," 399–400 (arguing that this stereotype is unfounded).

35. See 42 U.S.C. § 601(a), stating that the purpose of TANF is, inter alia, to "provide assistance to needy families so that children may be cared for in their own homes."

36. Gais and Johnson, "Welfare Reform," 1329.

37. Gais and Johnson, "Welfare Reform," 1330–32.

38. Gais and Johnson, "Welfare Reform," 1336.

39. Gais and Johnson, "Welfare Reform," 1346.

40. See Rebecca M. Blank, *It Takes a Nation: A New Agenda for Fighting Poverty* (New York: Russell Sage Foundation; Princeton, NJ: Princeton University Press, 1997).

41. Gais and Johnson, "Welfare Reform," 1353.

42. Gais and Johnson, "Welfare Reform," 1353.

43. Gais and Johnson, "Welfare Reform," 1334–35.

44. See Ward Doran and Roberts, "Welfare Reform and Families," at 411–16.

45. Ward Doran and Roberts "Welfare Reform and Families."

46. See Gais and Johnson, "Welfare Reform," 1351.

47. Gais and Johnson, "Welfare Reform," 1351.

48. Ramsey, "Children in Poverty," 449–52.

49. Ramsey, "Children in Poverty," 453.

Appendix to Chapter 3
Illustrative Service Organizations
That Address Welfare Issues

National

National Center for Children in Poverty (NCCP)
215 W. 125th Street, 3rd Floor
New York, NY 10027
Phone: 646-284-9600
Fax: 646-284-9623
E-mail: info@nccp.org
Web site: http://www.nccp.org

In conjunction with Columbia University's Mailman School of Public Health, the NCCP provides research and data related to poverty and its effect on children. Its Web site provides detailed information that should help families in poverty navigate the welfare system, as well as understand what effect any change in their location or lifestyle might have on their income or public support.

Homes for the Homeless
36 Cooper Square, 6th Floor
New York, NY 10003
Phone: 212-529-5252
Fax: 212-529-7698
E-mail: info@homesforthehomeless.com
Web site: http://www.homesforthehomeless.com

Homes for the Homeless is a New York City organization charged with the administration of the largest network of homeless centers in the country; these centers, called American Family Inns, provide not only shelter but services to homeless families. While it is only available in New York, many other organizations like it exist throughout the country.

The National Law Center on Homelessness & Poverty
1411 K Street, N.W., Suite 1400
Washington, DC 20005
Phone: 202-638-2535
Fax: 202-628-2737
Web site: http://www.nlchp.org/

The National Law Center on Homelessness & Poverty serves as the legal arm of the movement to end homelessness. Using both legislative advocacy and direct litigation assistance, the center works on a variety of issues such as housing, education, and civil rights.

National Center for Youth Law
405 14th Street, 15th Floor
Oakland, CA 94612-2701
Phone: 510-835-8098
Fax: 916-551-2195
E-mail: info@youthlaw.org
Web site: http://www.youthlaw.org/

The National Center for Youth Law provides services to at-risk and low-income children, using the law to improve their lives. It focuses on financial stability for low-income families, appropriate health care and mental health services, and transitions to adulthood for at-risk youth.

Examples of Law School Programs and Clinics

New York University School of Law Civil Legal Services Clinic
245 Sullivan Street, 5th Floor
New York, NY 10012
Phone: 212-998-6446
Web site: http://www.law.nyu.edu/clinics/year/civilservices/index.html

The NYU Civil Legal Services Clinic represents clients in a variety of areas, including housing and government benefits.

Stanford Community Law Clinic
2117 University Avenue, Suite A
East Palo Alto, CA 94303
Phone: 650-475-0560
Fax: 650-326-4162
Web site: http://www.law.stanford.edu/clinics/sclc/

The Stanford Community Law Clinic provides people in need with legal assistance in a variety of situations, such as eviction proceedings, government benefits, and employee rights.

Examples of Local Organizations in an Urban Community (Pittsburgh)

ACTION Housing, Inc.
425 Sixth Avenue, Suite 950

Pittsburgh, PA 15219
Phone: 412-281-2102
Fax: 412-391-4512
E-mail: ahi@actionhousing.org
Web site: http://www.actionhousing.org

ACTION Housing provides multiple forms of services to financially vulnerable families. The organization is not affiliated with Pennsylvania's TANF program.

East End Cooperative Ministry
250 N. Highland Avenue
Pittsburgh, PA 15206
Phone: 412-361-5549
Fax: 412-361-0151
E-mail: eecm@usaor.net
Web site: http://www.usaor.net/users/eecm/index.html

This organization provides a homeless shelter and food pantry.

Neighborhood Legal Services Association
928 Penn Avenue
Pittsburgh, PA 15222-3799
Phone: 412-255-6700
Fax: 412-355-0168
Web site: http://www.nlsa.us/

Neighborhood Legal Services Association is a nonprofit corporation that provides legal services to low-income individuals. The legal services range from telephone advice to actual representation in the court system, and cover guardianship, housing, and economic stability.

Thomas Foerster Family Support Training Center
University of Pittsburgh Office of Child Development
400 N. Lexington Avenue
Pittsburgh, PA 15208
Phone: 412-244-5026
Fax: 412-244-5425

There are thirty-three neighborhood-based family support centers in the greater Pittsburgh area, providing essential counseling and services to families in need. The Family Support Training Center serves as the central coordinator of training and networking between these local support centers.

4
Children's Criminal Behavior

On October 29, 2004, at 6:17 P.M., two teenagers were walking from the parking lot of their high school to the cafeteria. They were at the school to set up the ticket sales desk for the school play. No one else had arrived at the school yet.[1]

Upon closing their car doors, three other teenagers confronted them. One of the three wore a monster mask. They surrounded one of the teen victims and demanded money, letting the other run to the school. When the surrounded victim tried to keep walking into the school, the assailant with the mask pinned him against the car and stated, "You feel this? This is a gun." The other two assailants began to search the victim for money by reaching into his pockets. When the victim again tried to enter the school, he was restrained. Ultimately, the victim broke free, ran to the school, and called the police.

The three assailants ran into the woods next to the parking lot, laughing about their escapade. They were extremely excited by the thrill of scaring other kids their age with the threat of violence. They didn't really need any money. All they wanted was a thrill that cemented their relationship. They were a gang, true partners in crime.

The teenager with the mask took it off and laughed with the other two as they began planning their next move. One of the boys wanted to head home. But the other two wanted one more thrill. They pressured the other boy to stay for one more assault.

Approximately twenty minutes after the first incident, the three boys regrouped at the edge of the school parking lot. The one boy put his mask back on and confronted a teenage girl as she locked her car door and turned to go into the school. The three boys demanded money from the girl. She tried to walk away, but they surrounded her. One of the boys said, "We have a gun. Give me your money." Now truly frightened, the girl handed over $17. The three boys immediately ran into the woods. The girl went into the school and called the police to report the crime.

The police responded to the calls from both victims by searching the woods surrounding the school. Two officers involved in the search stopped John C. and two other boys when they emerged from the woods onto a street in the nearby housing development. The three boys matched the description given by both victims. The police officers detained the boys.

During the ride to the police station, the boys spoke with the police officers. The officers did not advise them of their right to remain silent or their right to an attorney. However, the officers also did not question the boys about the incidents in the parking lot. One of the boys did state that they had been at the school parking lot earlier in the evening, but he did not elaborate. The officers and the boys discussed where the boys lived, where their parents were, and what sports they played at school.

At the police station, the officers searched the boys. They found $17 in John C.'s coat pocket. They did not find a mask or a gun.

The officers arrested John C. and charged him with two counts of robbery in the first degree and two counts of conspiracy to commit robbery in the first degree. The next day, October 30, 2004, John C. appeared in juvenile court. The juvenile court judge automatically transferred the case to the adult criminal court docket.

Later that day, John C. was arraigned on the adult docket of the state district criminal court. The arraignment judge reviewed the sworn police reports and found that there was probable cause that John C. had committed the alleged crimes. She ordered officials to hold John C. for trial.

The state's legislature had recently made major changes to the juvenile justice system. With respect to juvenile transfers, the legislators had enacted a legislative transfer mechanism. The law now designated certain crimes for which a transfer to adult court was automatic. This mechanism, at least in part, replaced the prior judicial transfer mechanism that required juvenile court judges to assess an individual juvenile's amenability to treatment and rehabilitation, and to exercise their discretion in deciding whether to transfer the matter to adult criminal court. The legislative transfer scheme left no room for the exercise of judicial discretion.

The new juvenile transfer statute provides:

> The court shall automatically transfer from the docket for juvenile matters to the regular criminal docket of the superior court the case of any child charged with the commission of a capital felony or a Class A or B felony, provided such offense was committed after the child attained the age of fourteen years. A state's attorney may, not later than ten working days after a child's arraignment in the superior court, file a motion to transfer the case of any child charged with the commission of a Class B felony to the docket for juvenile matters.[2]

Because John C. was fourteen years old and the state charged him with four Class B felony counts, his case was automatically transferred to the regular adult criminal docket. The state's attorney did not intend to file a motion to transfer the case to the juvenile docket within the ten-day period provided by the statute.

Two days after his arraignment, John C. participated in a psychological evaluation. John C.'s parents, on the advice of John C.'s court-appointed attorney, arranged for the evaluation with a licensed psychologist for a fee of $500. The evaluation provided detailed information on John C.'s situation and presented a favorable review concerning his potential for successful rehabilitation within the juvenile system. Specifically, the evaluator noted that this was only John C.'s second alleged criminal act. He also noted that John C. had a supportive family, good school attendance, and a positive attitude toward treatment and counseling.

John C.'s attorney assured John C. and his parents that he would present the evaluation to the prosecutor and argue forcefully for a motion to transfer the case to the juvenile docket. The attorney knew that he had to present this information to the state's attorney quickly because the motion had to be filed within ten days. Despite his knowledge of the time requirements and his assurances, John C.'s attorney failed to present the evaluation to the state's attorney within ten business days from the arraignment. Upon receiving the evaluation fifteen days after the arraignment, the prosecutor informed John

C.'s attorney that it was too late to file a motion transferring the case to juvenile court. Additionally, the prosecutor stated that the evaluation would have made no difference because her office never seeks a transfer to juvenile court in robbery cases that involve the threatened use of a firearm.

Once in the adult criminal system, John C. took the advice of his attorney and his parents to plead guilty, provide evidence against the two other boys involved in the robberies, and accept the judge's sentencing decision. In exchange, the state's attorney agreed to recommend a sentence of five to seven years. John C. would serve the first two years of his sentence in a high-security juvenile facility and the last three to five years in an adult prison. John C. would be housed in a separate, young-offender section of the adult prison but otherwise would be treated like any other prisoner. The trial judge accepted the prosecutor's recommendation, noting John C.'s threat to use a gun and the need to treat him like an adult.

On appeal, John C. challenged the transfer of his case to adult criminal court. The attorney who took over John C.'s case following his sentencing worked closely with John C. and his parents. She was a public defender who handled only criminal appeals and who had been looking for a good case to challenge the automatic transfer statute. She felt very strongly that the state legislature had overreached, violated the United States Constitution, and harmed delinquent youth in adopting the statute.

Before reaching the constitutional issues, the appellate attorney felt that she had to bring an ineffective assistance of counsel claim. John C.'s attorney had made a serious mistake in not presenting the psychological evaluation to the state's attorney in a timely manner. Although she felt that this claim would likely fail, the trial attorney's error was too glaring to ignore. If the claim succeeded, it would give John C. a chance to gain a transfer to juvenile court. More important, presenting this information could help the appellate attorney in making the constitutional claims. The facts surrounding the evaluation would establish that John C. was a sympathetic youth who was a victim of the automatic transfer statute.

The appeals court did reject John C.'s ineffective assistance of counsel claim. The court began its analysis by noting that John C. had a right to counsel, and in matters as important as criminal proceedings and juvenile transfers, counsel had to provide effective assistance. But in order to establish that counsel's errors rendered the performance constitutionally ineffective, the defendant must show two things. First, counsel's performance had to be deficient as measured according to a standard of reasonableness under prevailing professional norms. Second, without counsel's deficient performance, there is a reasonable possibility that the result would have been different; in other words, counsel's errors had to undermine confidence in the outcome.

The court did not address the first element of the ineffective assistance of counsel claim even though John C.'s attorney probably failed to live up to prevailing professional norms. There was no reason to embarrass counsel with this finding when the second element was lacking. The court expressly found that counsel's errors did not cause John C.'s transfer to adult court. The prosecutor clearly and strongly asserted that the transfer was automatic and that her office consistently refused to move for transfer back to juvenile court in any case involving the threat of gun violence. Thus, even if John C.'s counsel had presented the prosecutor with a favorable psychological evaluation in a timely manner, it would have made no difference in the case.

In presenting the ineffective assistance claim, John C.'s attorney provided the court with information about John C.'s amenability to treatment. This information indicated that John C. was a juvenile defendant for which rehabilitation was possible—a goal that fits much more within the charge of the juvenile court as opposed to the adult court. In addition, the motion presented the court with the arbitrariness of the automatic transfer statute, especially the large degree of discretion granted to prosecutors. Based on individual case biases or harsh policy decisions, prosecutors had the unilateral power not to seek transfer of a case to juvenile court.

The attorney believed that presenting information on her sympathetic client and on the system's harsh approach in this case provided a strong foundation for challenging the constitutionality of the automatic transfer statute. She raised three constitutional claims. First, the automatic transfer mechanism does not comport with the requirements of due process. Second, the transfer statute violates the equal protection provisions in that similar defendants are treated unequally as a result of unchecked prosecutorial discretion. Third, the transfer statute gives the prosecutor sole discretion to return a case to the juvenile court, thereby violating due process and the constitutionally required separation of powers.

The appellate court found that each of John C.'s constitutional claims fails. In making the basic due process claim, John C. asserted that the automatic transfer mechanism violates a prior U.S. Supreme Court decision[3] because it does not provide the juvenile defendant with a pretransfer due process hearing. The Court had addressed a transfer statute that authorized a juvenile court judge to waive jurisdiction and order a child held for trial as an adult after full investigation of the particular juvenile's situation. However, the juvenile court judge had ordered transfer of the juvenile defendant to adult court without a hearing, without an opportunity to be heard, and without any stated reasons. The Court found that this procedure violated both the transfer statute and the constitutional requirements of due process.

The Court also discussed a list of factors that are relevant to a juvenile judge's assessment of a juvenile defendant's situation when deciding whether to transfer a particular case to adult criminal court. Either through statutory law or judicial decisions, numerous states have adopted the Supreme Court's factors in order to guide juvenile court judges in exercising their discretion. However, numerous state legislators have also enacted transfer schemes that do not involve the exercise of judicial discretion. These schemes involve either the exercise of discretion by prosecutors or direct mandates from the legislature. The automatic transfer statute at issue in John C.'s case is an example of the latter approach, one that includes a role for prosecutorial discretion.

In addressing John C.'s basic due process claim, the appellate court distinguished the Supreme Court case. The court pointed to a series of case decisions that distinguished the Supreme Court case and found that a hearing is not required before a juvenile is transferred to adult criminal court. The Supreme Court had addressed a situation in which the goal is to prevent the arbitrary transfer of juveniles to the adult system by juvenile court judges charged with assessing the individual juvenile's situation. This concern is not present in a statutory scheme that mandates adult treatment based on the crime charged and does not require the exercise of judicial discretion. Because John C.'s situation involved such a statutory scheme, due process did not require a transfer hearing.

John C. also asserted that the automatic transfer statute impermissibly creates two classes of defendants: those charged with Class B felonies who are prosecuted as adults and those charged with Class B felonies who are transferred back to juvenile court. The statute vests the state's attorney with sole discretion to determine within which class a particular defendant fits. The prosecutor, on his or her own and without any statutory standards or guidance, must determine whether to file a motion seeking juvenile court jurisdiction over a particular defendant. John C. argued that the lack of statutory standards for the exercise of this prosecutorial discretion violates the equal protection clause of the Fourteenth Amendment.[4]

The appellate court noted at the outset that there is no constitutional right to treatment as a juvenile. Therefore, the statutory classification involves neither a suspect classification nor a fundamental right. In such a situation, the defendant must establish that the statutory distinction is without a rational basis.[5]

In finding that John C. failed to meet this burden, the appellate court distinguished a case that found a juvenile transfer statute violated the equal protection clause of the Utah constitution. The Utah statute allowed the prosecutor, in the first instance, to decide whether a particular juvenile should be transferred to adult court. Thus, it could operate to charge some juveniles in adult court and leave others in juvenile court for the same offense. The automatic transfer statute in John C.'s case did not allow for this type of prosecutorial discretion or disparate treatment.

The appellate court also pointed to a list of cases from other states that found that the exercise of prosecutorial charging discretion does not violate the equal protection clause of the U.S. Constitution in the absence of suspect factors such as race, religion, or other arbitrary classification. In addition, the court noted a New York decision that upheld a statute requiring juveniles to be tried as adults unless the district attorney requests that the case be handled in juvenile court. The appellate court found the New York case to be conceptually the same as John C.'s case and concluded:

> The equal protection issue comes down to whether the automatic transfer of juveniles charged with Class A and B felonies to adult court furthers a legitimate governmental interest in protecting the public from serious juvenile crimes. The legislature's decision to further that interest by mandating the adult prosecution of Class A and B felonies is reasonably related to the pursuit of that legitimate goal. In short, there exists a rational basis for the statutory classification and therefore it does not violate equal protection.[6]

The court also held that the fact that a juvenile's classification is affected by the prosecutors' discretion does not violate equal protection.

In raising the third constitutional issue, John C. claimed that the automatic transfer statute violates the constitutional mandate for separation of powers. Specifically, the statute authorizes prosecutors to control the docketing of juvenile transfer cases. John C. asserted that the legislature's grant of authority to an executive branch officer impermissibly infringes on the inherent and exclusively judicial authority of the court.[7]

The appellate court easily rejected this claim. It noted that other courts had rejected similar claims because treatment as a juvenile is a creation of the legislature. Therefore, modification and restriction of such treatment are within the legislature's purview as well. Only laws that attempt to exercise power that lies exclusively under the courts' control violate the separation of powers mandate. Juvenile court transfer is not a power exclusively under the court's control.

Based on its reasoning in addressing John C.'s claims, the appellate court affirmed John C.'s conviction. The court upheld his sentence of five to seven years. John C. would likely serve time in an adult prison. He would likely be held beyond age nineteen, the maximum age that he could be held within the juvenile court system. More important, he would not receive the rehabilitation services available in the juvenile system. He would be at a higher risk of committing another crime upon release and failing to become a productive adult within American society.[8]

The criminal proceedings did not end with John C.'s conviction and sentence. The state's attorney decided also to charge John C.'s parents under the state's Parental Responsibility Act. This statute asserts that parents have a duty to control their children because they have the authority to do so. The law then provides that once a child is adjudicated delinquent, and the court finds that a parent's failure was the proximate cause of the child's delinquent act, the court can order the parent to exert control over the child to ensure that the child complies with the conditions of probation and treatment. If the child commits another delinquent or criminal act as the result of the parent's willful failure to exercise appropriate control over the child, the court can convict and punish the parent.[9]

Six months before the incident in the school parking lot, a police officer and an employee of the city council had spoken with John C.'s parents and told them that their son was rumored to be a thief in the neighborhood. After two more thefts in the neighborhood, two neighbors spoke with John C.'s parents, telling them that they and others believed that John C. was involved in the burglaries. John C.'s parents said that they had no reason to believe that their son was involved, but they would check their home for suspicious items and report any found. They failed to do this.

Several weeks later, police obtained a search warrant for John C.'s home. They found and confiscated two stereo speakers and a turntable that had been reported as stolen. The items were in plain view in John C.'s room. His parents denied any knowledge of the stolen equipment. The juvenile court placed John C. on probation, requiring him to participate in a treatment program under his parents' supervision.

John C.'s parents failed to make sure that he attended the treatment program. When the state's attorney charged John C. in the parking lot robberies, he decided to charge John C.'s parents under the Parental Responsibility Act. Upon hearing the evidence of the parents' failure to supervise John C.'s probation and treatment, the judge found that this failure was the proximate cause of John C.'s criminal acts. The judge fined John C.'s mother and father $1,000 and sentenced each of them to six months in the county jail.[10]

In a posttrial motion, John C.'s parents challenged the Parental Responsibility Act as unconstitutionally vague and overbroad. They asserted that the statutory requirement that parents exercise "appropriate and necessary control" over their children did not adequately inform parents of the type of behavior being prohibited. The judge rejected this argument, noting that John C.'s parents had previously been given a court order and notified that failure to comply could result in criminal sanctions. The parents knew what they had to do, the requirements did not overly restrict or control their conduct, and the parents willfully failed to meet the requirements. In this situation, the Parental Responsibility Act was not vague or overbroad.[11]

John C.'s parents also asserted that the statute violated their due process rights. They claimed that their parental right to raise their son as they see fit is fundamental and that the statute impermissibly infringes on this fundamental right. The act unduly interferes with the parent-child relationship.

The court rejected the parents' argument, refusing to find that the right to bear and raise children has been interfered with merely because parents are held responsible for their child's delinquent or criminal behavior. The judge stated that "with the right to raise children comes the responsibility to see that one's children are properly raised so that the rights of other people are protected."[12] The judge also noted that deterring juvenile crime is a legitimate governmental purpose. In addition, the means chosen by the state—namely, assigning responsibility to parents for their children's behavior—are reasonable and rational. The means constitute a valid exercise of the state's police power and do not violate constitutional limits.

In the end, John C. was required to serve a five- to seven-year sentence. He served two years in a juvenile facility; then state officials transferred him to an adult prison facility. John C.'s parents had to pay a $1,000 fine and serve six months in jail. As a result of their son's criminal behavior and their jail terms, they lost their jobs and their publicly subsidized housing. The state placed John C.'s siblings in foster care and began a long-term plan designed to reunify the family.[13]

The Juvenile Court Movement

The juvenile court/adult court process constitutes a dual system for addressing criminal behavior. Before the formal creation of juvenile courts in the early 1900s, the state treated children and adults who committed criminal acts similarly. By the late 1800s, some differences in treatment had emerged. Reformers secured the construction of houses of refuge that operated much like prisons whose population consisted exclusively of children. They introduced the concept of a formal age distinction between juveniles and adults, the idea of institutional separation between juveniles and adults, and the approach of using indeterminate sentences for juveniles that depended on the particular juvenile's rehabilitation. These elements provided the foundation for the creation of the juvenile court.[14]

Those in the juvenile court movement lobbied for specialized courts that would hear all cases involving children, including adolescents. The movement's foundational belief was that children are qualitatively different from adults. Namely, children do not possess the cognitive abilities necessary for full criminal responsibility. In addition, children are more susceptible to treatment because their cognitive skills and personality traits are still undergoing development. In other words, there is more hope for their successful rehabilitation.[15]

These differences provide strong support for treating juveniles differently. The juvenile court movement used them to assert that judges need a great deal of discretion to apply individualized treatments rather than predetermined punishments. Juvenile court professionals could use a treatment approach rather than a punitive approach. As Barry Feld has summarized, this child well-being approach had serious consequences for the judicial system and for children accused of delinquent behavior:

> Under the guise of *parens patriae*, the juvenile court emphasized treatment, supervision, and control rather than punishment. The juvenile court's "rehabilitative ideal" envisioned a specialized judge trained in social science and child development whose empathic qualities and insight would enable him or her to make individualized therapeutic dispositions in the "best interests" of the child. Reformers pursued benevolent goals, individualized their solicitude, and maximized discretion to provide flexibility in diagnosis and treatment of the "whole child." They regarded a child's crimes primarily as a symptom of his or her "real needs," and consequently the nature of the offense affected neither the degree nor the duration of intervention. Rather, juvenile court judges imposed indeterminate and nonproportional sentences that potentially continued for the duration of minority.[16]

The original juvenile court approach rejected the criminal law's jurisprudence. The criminal law emphasized the defined rule of law, the accused's competence and free will, and the appropriateness of punishment. In contrast, the juvenile court movement stressed the indeterminancy of judicial discretion, the juvenile's lack of full competence, the deterministic nature of juvenile behavior, and the need for treatment and rehabilitation.[17]

The juvenile court movement also rejected the criminal law's procedural safeguards. The proceedings resembled problem-solving meetings or treatment planning sessions more than adversarial contests concerning the formal presentation of facts and the determination of punishment. Juveniles did not have lawyers. The juvenile courts did not use juries. The rule was informality rather than formality, with a treatment approach that could extend only until the juvenile reached the age of majority.[18]

Illinois led the way in establishing a juvenile court system, granting the juvenile court original and exclusive jurisdiction over all cases involving juveniles. There were no exceptions to the principle that cases involving minors should be heard in the juvenile court. Even cases involving serious and violent offenses were to be heard within the juvenile court system.[19]

This broad and seemingly inflexible scope of juvenile court jurisdiction began to erode almost immediately. Fearful of an attack on the new system, juvenile court judges gave the state's attorney the opportunity to prosecute selected cases in the adult criminal justice system. The result was an informal system of concurrent jurisdiction over juvenile cases, "using a form of 'passive transfer,' in which, by doing nothing, the court allowed for a child to be tried as an adult."[20] In addition, juvenile judges actively transferred a few cases each year to criminal court because they involved "vicious" and "repeat" offenders. But even with the passive and active transfer mechanisms, the juvenile court heard the vast majority of cases involving juveniles, including those of juvenile homicide.

The juvenile process was flexible in nature, even in cases involving serious violence and homicide. The central idea was individualized assessment and treatment, not general concepts of punishment as a result of an adversarial process. The treatment approach called for a cooperative, informal approach that involved interested parties such as the juvenile, parents, state officials, community service providers, and the judge. These participants could work as a team to achieve rehabilitation and avoid branding a child a criminal and condemning a child to incarceration with criminal adults.

Unfortunately, this informal treatment approach failed in many instances. Because of a lack of resources and the inclination to punish juvenile offenders, treatment programs took on a punitive character. These programs did not appear capable of achieving rehabilitation. They appeared to be warehouses for youthful offenders, modeled after adult prisons. In the end, juvenile processes frequently resulted in punishment rather than rehabilitation.

Transformation of the Juvenile Court

Exposing juveniles to serious punishment led the Supreme Court to require a more formal juvenile court process—one that would recognize rights of juvenile offenders. In a 1967 decision, the Court required formal procedures at juvenile trials and fostered a procedural and substantive convergence with adult criminal courts.[21] For example, juvenile offenders were granted the right against self-incrimination and to legal representation. Barry Feld has succinctly summarized the ramifications of the Court's decision, noting that the Court's "emphasis on procedural formality shifted the focus of delinquency proceedings from a child's best interests to proof of legal guilt in adversary proceedings, highlighted the connection between a youth's crimes and subsequent sanctions, and ironically may have legitimated more punitive dispositions for young offenders."[22] The formal procedures and rights adopted by the Court for juveniles conferred on them an adultlike status and increased their exposure to adultlike punishment.

In recognizing this trend to extend adult rights and procedures to juvenile cases, it is important to note that the courts have refused to grant all legal rights to juveniles. For example, in a 1971 decision, the Supreme Court denied to juveniles the right to jury trials in delinquency proceedings.[23] The Court expressly noted the differences between the juvenile and adult systems. The treatment rationale of the juvenile process contrasted with the punitive purposes of the adult criminal system and justified procedural differences between the two systems.

This type of selective distinction exposes juveniles to significant risks of punishment without full procedural rights. More and more, the state treats juveniles as adults, both within a juvenile system that does not have adequate resources to fulfill the mission of rehabilitation and through the transfer of juveniles to the adult criminal system. Yet their status as children keeps the sentiment of treatment and rehabilitation alive in the minds of public actors. This sentiment leads to a diminishment of procedural safeguards and individual rights as juveniles are effectively processed as adults. In a very real sense, juveniles experience aspects of both systems that, when combined, place them at significant risk of punishment without full legal protections.[24]

The Family Metanarratives

The reasons for this predicament relate to the primary metanarratives surrounding children and families. The public's initial reaction is captured by the metanarrative of child well-being. Particular children may commit serious delinquent or criminal acts, but they are still children. The public holds out hope for these children and wants to help them. These children are impressionable and treatable and can be rehabilitated. Society and public actors should not brand them as hopeless criminals and condemn them to serious punishment.

This initial embrace of the metanarrative of child well-being explains the juvenile court movement. The public believed it could save these children from the social and personal circumstances that led to their delinquent behavior. Attentive, flexible, individual adjudication and treatment approaches would allow for successful salvage operations, transforming delinquent juveniles into competent adult citizens.[25]

The child well-being approach to juvenile crime existed in tension with a punitive approach from the outset. The other primary meta-narrative surrounding children and families, the private family, provided the foundation for this alternative approach. Its base concepts are family autonomy and individual responsibility. The private family is to be self-sufficient and autonomous. The members of the family association are supposed to take care of each other and themselves without burdening the public.

When the family and its individual members fail to live up to these expectations, the public assigns blame. Delinquent or criminal behavior by teenage family members calls for the assignment of blame and for punishment designed to protect the public rather than treatment aimed at securing child well-being and rehabilitation.[26] The primary target for blame is the juvenile actor, with the juvenile's parents as secondary targets.

The juvenile court movement resolved this tension in favor of securing child well-being, with limited exceptions allowing for adultlike punishment for and protection of the public from especially serious or chronic juvenile offenders. This resolution fell apart in the 1980s and 1990s. Juveniles have always committed a disproportionate amount of crime, but the arrest rates of children for violence, especially homicide, exploded beginning in the mid-1980s.[27] Juveniles in the early to late adolescent phase were committing an increasing share of violent crimes.

The increase in juvenile violent crimes coincided with an increase in handguns possessed by adolescents. It also coincided with a marked increase in the distribution of illegal drugs, especially crack cocaine. The drug distribution industry attracts adolescents, especially those without economic opportunities. Youths take more risks than adults in distributing drugs, and they tend to arm themselves for self-protection and to make threats during inevitable disputes. The result was a diffusion of guns to the youth population that resulted in a surge in violent juvenile offenders.[28]

The media covered this rise in violent juvenile crime, often profiling the typical offender as an urban African American teenage male—the juvenile "superpredator." Even academics predicted a tidal wave of remorseless, morally impoverished youth.[29] The public perceived danger and questioned the capacity of the juvenile court system to deal with serious and violent juvenile offenders.

State legislators and local prosecutors joined the call for tougher laws that would make it easier to prosecute juveniles as adults. Forty states passed such laws.[30] The result was a criminal justice system that provided less individualized justice for juveniles. Instead of dispositions aimed at treatment and rehabilitation, judges would impose sentences based solely on the nature of the offense. The laws emphasized characteristics of the offense rather than the offender.

Once an atmosphere of fear and punishment of youth defined the public response to juvenile crime, the significant decline in juvenile crime experienced in the late 1990s had no impact. (In fact, even for the peak years of the early 1990s, there was no evidence that violent juvenile offenders were more frequent or vicious offenders than youth in previous years.)[31] The call for tougher juvenile laws continued. Although many increasingly recognized the juvenile superpredator as a myth, legislators, prosecutors and judges continued to face pressure to get tough on juvenile offenders. The myth continued to drive juvenile justice policy, with the public viewing juvenile offenders not as children but as predators. The state now prosecutes growing numbers of children as adults and sentences them to terms in adult prisons.[32]

This belies the shift in the dominant metanarrative affecting the juvenile justice system. The driving force of child well-being has been displaced. It is extremely difficult to sustain the power of this narrative when the public perceives juvenile offenders not as children but as superpredators. This perception lends itself to a much different narrative. The rhetoric of autonomy and responsibility takes over and becomes dominant. Individual children and their families are responsible for juvenile criminal behavior. If they do not live up to their responsibility, the public should impose punishment based on the nature of their criminal behavior. Accordingly, the metanarrative of the private, autonomous family dominates the public discussion of juvenile offenders and juvenile justice.

Transfer to Adult Court

For juveniles, this shift has resulted in the increased ease of transfer to the adult criminal system. From the inception of the juvenile court system, judges could exercise discretion to deny a particular child offender the protection of the juvenile system and transfer a case to the adult criminal system.[33] In doing so, the juvenile court judge has to make an individualized assessment of the child, using a formal hearing process. The judge's assessment focuses on the juvenile's amenability to treatment as reflected in clinical evaluations and dangerousness as determined by the nature of the present offense and prior record. The child's age in relation to how long the juvenile system can retain jurisdiction in the case is also an important factor. A judge is less likely to waive jurisdiction if the child is relatively young, and the juvenile system can retain jurisdiction to age twenty-one rather than age eighteen or nineteen. In fact, some states limit judicial waivers to children over a specified age (e.g., fourteen or fifteen) and to felony offenses. However, other states impose no limits.[34]

Although the scheme of judicial waiver is appropriately individualized and treatment oriented, it is highly subjective. There is an absence of operative guidelines or assessment tools that would allow judges to make decisions that are consistent from case to case. As a result, the judicial waiver system is arbitrary in nature, with widely divergent outcomes for juveniles in similar situations.[35]

Despite its subjectivity and arbitrary nature, judicial waiver remains the most common process for transfer to the adult system. However, desiring a more uniform process that relies less on individual treatment assessments and more on the nature of the juvenile's offense, many state legislatures have adopted two other waiver mechanisms. *Prosecutorial waiver* empowers prosecutors to choose the appropriate system in which to try a juvenile offender.[36] Without a judicial hearing, the prosecutor assesses the juvenile's situation and makes a unilateral decision on forum. This mechanism does not reduce the arbitrariness inherent in judicial waiver, but it does allow prosecutors to implement a "get-tough" approach that focuses on the nature of a juvenile's offense. *Legislative waiver* excludes from the juvenile system young offenders who have reached a specified age and have allegedly committed specified types of offenses or have certain prior records.[37] This mechanism stands in stark contrast to judicial waiver, adopting a uniform approach based on age and offense categories that largely eliminates discretion based on assessments of individual offenders. Powered by the myth of the juvenile superpredator, state legislatures have adopted this inflexible mechanism in order to treat a large number of juvenile offenders as adults.

The strong trend to legislative waiver reveals the shift from a flexible, individualized treatment approach to a generalized, punitive, offense-oriented approach. It gives this shift in approach an immediate, stark impact on the lives of juvenile offenders. Yet these offenders are still children. When the public views them as children, the impulse to provide treatment and to seek rehabilitation reemerges.

This was evident in the case of twelve-year-old Lionel Tate whom a Florida trial court sentenced to life in prison for the murder of a six-year-old girl.[38] The prosecutor had offered a treatment-centered plea bargain deal that Lionel, his mother, and his attorney rejected. The jurors were angry and upset that the case was in adult court and that they had to treat Lionel as an adult. Upon the imposition of sentence, the prosecutor recommended that the governor commute the sentence. Legislators questioned whether the legislative transfer mechanism was too inflexible, with one stating, "we sit here and create laws in a vacuum: this crime gets this punishment. . . . But you know something? Sometimes there are extenuating circumstances."[39] The tension between the metanarrative of family and individual autonomy and responsibility and that of child well-being remains in the background even as the law moves strongly in the direction of the private family narrative.

The Practical Implications for John C.

John C.'s situation illustrates important aspects of the trend to a punitive approach. The most dramatic impact is the exclusive focus on the offenses charged by the prosecutor, namely, robbery in the first degree. By making this charging decision, the prosecutor precludes juvenile court jurisdiction. The legislative waiver mechanism automatically sends John C.'s case to the adult criminal system. The only hope John C. has for an individualized treatment approach is if the prosecutor decides to seek transfer of the case to juvenile court. Although not out of the question, this type of move by the state's attorney seems unlikely in light of the original charging decision.

The courts have consistently affirmed state legislatures' authority to send juveniles to the adult system. They have denied the claim that young offenders have a due process right to a hearing within the juvenile system. The courts note that the array of special treatments accorded to juvenile offenders are, at their root, a matter of legislative grace.[40] The juvenile system has not been created to satisfy some form of children's rights. Rather, legislatures created the dual juvenile/adult systems in order to actively address the situations of child offenders and protect society. They were in no way compelled to take this course of action. And they can change it at their will, with the only restrictions being applied by the political process and possibly by judges in determining whether the particular legislative action has a rational basis. However, the legislature provides a rational basis when it believes that certain criminal conduct poses such a significant risk to public safety that it is appropriate to adjudicate juvenile offenders in the adult criminal system. In this situation, the concern about an arbitrary transfer to the adult system because of a failure to provide a juvenile court hearing is absent. The statutory scheme simply mandates adult treatment at the outset.[41]

The state permissibly swept John C. into the adult criminal system because of the nature of his alleged offenses. The courts did not have an opportunity to assess his amenability to treatment. John C.'s only hope was the unilateral grace of the prosecutor. Absent such grace, the system would treat him as an adult offender and focus on his punishment.

But despite this formal, punitive approach, John C. is a child. Although the spirit of treatment and rehabilitation has been denied by the justice system, individual actors within the system are likely to treat juveniles like John C. differently than true adult offenders. The informal discussion the police officers had with John C. and the other youth offenders on the ride to the police station indicates this inclination. Without a formal reading of warnings and rights, the police engage the children in discussion. It is a relaxed atmosphere that does not seem like a formal adult process that places youth in serious danger of facing severe adult punishment.[42]

In such a natural, informal setting, juvenile offenders could easily lose the legal protections normally accorded to adults. This risk of loss carries through to the type and level of legal advocacy that juveniles receive. Often, public defenders who represent juvenile offenders are inexperienced and overwhelmed by a large volume of cases.[43] These conditions lead to inadequate representation like that John C. experienced. His attorney failed to aggressively pursue a transfer back to juvenile court. The attorney may have been able to convince the prosecutor to seek juvenile court jurisdiction, but he did not present the evidence or make the case on John C.'s behalf. This lax form of advocacy is a significant problem for juvenile offenders.

The combination of the dual system design, the status of the offender as a child, and the shortage of public resources exposes juvenile offenders to numerous legal dangers. During interrogations and other police procedures, officials tend to treat the offender as a child, failing to fully assess competency or afford full legal rights. During formal legal proceedings, the juvenile offender often experiences inadequate legal representation. Yet the juvenile faces adult punishment, often receiving sentences as harsh, if not harsher, than those imposed on adults for the same offense.[44]

Another danger to juvenile offenders posed by transfer to adult court is the lack of effectiveness of adult punishment. Researchers have compared the experiences of juvenile offenders in the juvenile system with those in the adult system. They have found that juveniles transferred to the adult system experience higher rates of rearrest and incarceration. In one study, based in the New York–New Jersey area, 76 percent of juveniles in the adult system were rearrested and 56 percent were incarcerated, whereas 67 percent of juveniles processed for similar offenses in the juvenile system were rearrested and 41 percent were incarcerated. In another study based in Florida, 30 percent of transferred juveniles were rearrested compared with 19 percent of those handled in the juvenile system. The transferred youth were also more likely to commit more serious offenses more frequently. In addition, transferred juveniles were likely to reoffend more quickly (135 days vs. 227 days).[45] This comprehensive failure of the transfer mechanism endangers society and places juvenile offenders in peril of becoming repeat offenders.

Parental Responsibility Laws

Along with the trend to transfer juvenile offenders to adult court, there is a strong trend to hold the parents of juvenile offenders responsible for the criminal behavior of their children. The basic assumption of parental responsibility laws is that parents can exercise control over their adolescent children's behavior. Consequently, it is believed that juvenile delinquency is the result of improper parental care and supervision. Because of this supposed causal connection between parental failure and juvenile delinquency, state legislatures have viewed it as appropriate to hold parents criminally responsible for their children's delinquent acts.[46]

Many states now have laws designed to sanction parents for the delinquent behavior of their children. These laws come in three basic forms. The first is based on parental culpability for actions that affect their children. This type of law requires the highest level of parental culpability. Through severe abuse, rejection, or encouragement of criminal activity, parental conduct has played a significant role in causing a particular child's delinquent acts. This type of law is the current form of the "contributing to minors laws" that have been on the books in some states for a very long time.[47]

The second type of parental responsibility law is based on the inaction of parents. They fail to properly supervise their children through neglect or inattention. When a child commits a delinquent act, the particular parent's improper supervision is presumed to contribute to the juvenile's delinquent behavior. This omission provides the basis for criminal prosecution and sanctions.

The third type of law imposes liability without fault. A child's delinquent acts, in and of themselves, justify criminal prosecution of parents. Traditionally, this type of law has been used to address juvenile status offenses such as curfew violations or truancy. Status offenses are rather minor in nature because they are treated as illegal only because the individual is a child. The same behavior would not be criminal if the actor were an adult. The main goal in these situations is to compel parents to work with school and community officials to help the juvenile offender.[48]

James Herbie DiFonzo has examined in detail contemporary laws that criminalize parental supervision. He notes two emerging traits. First, the laws increasingly specify certain forbidden actions that will expose parents to liability. For example, one state statute punishes parents for permitting their child "to habitually associate with vicious, immoral, or criminal persons, or to grow up in ignorance, idleness, or crime, or to wander about the streets of any city in the nighttime without being in any lawful business or occupation."[49] Second, the laws increasingly employ strict liability concepts, abandoning any criminal intent requirement on behalf of parents. The parents have a duty to supervise and control their child so that other persons and society in general are protected from the child. Those who neglect their duties, as evidenced by their child's delinquent behavior, must "be encouraged to be more diligent through criminal sanctions, if necessary."[50] For example, DiFonzo notes a statute that reflects this approach: "In 1995 Oregon enacted an 'improper supervision' statute that imposed criminal liability on a parent whose child either 'commits an act that brings the child within the jurisdiction of the juvenile court,' 'violates a curfew,' or 'fails to attend school.' The statute provided for no-fault culpability unless the parent established certain affirmative defenses."[51]

The statute used to prosecute John C.'s parents approaches a strict liability regime. The prosecutor had to establish that the parents' failure to supervise John C. was a proximate cause of his delinquent acts, but the court largely inferred the proof of causation. His parents had knowledge of his delinquent behavior, and he then committed more criminal acts. This was enough to establish their failure to supervise John C. adequately and to support their criminal conviction. The law essentially required them to monitor John C. actively and prevent him from engaging in criminal behavior. When John C. committed a robbery, public officials could infer that they had failed to meet their parental responsibility and that this failure was a proximate cause of John C.'s offenses. They then could punish the parents, likely doing irreparable harm to the family, both economically and emotionally.

This approach is another reflection of the dramatic shift in the dominant narrative. The recently enacted parental responsibility laws focus on protecting society from dangerous juveniles. The concern for child well-being is significantly diminished. DiFonzo describes this shift:

> The new generation of parental responsibility laws have refocused the criminal law's treatment of parental involvement in juvenile delinquency. The legal spotlight has shifted from the problem of child protection to seeking protection from the problem child. Accordingly, the new laws governing parenting evince only passing reference to the traditional rehabilitative foundations of juvenile justice, in which both the parents and the broader society were primarily concerned with the welfare of the child. Instead, they focus on the failure to comply with parental duties. They are intended to induce action, and to punish parents for failure to act, with the hope of preventing further injury to those whom the parent's child has already harmed and to other potential victims.[52]

The aim of the laws is truly future prevention and protection, not to encourage child well-being or even to provide financial compensation or other vindication for victims.[53]

Once again, the narrative of the private family becomes dominant. Parents are to take care of their own children. This means that they are to control their children's behavior. As autonomous individuals, juvenile offenders, in the first instance, are responsible for themselves. However, these juveniles are situated in an autonomous family that, in the second instance, is responsible for the behavior of juvenile members. The essential public goal is to protect society, not to secure child well-being.[54]

The Need for a Zealous Advocate

Embracing the narrative of the private family and individual autonomy in dealing with both juvenile offenders and their parents gives rise to a fundamental contradiction. On one hand, the public views adolescents as self-determinative individuals who, like adults, are fully responsible for their criminal behavior. On the other hand, the public views juveniles as being under the control of their parents. The inherent contradiction in these simultaneous views indicates that the public's overall approach is based on ideological oversimplifications that do not reflect reality.[55]

The reality for adolescents and their parents is complex. Adolescents do not have the mental capacities of adults. They are in the midst of developing self-control and a sense of social responsibility that allows them to fully distinguish the nature of their acts. They are resisting parental influences and certainly control.[56] Because of this complex phase of development, adolescents demand understanding and care, not severe punishment. Despite the strong movement to punish juveniles as adults, many recognize, even if not consciously or expressly, that juvenile offenders need help and still have hope for responsible maturation. This recognition, even if latent, provides an opportunity for child offenders and their families. In many instances, they can successfully call on and revive the narrative of child well-being to secure help.

For juvenile offenders themselves, this means understanding that they are involved in a serious adversarial process. The police and other public officials are not on their side, at least not initially, under the current punitive approach. Thus, juveniles must recognize that they need help. Within the current system, the help they need is provided by a legal professional. They need an advocate who can protect all of their legal rights.[57] Ideally, this advocate would also pursue assessment and treatment services for the juvenile. The advocate must make the individual child's situation and hope come alive for public decision makers. Those who hold power over the case, whether it is a prosecutor or judge, must see the child offender as salvageable. If this regard is achieved, it is much more likely that the child will be treated within the juvenile system and, even if dealt with in the adult system, will be treated to some degree, rather than just punished. In summary, the juvenile caught up in the criminal justice system needs a zealous legal advocate who can effectively access mental health and other support services that provide the individual assessment necessary to powerfully activate the narrative of child well-being for a particular child.

Of course, a better approach is for the public to provide services to families that help prevent juvenile offenses. Several commentators have argued strongly for this approach in connection with parental responsibility laws.[58] Instead of punishing parents, these laws could focus judges, attorneys, and others on providing services to support the particular parents and juvenile. Rather than disabling or destroying a family through fines and imprisonment, public officials could procure outreach services that will help the family in the long run.

In light of the current system's punitive approach, parents and juveniles at risk need assistance from knowledgeable advocates. They can direct parents to community service groups that provide education concerning child development, parenting practices, and communication skills. They can also invite parents and children to conflict resolution classes that improve family communications and provide an alternative to delinquent behavior. In addition, they can involve youth in structured after school and extracurricular activities. These types of services, classes, and activities are likely to be much more effective than fines or imprisonment that only damage and tear apart viable family associations.[59]

Locating Support Services

Parents and youth need to recognize their need for active support and advocacy. Only in this way can they effectively tap into the narrative of child well-being and secure the public support they need.

However, finding appropriate advocates in this area is difficult. Local youth and family support programs are a good place to start. Neighborhood community centers are often helpful in engaging youth and addressing delinquent behavior. On a national level, the American Bar Association's Child Law Center has identified and profiled several programs that target families with high-risk factors for juvenile delinquency, including the following:

Family and Neighborhood Services Programs, South Carolina: The delinquent and family are provided services and treatment in the context of their individual family and community issues. Caseworkers usually see the delinquent once a day at the delinquent's home. Youth in this program tend to be repeat offenders. (For more information, see *Guide for Implementing the Comprehensive Strategy for Serious, Violent, and Chronic Juvenile Offenders*, 60, http://www.ncjrs.org/pdffiles/guide.pdf.)

After Care Program, San Diego, California: This program enables probation officers to continue to supervise recently released delinquents and visit them regularly for several months after they are put on probation. Additionally, officers help the family apply for financial subsidies and address child care needs. (For more information, see Naomi R. Cahn, "Pragmatic Questions about Parental Liability Statutes," *Wisconsin Law Review* (1996): 443–44.)

Project S.A.F.E. (Strengthen Adolescents/Family Enrichment), Passaic County, New Jersey: First-time juvenile offenders and their families are taught skills for positive communication and responsible behavior in and out of the home. (For more information call 973-3055742.)

All Children Excel, St. Paul, Minnesota: This program works with young high-risk youth and their families to reduce risk factors for delinquent behavior, improve social skills, and school success. (For more information see http://promise.umn.edu/database/fullrecord.asp?progID=91; or call 651-7711301.)

Families and Schools Together (FAST), Madison, Wisconsin: The goals of this nationwide program, initiated in Wisconsin, include early intervention to help high-risk youth avoid becoming involved in the delinquency system. Families, schools, and communities are involved to help provide the youth with a protective safety net. (For more information, see http://www.ncjrs.org/html/ojjdp/9911_2/contents.html; 608/2639476.)[60]

Conclusion

In the long term, the key is to educate legislators and society at large about juvenile crime rates and juvenile offenders. Juvenile crime has not exploded. The juvenile "superpredator" is largely a myth. Laws and policies designed to respond to these mistaken beliefs are fundamentally flawed. They lead to the dominance of the metanarratives of the private family and the responsible, autonomous individual in an area that calls for a more balanced approach that draws most heavily on the metanarrative of child well-being. More pragmatically, these laws and policies lead to increased recidivism by juvenile offenders. Public officials treat them like adults, increasing the likelihood that they will become adult criminals. In addition, these laws punish parents. Public officials fine and imprison parents whose children commit crimes, damaging or destroying any possible family support for the juvenile offender and his or her siblings.

Society must face this situation and revive the narrative of child well-being that powered the original juvenile court movement. But this will likely not happen soon. Right now, each child and family involved in the current justice system need to work hard to secure a strong, zealous advocate who can protect their rights and secure effective support and treatment.

Notes

1. This story is based on two unrelated cases: *Connecticut v. Jose C.*, 1996 Conn. Super. LEXIS 754, *1 (1996); *In re Appeal in Maricopa County Juvenile Action* No. JV-511576, 925 P.2d 745, 746 (Ariz. Ct. App. 1996). The names have been changed.

2. Conn. Gen. Stat. Ann. § 46b127 (West 2003).

3. *Kent v. United States*, 383 U.S. 541, 543 (1966).

4. *Jose C.*, 1996 Conn. Super. LEXIS 754, *23.

5. See, for example, *Romer v. Evans*, 517 U.S. 620, 632 (1996); *Heller v. Doe*, 509 U.S. 312, 319–20 (1993).

6. *Jose C.*, 1996 Conn. Super. LEXIS 754, *28–29.

7. *Jose C.*, 1996 Conn. Super. LEXIS 754, *29.

8. See Joshua T. Rose, "Innocence Lost: The Detrimental Effect of Automatic Waiver Statutes on Juvenile Justice," *Brandeis Law Journal* 41 (2003): 977, 987.

9. Courtney L. Zolman, "Parental Responsibility Acts: Medicine for Ailing Families and Hope for the Future," *Capital University Law Review* 27 (1998): 217, 248–50.

10. See Zolman, "Parental Responsibility Acts," 249; *State v. Hankerson*, 434 N.E.2d 1362, 1367 (1982).

11. Zolman, "Parental Responsibility Acts," 236–38.

12. *Watson v. Gradzik*, 373 A.2d 191, 192 (Conn. C.P. 1977).

13. See chapter 2 for a discussion of the public child welfare system.

14. Barry C. Feld, "Juvenile and Criminal Justice Systems' Responses to Youth Violence," *Crime & Justice* 24 (1998): 189, 192–93.

15. See Rose, "Innocence Lost," 986; David S. Tanenhaus and Steven A. Drizin, "Criminal Law: 'Owing to the Extreme Youth of the Accused': The Changing Legal Response to Juvenile Homicide," *Journal of Criminal Law & Criminology* 92 (2002): 641, 678–81; David O. Brink, "Immaturity, Normative Competence, and Juvenile Transfer: How (Not) to Punish Minors for Major Crimes," *Texas Law Review* 82 (2004): 1555, 1559.

16. Feld, "Juvenile and Criminal Justice Systems' Responses," 192–93 (citations omitted).

17. Brink, "Immaturity, Normative Competence, and Juvenile Transfer," 1559.

18. Brink, "Immaturity, Normative Competence, and Juvenile Transfer," 1559–60.

19. Brink, "Immaturity, Normative Competence, and Juvenile Transfer," 1559; Tanenhaus and Drizin, "Criminal Law," 646–49.

20. Tanenhaus and Drizin, "Criminal Law," 647.

21. *In re Gault*, 387 U.S. 1 (1967).

22. Feld, "Juvenile and Criminal Justice Systems' Responses," 193.

23. *McKeiver v. Pennsylvania*, 403 U.S. 528 (1971).

24. Feld, "Juvenile and Criminal Justice Systems' Responses," 191.

25. Rose, "Innocence Lost," 985–86; but see Feld, "Juvenile and Criminal Justice Systems' Responses," 237 ("[A] comprehensive assessment of rehabilitation research conducted by the National Academy of Sciences questioned . . . the assumption that youths manifest greater treatment responsiveness").

26. Brink, "Immaturity, Normative Competence, and Juvenile Transfer," 1555; Feld, "Juvenile and Criminal Justice Systems' Responses," 194–95; Tanenhaus and Drizin, "Criminal Law," 642–43.

27. Tanenhaus and Drizin, "Criminal Law," 642; Feld, "Juvenile and Criminal Justice Systems' Responses," 194.

28. Feld, "Juvenile and Criminal Justice Systems' Responses," 194.

29. Tanenhaus and Drizin, "Criminal Law," 642.

30. See, for example, Pa. Cons. Stat. Ann. § 6355 (West 2004); Va. Code Ann. § 16.1-269.1 (West 2004); Ohio Rev. Code Ann. § 2152.12 (Anderson 2005).

31. Tanenhaus and Drizin, "Criminal Law," 643.

32. Tanenhaus and Drizin, "Criminal Law," 664.

33. Feld, "Juvenile and Criminal Justice Systems' Responses," 196.

34. Brink, "Immaturity, Normative Competence, and Juvenile Transfer," 1563.

35. Feld, "Juvenile and Criminal Justice Systems' Responses," 200.

36. Feld, "Juvenile and Criminal Justice Systems' Responses,"197.

37. Feld, "Juvenile and Criminal Justice Systems' Responses,"196–97.

38. Tanenhaus and Drizin, "Criminal Law," 678–80.

39. Tanenhaus and Drizin, "Criminal Law," 680.

40. *Kent*, 383 U.S., 554–55.

41. *Jose C.*, 1996 Conn. Super. LEXIS 754, *5–*7.

42. See, for example, *McKeiver*, 403 U.S. 528 (jury trial not required); Tanenhaus and Drizin, "Criminal Law," 678–80 (discussing the Lionel Tate case).

43. Patricia Puritz et al., *A Call for Justice: An Assessment of Access to Counsel and Quality of Representation in Delinquency Proceedings* (Washington, D.C.: ABA Juvenile Justice Center, 1995), 7.

44. Tanenhaus and Drizin, "Criminal Law," 665.

45. Tanenhaus and Drizin, "Criminal Law," n. 235; James Herbie DiFonzo, "Parental Responsibility for Juvenile Crime," *Oregon Law Review* 80 (2001): 1, 37.

46. See, for example, Or. Rev. Stat. § 163.577 (1999); Ohio Rev. Code Ann. § 2919.24 (Anderson 2005).

47. Tammy Thurman, "Parental Responsibility Laws: Are They the Answer to Juvenile Delinquency?" *Journal of Law & Family Studies* 5 (2003): 99, 103.

48. Thurman, "Parental Responsibility Laws," 103–4.

49. DiFonzo, "Parental Responsibility for Juvenile Crime," 54; R.I. Gen. Laws § 1194 (1994).

50. DiFonzo, "Parental Responsibility for Juvenile Crime," 60; Salt Lake City Ordinances 11.16.010 (1995).

51. Difonzo, "Parental Responsibility for Juvenile Crime," 60; Or. Rev. Stat. 163.577 (1999).

52. Difonzo, "Parental Responsibility for Juvenile Crime," 49–50.

53. Difonzo, "Parental Responsibility for Juvenile Crime," 53 (noting significant limits on the amount of civil penalties).

54. Difonzo, "Parental Responsibility for Juvenile Crime," 49–50.

55. Difonzo, "Parental Responsibility for Juvenile Crime," 42–44.

56. Difonzo, "Parental Responsibility for Juvenile Crime," 44.

57. Puritz et al., *A Call for Justice*, 29–40.

58. See Howard Davidson, "No Consequences—Re-examining Parental Responsibility Laws," *Stanford Law & Policy Review* 7 (1995): 23, 24; Zolman, "Parental Responsibility Acts," 218; Thurman, "Parental Responsibility Laws," 109.

59. American Bar Association, "The Federalization of Family Law," *Family Advocate* 23, no. 4 (2001): 63.

60. American Bar Association, "The Federalization of Family Law," 61.

Appendix to Chapter 4
Illustrative Service Organizations That Address Juvenile Criminal Behavior

National

Juvenile Law Center
The Philadelphia Building, 4th Floor
1315 Walnut Street
Philadelphia, PA 19107
Phone: 215-625-0551
Fax: 215-625-2808
Web site: http://www.jlc.org/index.php

The Juvenile Law Center describes itself as a public interest law firm dedicated to protecting and advancing the rights and well-being of children in jeopardy. Its work ranges from abused and neglected children to delinquent youth and children with special education needs.

Youth Law Center
417 Montgomery Street, Suite 900
San Francisco, CA 94104-1121
Phone: 202-637-0377
Fax: 202-379-1600
E-mail: info@ylc.org
Web site: http://www.ylc.org

The Youth Law Center is a nonprofit legal office dedicated to protecting abused and at-risk children. Its staff investigates reports of abuse, protects the children assigned to foster care, and monitors system reform.

National Center for Youth Law
405 14th Street, 15th Floor

Oakland, CA 94612-2701
Phone: 510-835-8098
Fax: 916-551-2195
E-mail: info@youthlaw.org
Web site: http://www.youthlaw.org/

The National Center for Youth Law provides services to at-risk and low-income children, using the law to improve their lives. It focuses on financial stability for low-income families, appropriate health care and mental health services, and transitions to adulthood for at-risk youth.

Examples of Law School Programs and Clinics

University of North Carolina Law School Criminal Law Clinic
Van Hecke–Wettach Hall
100 Ridge Road
CB #3380
Chapel Hill, NC 27599-3380
Web site: http://www.law.unc.edu/Centers/details.aspx?ID=50&Q=4#two

The Criminal Law Clinic focuses on delinquency proceedings in a wide variety of felony and misdemeanor charges. Students and their practicing partners represent children at every stage of proceedings, ranging from undisciplined children and truancy to assault and drug distribution.

Criminal and Juvenile Justice Project
The University of Chicago Law School
Mandel Legal Aid Clinic
6020 S. University Avenue
Chicago, IL 60637
Phone: 773-702-9611
Fax: 773-702-2063
Web site: http://www.law.uchicago.edu/mandel/criminal/

The Criminal and Juvenile Justice Project provides quality representation to juveniles accused of crime. Its primary clients are youths from Chicago's South Side. The project also promotes a multidisciplinary approach to dealing with juvenile criminal behavior.

Youth and Education Law Clinic
Stanford Law School
Crown Quadrangle
559 Nathan Abbott Way
Stanford, CA 94305

Phone: 650-723-2465
Fax: 650-725-0253

The Youth and Education Law Clinic at Stanford provides representation in juvenile and education law cases to families in need. Realizing the connection between inadequate educational resources for low-income children and the risk for involvement with the juvenile justice system, it works in areas ranging from school discipline to the special education needs of those incarcerated in the juvenile justice system.

Example of a Local Organization in an Urban Community (Pittsburgh)

Office of the Public Defender, Allegheny County
400 County Office Building
542 Forbes Avenue
Pittsburgh, PA 15219
Phone: 412-350-2401
Fax: 412-350-2390
Web site: http://www.county.allegheny.pa.us/opd/

Public defenders' offices such as this one often have staff experienced with serving juvenile defendants. While the caseload for such attorneys is often very high, this office is an excellent place to start seeking legal advice.

Part II

Public Resistance to a Comprehensive Child Well-Being Approach

Several areas of law and public policy that affect children call for the dedication of substantial public resources if society is to realize a comprehensive vision of child well-being and justice. This substantial need is apparent and daunting. The general reaction of citizens, legislators, judges, and other policymakers in these areas has been to reject the vision of comprehensive child well-being. In contrast to the situations addressed in Part I, the situations examined in this part do not elicit even an initial widely held commitment to secure comprehensive child well-being and justice. Even at the outset, the narrative of the private, autonomous family dominates in a way that relieves the public from seeking a goal that appears unattainable.

The three chapters in this part describe specific situations that fall into this category. As in Part I, each chapter begins with a story drawn from actual case experiences. The story provides a platform for the description of a specific area of potential public obligation to children. The story also reveals public actors' failure to make the seemingly daunting commitment to secure comprehensive child well-being in the particular area. Through their actions, these actors indicate their comfort in leaving many families to their own means in addressing particular areas of need. Each chapter will suggest pragmatic strategies and contacts to help children and families experiencing the type of situation addressed in the chapter.

5

Public Education

Elizabeth Brown lives in the northwest section of Detroit, Michigan.[1] She is a single mother of two children. Dana and Dale are twelve and thirteen, respectively. Elizabeth is thirty. She works hard, holding down two jobs. She is a full-time restaurant manager and part-time waitress. A former welfare recipient, she is a model of success for the new federal welfare law's work requirements. She now makes significantly more than the average person who has left welfare, but substantially less than that required to meet the needs of her family.

Elizabeth worries about both of her children for different reasons. Dana is her most immediate concern. Although she is dependable and has provided good care for her brother while Elizabeth works, Dana is having difficulty at school. She enjoyed school at the beginning, earning straight A's for the first three years of elementary school. However, she seemed to lose interest in fourth grade and earned mostly C's as she entered middle school. Elizabeth feels that she must keep Dana interested in school if Dana is to avoid her own fate of teenage motherhood.

However, the schools are a real problem. There was a time that the public schools in Detroit were quite strong, if not outstanding. But once white, middle-class families moved out to the suburbs and African American and Latino families remained or moved into the area, the school system deteriorated. Now, a child entering a typical middle school in the Detroit system has only a 30 percent likelihood of graduating from high school. Even for children who manage to graduate from high school, 25 percent read only at the eighth grade level or below.[2]

Aware of these dismal statistics, Elizabeth initially investigated the five publicly funded charter schools in her area. One was clearly superior and seemed especially attractive, providing a slick brochure produced by the private company that managed the school. Elizabeth met with the principal, who was very optimistic about the school's programs and its projected student outcomes. Impressed, Elizabeth planned to enroll Dana in the charter school.

Fortunately, Elizabeth spoke with a parent of one of the current students in the charter school before she enrolled Dana. This parent told Elizabeth that within the first three months, her child had three different teachers. The school just could not retain teachers. Her child reported seeing rats in the school and being bored with his classes. He told her that students in the school often just sat at empty desks staring into space as the teacher did nothing other than make sure the students remained quiet. When Elizabeth looked at the boy's spelling book, it contained words such as *log*, *dog*, *hat*, and *cat*. She realized that Dana would gain nothing from such lessons.

This parent told Elizabeth that she had tried to become active with the parents' governing board that the school's charter required. The board consisted of fifteen parents, but only three regularly participated in meetings. The others were too busy or not really interested. Officials from the school's management company set and controlled the board's agenda. The focus was always on school finances and the development of strategies for pressuring public officials for more funds. They largely ignored issues of quality education and student experiences. Based on her conversation with this parent, Elizabeth realized that she could not send Dana to this school.

Elizabeth then petitioned public school authorities to have Dana assigned to a school other than the Dodge Middle School in her neighborhood. She wanted officials to allow Dana to enter a magnet middle school in the Palmer Park area of the city. This school has a diverse student population, by both race and income level, and its students have achieved strong achievement test scores. Unfortunately, this school has a long waiting list for children who live outside the relatively affluent Palmer Park neighborhood. Elizabeth had to settle for sending Dana to Ford Middle School near Wayne State

University. It would require a long bus ride for Dana, at least a half hour each way, but it was better than Dodge.

Students at Ford do better on standardized tests than students at Dodge, but that does not mean that they do well. Ford had had a tough principal who was adept at developing students' reading skills. Unfortunately, she had taken a job in a suburban district that could double her salary. This was a devastating loss of leadership at Ford, and now over one-fourth of the students at the school tested as illiterate.

Dana enrolled at Ford to begin seventh grade. The school building is wedged into a city block neighboring a collection of vacant, decrepit homes. The school's asphalt grounds seem more like a parking lot than a playground.

Once inside, the condition of the fifty-year-old school building is apparent. The air is heavy and musty. Metal lockers line the hallway. Most are severely dented, with doors ajar and broken locks. The low-hung ceiling is stained from rainwater that seeps through the leaky roof. The halls are dark and gloomy, with most overhead lights burned out.

The halls are also very crowded. With the population in the city declining during the past ten years, school officials have closed numerous school buildings in order to cut an operations deficit. This has meant consolidation of schools, long bus rides for students, and overcrowding. Ford Middle School was designed to accommodate seven hundred students and now houses over one thousand. As a result, the school's gymnasium and auditorium have been converted into makeshift classrooms. Several classes meet in these areas, separated only by plastic room dividers that allow noise from neighboring classes to significantly distract students as they study.

There is also a shortage of teachers. Teacher salaries in the Detroit school district are significantly lower than those in most suburban districts. In addition, the working conditions are much more stressful. As a result, it is extremely difficult to maintain a full teaching staff. The district regularly uses substitutes to cover all the classes. The district does not have to commit to long-term employment of these substitute teachers, and they do not demand high salaries. However, even with the pervasive use of substitute teachers, class sizes range from thirty to forty students each. This is much higher than the typical eighteen to twenty-five students in suburban district classes. Compounding this problem of a short supply of teachers is the lack of quality. The district regularly loses its most talented teachers to the suburban districts. The poor to mediocre teachers remain in the city schools. The combination of high student numbers and low-quality teachers has a significant detrimental effect on educational quality and outcomes.

Dana experienced these conditions at Ford. On a typical day, one or two of her classes would not be held because her teachers failed to report for work. When this occurred, school officials let Dana and her classmates talk with each other. Dana regularly spent one-third of her school day doing nothing because substitute teachers were in short supply.

Even in the classes with permanent teachers present in the classroom, Dana was not challenged. The teachers often let the students play games and talk to each other. This was especially the case in her science class because there was no functioning lab equipment. The students had no opportunity to conduct experiments that would bring their learning to life, so they simply put in their time until the bell rang.

At the end of each class, Dana and her classmates must return their textbooks to the teacher. Not every student has their own textbook — not enough books are available. Because school officials feel it would be unfair to let some students have books outside class while others could not and because they worry that they would lose many textbooks, the school does not allow students to take books outside the classroom. This means that students must complete most of their reading assignments during class, often reading the book in groups of two or three. Numerous days of instruction are lost as a result.

One method Elizabeth uses to keep Dana engaged and out of trouble is to involve Dana in extracurricular activities. Unfortunately, the school does not offer academic activities. Therefore, Dana joined the track team.

The track they use is the field at a local community center. It is a simple asphalt oval that does not have any lane lines. It is about four runners wide. Because it is such a poor facility, all of Ford's meets take place at other schools. Despite these conditions, the team is successful.

Dana likes traveling to other schools for track meets. These meets take place at some of the best suburban public schools. One was at Maplefield High School, which had a nine-lane, rubberized surface track that compared favorably to most college tracks. Not only was the track outstanding, the entire school simply gleamed in Dana's eyes. Everything was clean and bright. There was enough space and books for everyone, with class sizes ranging from twenty to twenty-five students. The science labs included all the latest equipment. Their teachers and coaches were well paid and seemed very bright and engaged. The school was surrounded by green playing fields, and one wing of the school contained two large gyms, an Olympic pool, a fencing room, a wrestling room, and studios for dance instruction. Everyone seemed to have everything.

Dana didn't speak with the Maplefield students. If she did, she would be even more amazed. They could tell her about all their elective courses. They can concentrate their studies in areas such as music, art, or drama in addition to completing their challenging academic courses. The school also operates a student-run television station.

Maplefield can support this type of public school because the district provides a high value of taxable property for each child. In contrast, the taxable property in the Detroit district provides only 25 percent of that in Maplefield. As a result, and in spite of a much higher tax rate in the city, spending per student in Detroit is less than half the amount in Maplefield. The difference in teacher salaries is striking. At each level of seniority, teachers in Maplefield make 50 percent more than teachers in Detroit. Even more striking is the difference in student outcomes. The graduation rate in Detroit is 25 percent of those who enter high school, with only 20 percent of high school seniors engaged in any type of college preparation program. Most students are engaged in vocational training in low-wage fields. In contrast, the graduation rate in Maplefield is over 95 percent, with 95 percent of seniors preparing for college.[3]

Dana enjoys her trips with the track team. She gets to see another world, one that offers exciting opportunities. But upon her return to Ford, she is always sad and angry. She realizes that she is trapped in a very poor school that offers her little and expects her to fail. The only opportunity for her is to limp to graduation and find some low-level job. She does not understand why her life has to be so different from her peers who go to school in the suburbs, but she is aware that her situation is unlikely to change.

Elizabeth had a somewhat more positive experience with her oldest child Dale. Dale had a real talent for art but had also been diagnosed as dyslexic in third grade. His elementary school had placed him in the school's special education classroom, where teachers either ignored him or treated him harshly for misbehavior.

The public school system resisted Elizabeth's efforts to get Dale appropriate educational services every step of the way. Initially, the school refused to assess his condition and capabilities. Elizabeth's neighbor directed her to a nonprofit agency that would assess Dale. Doing so was the only way that Elizabeth learned that Dale was dyslexic.

Fed up with Dale's experience in the school's special education classroom, Elizabeth went to the local legal services office to see whether she could get an advocate who would push the school system to address Dale's needs. One of the staff attorneys agreed to take Dale's case pro bono.

The attorney had the school system review Dale's case. School officials arranged for a comprehensive psychological evaluation. The psychologists found that Dale had pervasive developmental disorders. They concluded that the Detroit school system's special education programs were not meeting, and could not meet, his needs.

Responding to this evaluation, the school system proposed to place Dale in a special education institution. This was a school for children deemed to have no capacity to fulfill the requirements for high school graduation. Elizabeth was not satisfied. The legal services attorney advocated for Dale's placement in a private school in a Detroit suburb that served children with disabilities. Aware of the applicable special education laws and the duties it placed on school districts, she pushed the school system not only to arrange this educational placement but also to cover all the tuition costs. Fearful of a long court battle that they would likely lose, the school officials agreed.

The private school restricted all classes to eight students, a requirement that provided Dale with a comfortable environment. After several initial incidents of misbehavior involving stealing from teachers and other students, Dale began making significant progress. He improved his reading. More important, he began feeling at ease with his classmates. He learned to speak with less fear and even to form friendships. His classmates seemed to like him and to appreciate his artwork.

As Dale continued to make progress, it became apparent that he is actually very intelligent. His teachers now consider him to possess artistic and educational ambition. They believe that Dale will soon be ready to be mainstreamed into his regularly assigned public school.

Unfortunately, if Dale is mainstreamed, he will lose his teachers and therapists. Instead of a counselor who advises him and only eleven other students, he will be in a school with one counselor for four hundred students. He will also lose his small, intimate class-room. Instead of working in a class with only five other students, he will be in a class of thirty-five to forty. In addition, Dale will lose the benefits of diversity. Instead of learning with and from students from a very different suburban world, he will interact primarily with students of his own race and economic situation. The interactions that have broadened, softened, and opened up his mind and learning environment will be lost. This is a bigger loss than the pleasant facilities and grounds of the private school. He will be forced back to an impoverished educational environment like the ones experienced by his sister, who he has seen suffer.

Elizabeth would like to fight to keep Dale in the private school. However, the legal services attorney has advised her to work with the public school in order to arrange appropriate services for Dale as he is mainstreamed. He is no longer a student with a disability who requires a costly private school placement. This placement has worked, but it cannot be sustained on a permanent basis in Dale's case.

Elizabeth realizes that the attorney's advice is sound, but she is frustrated with the situation. Once again, both of her children will be trapped in dysfunctional public schools. They will not have the same opportunity as Dale's private school classmates or all the children who live in the suburbs. In fact, her children's educational opportunities will not even approach those of children outside the city system. Her children are destined to be ignored by public officials and to be trapped in dead-end jobs and lives. Elizabeth only hopes that one of her children will be extraordinary and escape the fate of educational neglect.

The United States Supreme Court and Equal Educational Opportunity

Equality of educational opportunity has a long and dramatic legal history that is both uplifting and frustrating. The guiding principle prior to the 1950s was separate but equal.[4] Public officials, policies, and laws officially separated society and its children by race. The Supreme Court held that this situation was not prohibited by the Constitution. Specifically, the Court held that black children could receive an adequate education while remaining separated from white children.[5] The Court deemed these separate educational opportunities as equal.

The Court dramatically changed course in 1954, holding that the concept of separate but equal actually denied black children equal educational opportunities.[6] When one examined the actual outcomes and real psychological impact of racial separation, it was clear that one could never deem separate education to be equal education within a society characterized by profound subordination of blacks. Schools made up of black children received far less resources. Students who attended and even graduated from these schools were largely prepared only for menial, low-wage jobs. In addition, they perceived themselves as somehow inferior and socially handicapped.

The Court's finding appeared to ensure equal educational opportunities for all children. Despite the unusually slow implementation of actual remedies,[7] the tide had turned and separate, unequal educational settings were now unacceptable. The decision called for black and white children to attend school together. The courts perceived integration as the means that would secure equal educational opportunities. Parents of white children would not allow the public to abandon or underfund the schools their children attend. Because black students would attend the same schools, they would receive equal educational benefits.

However, as formal racial separation ended and school districts implemented integration plans, many parents of white children moved to districts that included very few black students. This white flight thwarted the practical impact of the Court's decision. Using school district boundaries as legally impenetrable barriers, parents of white children regained their racially separate educational environment. Although separation, and the resulting disparity in school finances, did not occur primarily within a particular school district, it did occur across districts.[8]

There were now poor school districts, usually encompassing central urban areas and relatively remote rural areas, and rich school districts, mainly located in suburban areas. The disparity in financial resources resulted from the perceived need to fund schools primarily from local resources in order to maintain local control of educational decisions.[9] Many viewed local control as desirable and essential. Only if residents within the specific school district, through their elected school boards, could make fundamental decisions about children's education would the quality and appropriateness of education be assured. And the only way to secure this power for local residents was to have them control school finances. They could then spend as much or as little as they wanted and be free to decide what type of educational experience they wanted to provide to district children. They could control both the design of their school system and their tax burden. Many embraced this form of local power even as states became more involved in controlling education and the actual extent of local power, and the supposed benefits, diminished. The final outcome is relatively weak school board decision-making power along with wide financial disparities among public school districts.[10]

The local tax system used to support school districts and perceived as necessary for local control is the root source of funding disparities. Urban and rural school districts often encompass areas with relatively low property values. In contrast, suburban school districts often consist of high-value properties. As a result, urban and rural districts must tax property at much higher rates than suburban districts in order to raise a similar amount of tax revenue. The tax burden per dollar of property value in these poorer districts is much higher and onerous.[11]

Because of this situation, poor urban school districts soon discover that the residents cannot pay higher local property taxes even if they value education very highly. Higher taxes would have an extreme chilling effect that would thwart economic growth and community health. In the end, higher taxes would only accelerate the relocation of wealth to suburban communities.[12]

As a result, poor urban school districts have no real option to increase educational resources. The local property tax system that many view as essential to beneficial local control robs these districts of control.[13] They are trapped in a situation of extremely high property tax rates and very poorly funded schools, with no realistic opportunity to increase educational resources while maintaining economically and socially viable communities.

The significant disparities in educational resources prompted citizens in poorer districts to challenge their state governments. They asserted that state-sanctioned funding systems denied them equal protection of the law. The state was denying their children an equal opportunity to learn and thrive.

In addressing the school funding system in Texas, the Supreme Court in 1973 denied an equal protection challenge.[14] For purposes of the federal constitution, citizens from poor districts are not members of a suspect class. The Court refused to recognize poverty as a suspect classification. In addition, the Court held that education does not constitute a fundamental right. Noting that the Constitution does not expressly articulate a right to an education, it refused to construct such a right as fundamental within our constitutional democracy.

In the absence of both a suspect classification and a fundamental right, the Court reviewed the state funding scheme only to determine whether the legislature had a rational basis in adopting it. The Court found the legislature's goal of securing local control of school districts to be rational and to satisfy constitutional requirements. It allowed the wide financial disparity among public school districts to continue.

In another means of attack, those in poor districts sought to achieve cross-district integration. The idea was that if children from suburban districts had to attend city schools, suburban parents and the state would work to ensure equal resources for those schools and equal educational opportunities for all children. The legal claim raised in a case involving the Detroit school district and surrounding suburban districts asserted that cross-district integration was necessary to secure equal protection of the laws.[15] If the courts allowed de facto segregation to persist because of white flight to the suburbs, the state would effectively deny black children in the city school district their equal protection rights.

In a 1974 decision, the Supreme Court rejected this claim.[16] It refused to order cross-district integration. For purposes of desegregation orders, the courts would not breach school district boundaries unless surrounding districts had affirmatively acted to cause the racial segregation in the central district. Proving such affirmative discriminatory action was virtually impossible when segregation resulted from numerous individual parents deciding to move to suburban districts. The Court allowed the suburban districts to claim that white flight was not their fault and that the courts should not be able to compel them to participate in a desegregation plan for the central city district.

These two Supreme Court decisions trapped a significant number of students in resource-poor, racially segregated schools. These students had no right to educational resources equal to those provided to students in other districts. The quality of their schools depended on the wealth of their local community, not on the concept of an equal, or even adequate, education. The Constitution did not place any obligation on the states to address educational inequities. In addition, these students had no right to learn with children of other races. If white flight left a city district with an overwhelming black or Latino student population, achieving desegregation seemed impossible. Again, the states and school districts had no constitutional obligation to address this situation. This left children in poor urban school districts in a situation arguably worse than before the Supreme Court's landmark decision striking down the separate but equal approach to education. In practice, and with the Court's express sanction, the rule became separate and unequal educational settings.[17]

The State Courts and Equal Educational Opportunity

Denied educational rights under federal law, students, parents, and school districts sought relief for funding disparities under state law. They sued in numerous states, pressing two primary claims. One claim is that the inequalities in public school finance violate the equal protection clause of the particular state constitution. They asked state courts to interpret their respective constitutions in a way that required equal school funding. The California Supreme Court accepted such a claim and ordered education finance reform. A few other state courts also accepted this argument.[18]

The second claim is that by relying on local funding, a state fails to provide the resources necessary to secure minimally adequate educational opportunities in poor districts. This failure violates state constitutional provisions concerning basic education. The New Jersey Supreme Court ruled in favor of this claim, finding that the state's local funding scheme failed to provide a "thorough and efficient" education as required by the state constitution. Several other state supreme courts followed New Jersey's lead on this issue.[19]

The first claim has not met with much success recently, possibly because a court may fear that a ruling based on the equal protection clause will have broad, unintended consequences in areas other than education. The second claim does not give rise to the same fears because it arises only in the context of basic education. This may explain why this second claim has been used extensively in recent public school financing cases.

A 1997 decision of the North Carolina Supreme Court provides an illustration of the legal trend in this area.[20] The primary plaintiffs were students and their parents from the state's relatively poor school districts. They sued the state, claiming that the defendant's current school funding system denied them adequate educational opportunities in violation of the state constitution. They also claimed that the state was denying them their right to educational opportunities equal to those of other North Carolina children in violation of the state constitution.

The plaintiffs pointed to the funding disparities caused by local control for giving rise to the constitutional violations. The state leaves the funding of capital expenses, as well as 25 percent of operating expenses, to local governments. The court described the plaintiffs' more specific complaints, ones that mirror the situation experienced by Elizabeth and her two children in Detroit:

> Plaintiffs complain of inadequate school facilities with insufficient space, poor lighting, leaking roofs, erratic heating and air conditioning, peeling paint, cracked plaster, and rusting exposed pipes. They allege that their poor districts' media centers have sparse and outdated book collections and lack the technology present in the wealthier school districts. They complain that they are unable to compete for high quality teachers because local salary supplements in their poor districts are well below those provided in wealthy districts. Plaintiffs allege that this relative inability to hire teachers causes the number of students per teacher to be higher in their poor districts than in wealthy districts.
>
> Plaintiffs allege that college admission test scores and yearly aptitude test scores reflect both the inadequacy and the disparity in education received by children in their poor districts. Plaintiffs allege that end-of-grade tests show that the great *majority of students in plaintiffs' districts are failing in basic subjects.*[21]

The court began its opinion by rejecting the reasoning of the lower court that had held that the right to education guaranteed by the state constitution only meant that each child was to have equal access to the existing system of education. The court then found that the state constitutional right entails a qualitative standard. Namely, the state is required to provide children with an education that meets a minimum standard of quality. This is a "sound basic education"[22] that must serve the purpose of preparing students to participate and compete in the society in which they live and work.

> For purposes of our Constitution, a *"sound basic education"* is one that will provide the student with at least: (1) sufficient ability to read, write and speak the English language and a sufficient knowledge of

fundamental mathematics and physical science to enable the student to function in a complex and rapidly changing society; (2) sufficient fundamental knowledge of geography, history, and basic economic and political systems to enable the student to make informed choices with regard to issues that affect the student personally or affect the student's community, state, and nation; (3) sufficient academic and vocational skills to enable the student to successfully engage in post-secondary education or vocational training; and (4) sufficient academic and vocational skills to enable the student to compete on an equal basis with others in further formal education or gainful employment in contemporary society.[23]

Based on this right to a minimally adequate education, the court allows the plaintiffs to proceed with their claim.

In contrast to this ruling, the court rejected the plaintiffs' claim based on a right to equal educational opportunity.[24] The plaintiffs asserted that inequalities in the facilities, equipment, student-teacher ratios, and test results arise from great variations in per-pupil expenditures from district to district and deny them equal educational opportunities. The court did not dispute the facts surrounding significant funding disparities, but it instead held that the state constitution did not provide relief from this situation. The original constitutional provision written in 1868 that required "a general and uniform system of free public schools" only intended that children have a right to a sound basic education. In addition, the provision adopted in 1970 that stated "wherein equal opportunities shall be provided for all students" ensured only that all children of the state would enjoy the right to a sound basic education. The education clauses of the state constitution provide nothing more.[25]

In reaching this conclusion, the court relied on basic concepts of local control. It noted that the state constitution expressly authorizes the legislature to require that local governments bear part of the costs of their local public schools. More tellingly, the constitution provides that local governments may use local revenues to supplement their school programs as much as they wish. Because of these provisions, the court stated that "there can be nothing unconstitutional about [additional local funding] or in any inequality of opportunity occurring as a result."[26] The court concluded, "We see no reason to suspect that the framers intended the substantially equal educational opportunities beyond the sound basic education mandated by the Constitution must be available in all districts."[27] In the end, the tradition of local control led the court to reject plaintiffs' claim that they had a right to equal educational opportunity, while the court upheld plaintiffs' claim that they had a right to a minimally sound basic education as defined by the court.[28]

It should be noted that the litigation process in this area is lengthy, providing no immediate relief. It has stretched out over ten years or more in some states.[29] And even when plaintiffs ultimately prevail, frustrations and funding inequities continue.

The North Carolina Supreme Court noted the difficulties experienced by many states in assuring the right to a sound basic education. Affected states have struggled to understand and implement court mandates. Thus, the result of successful litigation is often a failure to improve student performance. The problems are even worse when courts try to ensure a right to equal educational opportunities. The court feared protracted litigation that would yield only unworkable remedies. This process would pit the courts against the legislature in a struggle to realize an impractical or unattainable goal.[30] Because of these considerations, the North Carolina court recognized the right to a sound basic education and provided guidance on how to measure achievement in this area while it rejected the right to equal educational opportunities and equal funding among districts.

This has been such a struggle because many perceive the stakes as very high. Providing every child with a sound basic education may require a significant redistribution of resources to poor districts. Certainly fulfilling a right to equal educational opportunities would require significant redistributions. While poor districts may benefit,[31] wealthy districts will certainly suffer. This outcome affects the powerful, and their power is used to resist any fundamental change in the distribution of educational resources. They fight to keep their tax dollars within their own community for their children's benefit.

Those in wealthy districts use the rhetoric of local control of school districts to prevail in the fight. They expound on the supposed benefits of local control to educational systems.[32] They then assert that in order to achieve effective local control, communities must have the capacity to provide local funds to their schools. In essence, money is control. If they can generate the resources necessary to realize particular educational goals, they should have the authority to do so and the right to keep those funds within their district.

The Family Metanarratives

The argument for local control arises from the metanarrative of the autonomous, private family.[33] This narrative places the control of educational decisions in the hands of parents first and the local community, within which parents play an active and important role, second. If a family has the capacity and decides to live in a relatively wealthy community, they should be able to benefit. More specifically, they should be able to have their local tax dollars remain in the local community for the benefit of their children and schools. Individuals and families in poorer communities have the same right and authority to fund their own schools, but they should not expect resources from relatively wealthy communities. Therefore, the necessary corollary is that if a family decides to live in a poorer community, they will suffer. Specifically, their children will attend poor schools and receive less educational resources.

The bottom line is that the metanarrative of child well-being that supports equity among children throughout American society, and therefore equal educational opportunities, is overwhelmed by the metanarrative of the private family that supports local control of educational decisions and resources.[34] The relatively wealthy and powerful utilize the concepts of autonomy to prevail, to secure abundant educational resources for their children and their community, and to effectively reduce the educational and career opportunities for children in poorer districts, thus reducing the competition eventually faced by their children in the marketplace. In the end, our society leaves Elizabeth's children on their own, harmed and disabled by poor schools.

The Supreme Court decisions and the rhetoric of local control employed by the relatively wealthy and powerful explain why the experience of Elizabeth's children is typical. American society traps poor children in poor school districts. They cannot look to the federal Constitution for relief, either in equalizing funding or in desegregating their schools. They are dependent on the funds and degree of diversity that only their local community can generate. They cannot look for effective relief from outside their community, with state efforts to improve the situation hampered by a modest goal of securing only minimally adequate educational opportunities, vigorous political resistance, and eventual subversion.[35]

The Current Realities Concerning
Equal Educational Opportunity

The results of this situation have been extensively documented. First, there is a wide disparity in school funding. Relatively affluent suburban districts regularly spend significantly more per student than poor districts do, with some disparities exceeding 100 percent.[36] In other words, some suburban districts can spend double the amount on their students. As Dana observed in her trip to a suburban school, this difference means a great deal. Frequently cited differences include quality of books, access to computers, existence and availability of laboratories, higher achievement standards and goals, more qualified teachers, smaller class sizes, and the existence and condition of educational and athletic facilities.[37] Brian Marron has described the resulting conditions at urban public schools:

> Many common-place features of urban public schools contribute to providing an inadequate education to students. First, many urban schools are housed in old and poorly maintained buildings, some dating back to the nineteenth century. Second, many of these ancient dilapidated buildings are oversized and overcrowded. Third, inner-city children are also disproportionately likely to receive inexperienced teachers or teachers who lack the requisite credentials.[38]

These conditions significantly hinder educational achievement. The evidence lies in test score results. A comprehensive study found that only 40 percent of fourth and eighth grade students attending city schools met minimum basic standards on exams in reading, math, and science. In contrast, over 60 percent of students in suburban districts met the basic standards.[39] Students in city districts drop out of school at a much higher rate than those in suburban districts. Even among those who do graduate, many have not acquired a basic education. As Jonathan Kozol found in Chicago, "27 percent of high school graduates read at the eighth grade level or below." He also noted "that only 3.5 percent of students graduate and read up to the national norm."[40]

These conditions disproportionately affect minority children. There is a significant persistent and growing achievement gap between white children and minority children. A 2004 special report stated, "Last year, 6 of 10 black fourth graders who took the NAEP reading test had not even partially mastered grade-level skills. Only 25 percent of whites scored that low. In high schools, the situation is just as dismaying: Black and Hispanic seniors on average read and do math only as well as white eighth graders."[41] The report also revealed that even in the strongest of six urban school districts examined (Charlotte, North Carolina), 52 percent of black fourth graders were "below basic" in reading, while only 17 percent of white students were below basic.[42]

This disparity is not surprising in light of the failure to integrate schools. Our society increasingly abandons minority students to poor districts with poor schools. America's public schools became substantially more segregated during the 1990s, with the trend alarmingly toward increased segregation. Since 1988, the percentage of black students attending schools that have a majority of white students has continually declined. In 1988, 43.5 percent of black students attended majority white schools, but by 1998, this percentage had declined to 32.7 percent. Consequently, black students attending majority-minority schools increased over the same period from 62.9 percent to 70.2 percent.[43] The same trend holds for Latino students.

It is noteworthy that during the 1990s, the Supreme Court provided school districts with relief from desegregation orders, ending several successful programs and causing significant increases in segregation.[44] It ruled that as long as a school board has complied in good faith and the vestiges of past discrimination have been eliminated to the extent practicable, a federal court's desegregation order should end even if evidence showed that ending the court order would result in substantial resegregation. The lower federal courts followed the Supreme Court and ended desegregation orders affecting several major urban school systems.

The current law now supports school systems best characterized as separate and unequal.[45] The best predictors of student achievement are class and race. This is the current educational reality in the United States.

Academics and public policy experts have proposed various approaches to change the current reality. However, these approaches are largely unrealistic. For example, Erwin Chemerinsky proposes the creation of unitary public school systems that encompass large urban centers and the surrounding suburbs and in which every child must enroll.[46] These school systems could ensure desegregated schools because they would include a large number of majority-white suburban communities. They would also allow for equal allocation of funds throughout a large area and, hopefully, equal educational opportunities for students in inner-city and suburban schools. Chemerinsky recognizes the coherent logic and real advantages of his proposal, but he also realizes that it is not politically or legally viable.[47]

Another common proposal is to provide school choice for children in poor school districts. The progressive school choice movement is the most hopeful. It would target benefits only to children most in need—poor, minority children in resource-poor school districts. It would include a wide array of choices, including religious schools, and provide a great deal of information to parents. This movement would offer targeted children equal educational opportunities by empowering their parents to choose their school.[48]

While this proposal also makes a great deal of sense, it, too, is impractical under present conditions. There is great political resistance to school choice programs because many perceive them as threatening resources for public schools, teachers' unions, and integration goals.[49] In addition, it is extremely difficult to generate adequate choices in areas reachable by poor children. As Elizabeth found with Dana, there is no real choice when all your choices are bad. Finally, choice programs rely heavily on well-informed parents, a reliance that may be unrealistic.

The actual current plan for improving education is captured by the federal No Child Left Behind Act (NCLB).[50] Despite the continued rhetoric of local control, the federal government has taken the lead role in education reform. The core component of NCLB is to require school districts to demonstrate adequate yearly progress in student achievement regardless of race, disability, or class. NCLB requires each state to implement a single accountability system that meets federal guidelines and facilitates targeted support for student learning. Over a twelve-year period, the acceptable threshold rises incrementally until 100 percent of students reach proficiency measured both in the aggregate and by particular groupings based on race, disability, and class.[51]

NCLB specifies sanctions for schools that fail to meet their annual yearly progress goals. If a school fails for two years, the district must develop an improvement plan and receive technical assistance. In addition, public school choice becomes operational, providing funds to students to transfer to another school within their public school district. If a school fails three years in a row, the initial sanctions continue, and the district must provide supplemental education services to disadvantaged students. The fourth year of failure builds on the previous sanctions by requiring the school to replace staff, institute a new curriculum, decrease management authority and appoint an outside expert, extend the school day, or restructure. If the school fails a fifth year, it must restructure. This could involve transformation to a charter school or a state takeover of operations.[52]

NCLB has been both praised and criticized. On one hand, many view its overall goal of providing adequate educational opportunities to every child as appropriately ambitious. Many also note the improvement in information provided to parents. Hopefully, more information will lead to better educational choices and performance.[53]

On the other hand, many criticize the law for being too focused on achievement test results. Teachers are required to teach to a test in a rote or mechanical way. Creative educational approaches and learning must take a backseat as the tested knowledge and skills dominate. Critics also argue that the law establishes unachievable goals. Schools must eventually have 100 percent of their students at the proficient level for their grade. This is true for all subgroups, including students with disabilities. It is highly unlikely that even good schools will achieve this goal. Therefore, schools will face NCLB sanctions, with poorer schools confronting the sanctions first. These sanctions could severely damage, if not destroy, the schools that are most in need. This is especially true if the federal government continues to fail to provide the resources for needed improvements. The law will allow parents in these poor districts to exercise choice, but their choices may be limited to other poor public schools in their own districts. Overall, critics fear that the law may cause severe damage to some public schools, damage that may lead to permanent educational inadequacy and failure.[54]

The Special Case of Special Education

This is the current reality of educational opportunities in poor urban districts. Children like Dana and Dale are trapped in schools that are largely segregated by race and class, that lack basic resources, and that provide little opportunity for learning and eventual full participation in society. However, Dale's experience provides a glimpse at an immediate hope for children trapped in this situation. At least temporarily, he experienced a high-quality education that met his individual needs. He gained this experience because he fell within the ambit of special education law, a law that opens the door to special education services.

The federal Individuals with Disabilities Education Act (IDEA) requires states and school districts to provide a free and appropriate public education (FAPE) to students with disabilities.[55] The definition of what constitutes FAPE has changed over time. The IDEA checklist requires the provision of instruction at public expense and under public supervision, instruction that meets state educational standards and approximates the grade levels used in the regular education system, and instruction that fulfills a particular student's individualized educational plan (IEP).

The Supreme Court initially interpreted FAPE to require only that students with disabilities benefit in some way from the instruction provided, with IDEA only providing a basic opportunity for some type of educational benefit.[56] However, the states began to interpret their constitutions as requiring more, such as children's acquisition of sufficient skills to be successful in society.[57] As states implemented this type of substantive educational standard for all students, including those with disabilities, and began to adopt and publicize outcome measures, FAPE came to mean more. School districts had to provide disabled students educational opportunities that allowed them to meet state standards.[58] The NCLB reinforced this trend by including such students in the law's assessment measures and goals. In fact, even before the enactment of NCLB, Congress had amended the IDEA to explicitly mandate that states establish performance goals for students with disabilities that are consistent with goals and standards set for all students.[59]

IDEA is very supportive of students and, if implemented fully, can provide a high level of educational services and opportunities. Dale experienced this high level of service. But his mother had to fight to get these services. She needed an advocate, a good deal of tenacity, and a bit of luck.

Initially, parents and educators must recognize a child's need for special education services. Poor grades, lack of interest in school, behavior problems, and other educational problems may indicate a need for services. Upon recognition of need, a parent can seek a full evaluation of the child by making a written request to the child's school. The parent will serve as the key decision maker in the IDEA process and must consent to the evaluation. It should be noted that if the parent has sufficient resources and does not fully trust the school system to conduct a thorough evaluation, the parent can secure an independent evaluation before beginning the process with the school. This additional evaluation step may delay the process, but it also will allow the parent to have a specific goal in mind as he or she deals with the school.[60]

Federal law gives the school system a "reasonable period of time" to complete the evaluations and meet as a team with the parent to determine whether a child is eligible for special education services. IDEA provides that a "child with a disability" means a child

> (i) with mental retardation, hearing impairments (including deafness), speech or language impairments, visual impairment (including blindness), serious emotional disturbance (hereinafter referred to as "emotional disturbance"), orthopedic impairments, autism, traumatic brain injury, other health impairments, or specific learning disabilities; and (ii) who, by reason thereof, needs special education and related services.[61]

The law also provides that

> the term "special education" means specially designed instruction, at no cost to parents, to meet the unique needs of a child with a disability, including—
> (A) instruction conducted in the classroom, in the home, in hospitals and in other settings; and
> (B) instruction in physical education.[62]

The school must determine whether the child has one or more specified physical or mental impairments and if the child requires special education services by reason of one or more impairments.[63] Approximately 13 percent of current students meet the definition of a child with a disability and are eligible for special education services.[64]

The eligibility meeting has to include the parent and a team of qualified professionals. The school must provide a copy of any evaluation to the parent, hopefully before the meeting occurs. It may be worth delaying the meeting in order to allow the parent to review evaluations with an advocate or other professional. The professional team must determine whether the child has a disability and whether the child needs special education services.[65]

Once a school determines that a student is eligible, it must develop an Individualized Education Program (IEP) for the student. The IEP team includes parents, a regular education teacher, a special education teacher, a qualified school system representative, a psychologist or therapist who can understand the instructional implications of evaluation results, others with knowledge of the child (at the parents' discretion), and the student, if appropriate. The team must develop the IEP within thirty days of the eligibility decision.[66] An IEP describes in detail the child's needs and how the school will meet those needs. It must include measurable annual goals and designate who is responsible for monitoring the student's progress. The IEP must also identify the special education and related services to be provided and the detailed plan for service delivery (e.g., specialized instruction on reading skills in a separate classroom for two hours every Tuesday afternoon, occupational therapy for one hour every Friday). These services could extend beyond the school year and include the summer months.[67]

The parent should work with an advocate to prepare for the IEP meeting. Together, they should think about what the child should accomplish during the next year, prepare to inform the team of the child's special conditions and characteristics, and review all records and evaluations, noting points of agreement and disagreement. In the meeting, they should record major points of discussion, possibly taping the meeting, if allowed. The parent should not sign the IEP until he or she fully understands it and agrees. Services begin once the parent signs the initial IEP, but the parent should not sign if he or she disagrees with the proposed IEP.

If the parent agrees with the IEP, he or she needs to monitor the services provided and the child's progress. The parent should communicate regularly with the child's teachers and request an IEP meeting if problems come up. The school must review the IEP annually, with a reevaluation of the student at least every three years. The school cannot decide that the child is no longer eligible for special education services without first evaluating the child.[68]

If the parent disagrees with the IEP team initially or at any point in the process, he or she has three options.[69] The first is mediation. A qualified, impartial mediator will conduct the process, with the school bearing the cost. All information and discussions are confidential and cannot be used at a subsequent formal hearing. If the parties reach an agreement, it must be in writing.

The second option is a formal due process hearing, a trial-like administrative hearing. A hearing officer presides over the presentation of witnesses and other evidence. The hearing officer can order the school system to provide appropriate services and to pay the parents' attorney expenses. Because of the formal nature of the proceedings and the complexity of special education law, parents need an experienced advocate at the hearing even though this is not required by law.

The third option is to file a complaint with the state department of education. This option is less demanding on parents. The state investigates and makes decisions concerning special education services for the child. Unfortunately, the quality of state investigations varies widely, and relying on this option to pursue complex service issues may be unwise.

The best way to take advantage of the special education law is to prepare thoroughly for a high-quality eligibility determination and IEP meeting. This will allow parents and schools to avoid conflicts and to provide a proper array of supportive services that meet the particular student's needs. The importance of an alliance with an experienced and skilled advocate cannot be overemphasized. This is the type of person who can make the complex system work for the student. It made all the difference for Elizabeth and Dale. Because they had someone push for an appropriate evaluation and tailored service plan, Dale gained an educational opportunity that allowed him to blossom. The federal law provides a means to secure significant educational benefits for children with disabilities, as long as parents and educators monitor students closely so that special education services do not become an educational backwater where difficult children are hidden.[70] Vigilant parents, allied with zealous advocates, can provide some children in poor school districts with high-quality educational opportunities through the process and rights provided by the IDEA.

Conclusion

The special education law appears to be the current best hope for children trapped in poor school districts. This is unfortunate because this hope is not available to all children. Although relatively common conditions such as attention deficit disorder may constitute a "disability" or "handicap" entitling children to FAPE services, many children do not come within the federal law[71] and will remain trapped in dysfunctional schools.

However, special education law illustrates the powerful force unleashed when parents and students can appeal to the metanarrative of child well-being. In particular contexts, this metanarrative can overcome that of the private, autonomous family and the related metanarrative of local control of schools.[72] When society views a child as being in special need, it responds. The challenge is to have the public view every child as needing high-quality educational opportunities. The cost entailed in embracing and acting on such a view currently makes the public shy away. Education advocates, progressive legislators, and supportive judges must work to bring to life the metanarratives of child well-being and equal educational opportunity in a way that overcomes the rhetoric used to avoid public commitment. It will be a long battle, but it is the only way to free most poor children from educational segregation, despair, and failure.

Notes

1. This story is based on the following sources: Jonathan Kozol, *Savage Inequalities: Children in America's Schools* (New York: Crown, 1991), 40–82; Katherine Boo, "After Welfare," *New Yorker*, April 9, 2001, 93.

2. See Kozol, *Savage Inequalities*, 58, for a discussion of similar statistics in a major urban public school system.

3. See Kozol, *Savage Inequalities*, 63–69, for a discussion of similar statistics in a major suburban public school system.

4. See *Plessy v. Ferguson*, 163 U.S. 537 (1895).

5. See *Cumming v. Board of Education*, 175 U.S. 528 (1899); *Missouri ex rel. Gaines v. Canada*, 305 U.S. 337 (1938).

6. *Brown v. Board of Education*, 347 U.S. 483 (1954).

7. See *Brown v. Board of Education*, 349 U.S. 294 (1955) (holding that the remedy of Brown should be desegregation "with all deliberate speed"); *Cooper v. Aaron*, 358 U.S. 1 (1958).

8. See Erwin Chemerinsky, "Separate and Unequal: American Public Education Today," *American University Law Review* 52 (2003): 1461, 1468.

9. John C. Reitz, "Public School Financing in the United States: More on the Dark Side of Intermediate Structures," *Brigham Young University Law Review* (1993): 623, 626.

10. Reitz, "Public School Financing," 628–30.

11. Reitz, "Public School Financing," 630; Chemerinsky, "Separate and Unequal," 1470.

12. Chemerinsky, "Separate and Unequal," 1470.

13. Reitz, "Public School Financing," 630.

14. *San Antonio School Dist. v. Rodriguez*, 411 U.S. 1 (1973).

15. See *Milliken v. Bradley*, 418 U.S. 717 (1974).

16. *Milliken v. Bradley*.

17. Chemerinsky, "Separate and Unequal," 1463–64; David S. Broder, "Still Separate and Unequal," *Washington Post*, May 13, 2004, A29; Brian P. Marron, "Promoting Racial Equality through Equal Educational Opportunity: The Case for Progressive School-Choice," *Brigham Young University Education & Law Journal* (2002): 53, 61–62.

18. See Reitz, "Public School Financing," 632; *Horton v. Meskill*, 376 A.2d 359 (Conn. 1977); *Washakie County School Dist. No. 1 v. Herschler*, 606 P.2d 310 (Wyo. 1980), cert. denied, *Hot Springs County School Dist. v. Washakie County School District*, 449 U.S. 824 (1980).

19. See Reitz, "Public School Financing," 633; *Robinson v. Cahill*, 303 A.2d 273 (N.J. 1973); *Rose v. Council for Better Education, Inc.*, 790 S.W.2d 186 (Ky. 1989); *Helena Elementary School District No. 1 v. State*, 769 P.2d 684 (Mont. 1989); *Seattle School Dist. No. 1 v. State*, 585 P.2d 71 (Wash. 1978); Scott Rothschild, "State Officials to Appeal Judge's Order to Halt Spending on Schools," *Lawrence Journal-World*, May 11, 2004, http://www.ljworld.com/section/?breaking/story/169890.

20. *Leandro v. State*, 488 S.E.2d 249 (N.C. 1997).

21. *Leandro v. State*, 252.

22. *Leandro v. State*, 255.

23. *Leandro v. State*, 255.

24. *Leandro v. State*, 257.

25. *Leandro v. State*, 257.

26. *Leandro v. State*, 256.

27. *Leandro v. State*, 256.

28. The Court subsequently affirmed this right in *Hoke County Board of Education v. State*, 599 S.E.2d 365 (2004).

29. See *Leandro*, 488 S.E.2d at 249; *Hoke County Bd. of Education v. State*, 599 S.E.2d at 365; *Milliken*, 418 U.S. at 267; *Bradley v. Milliken*, 433 F.2d 897 (6th Cir. Mich. 1970); *Bradley v. Milliken*, 1990 U.S. App. LEXIS 20093, *1 (6th Cir. Mich. 1990). *Leandro* and *Hoke County* spent eight years at the appellate level alone (not counting time at or before trial); *Milliken* was argued before the courts, in some form, for over twenty years.

30. *Leandro*, 488 S.E.2d, 257.

31. *Leandro*, 257 (noting that even this benefit is in doubt).

32. Reitz, "Public School Financing," 626–27.

33. See Reitz, "Public School Financing," 626–32; Chemerinsky, "Separate and Unequal," 1473; *Wisconsin v. Yoder*, 406 U.S. 205 (1972).

34. See Marron, "Promoting Racial Equality," 66; Chemerinsky, "Separate and Unequal," 1474.

35. See Chemerinsky, "Separate and Unequal," 1473–75; Reitz, "Public School Financing," 626 (discussing "save harmless" provisions that prevent redistribution of state aid and other political loopholes to funding reform); *Leandro*, 257.

36. See Marron, "Promoting Racial Equality," 64; Reitz, "Public School Financing," 625–26; Chemerinsky, "Separate and Unequal," 1467–68.

37. Marron, "Promoting Racial Equality," 60; Kozol, *Savage Inequalities*, 63–69.

38. Marron, "Promoting Racial Equality," 62 (citations omitted).

39. Marron, "Promoting Racial Equality," 62–63.

40. Kozol, *Savage Inequalities*, 58.

41. Julian E. Barnes et al., "Unequal Education," *U.S. News & World Report*, March 22, 2004, 66.

42. Barnes et al., "Unequal Education."

43. Chemerinsky, "Separate and Unequal," 1463–64; Gary Orfield, "Schools More Separate: Consequences of a Decade of Resegregation" (Cambridge, MA: Harvard University, Civil Rights Project, 2001), available at http://www.civilrightsproject.harvard.edu/research/deseg/Schools_More_Separate.pdf.

44. Chemerinsky, "Separate and Unequal," 1464–65; *Board of Education of Oklahoma City v. Dowell*, 498 U.S. 237 (1991); *Freeman v. Pitts*, 503 U.S. 467 (1992).

45. See Chemerinsky, "Separate and Unequal," 1463; Broder, "Still Separate and Unequal," 17.

46. Chemerinsky, "Separate and Unequal," 1462.

47. Chemerinsky, "Separate and Unequal," 1473–75.

48. Marron, "Promoting Racial Equality," 70–81.

49. Marron, "Promoting Racial Equality," 85–87.

50. 20 U.S.C. § 6301 (2002).

51. George J. Petersen and Michelle D. Young, "The No Child Left Behind Act and Its Influence on Current and Future District Leaders," *Journal of Law & Education* 33 (2004): 343, 348.

52. Petersen and Young, "The No Child Left Behind Act," 350.

53. Petersen and Young, "The No Child Left Behind Act," 349; Marron, "Promoting Racial Equality," 81–85.

54. Petersen and Young, "The No Child Left Behind Act," 361.

55. 20 U.S.C. §§ 1401(3), 1401(25) (2000). The Rehabilitation Act of 1973, 29 U.S.C. § 794 (2000), may also provide relief for children with disabilities. See "Memorandum" from Robert R. Davila et al., Office of Special Education and Rehabilitative Services, Joint Policy Memorandum (ADD), September 16, 1991, 5.

56. *Board of Education v. Rowley*, 458 U.S. 176, 192 (1982).

57. See, for example, *In re John K.*, 170 Cal. App. 3d 783, 790–91 (Cal. Ct. App. 1985); *School Board v. Beasley*, 380 S.E.2d 884 (Va. 1989).

58. Scott F. Johnson, "Reexamining *Rowley*: A New Focus in Special Education Law," *Brigham Young University Education & Law Journal* (2003): 561, 567.

59. Johnson, "Reexamining *Rowley*," 567.

60. Kathleen McNaught, "Navigating the Special Education Process," *Child Law Practice* 23 (2004): 65, 65–78.

61. 20 U.S.C. § 1401(3) (2005).

62. 20 U.S.C. § 1401(29) (2005).

63. Davila, "Memorandum," 3.

64. T. D. Snyder, A. G. Tan, and C. M. Hoffman, *Digest of Education Statistics 2003* (NCES 2005-025) U.S. Department of Education, National Center for Education Statistics (Washington, DC: U.S. Government Printing Office, 2004).

65. 20 U.S.C. § 1414(b) (2005).

66. 20 U.S.C. § 1414(d) (2005).

67. See 20 U.S.C. §§ 1412(a)(1)(A), 1414(d)(1)(B) (2005); *J.P. v. West Clark Community Schools*, 230 F. Supp. 2d 910 (S.D. Ind. 2002) (discussing level of review given to extended school year IEPs).

68. 20 U.S.C. § 1414(a)(2) (2005).

69. 20 U.S.C. § 1415 (2005).

70. See Diana Jean Schemo, "School Achievement Reports Often Exclude the Disabled," *New York Times,* August 30, 2004, A10.

71. 20 U.S.C. § 1401(3); McNaught, "Navigating the Special Education Process," 77.

72. See McNaught, "Navigating the Special Education Process," 77; Marron, "Promoting Racial Equality," 70.

Appendix to Chapter 5
Illustrative Service Organizations
That Address Education Issues

National

Center for Law and Education
1875 Connecticut Avenue, N.W.
Suite 510
Washington, DC 20009
Phone: (202) 986-3000
Fax: (202) 986-6648
Web site: http://www.cleweb.org

A national league dedicated to education reform, its member organization, Community Action for Public Schools, offers members (including parents) telephone tips and information.

Council for Exceptional Children
1110 North Glebe Road, Suite 300
Arlington, VA 22201
Phone: 703-620-3660
Fax: 703-264-9494
E-mail: service@cec.sped.org
Web site: http://www.cec.sped.org/

The Council for Exceptional Children is a national organization dedicated to meeting the needs of exceptional or gifted children or children with disabilities. It publishes newsletters and journals on educational topics, as well as facilitating cross-training for education professionals.

Juvenile Law Center
The Philadelphia Building, 4th Floor
1315 Walnut Street
Philadelphia, PA 19107
Phone: 215-625-0551
Fax: 215-625-2808
Web site: http://www.jlc.org/index.php

The Juvenile Law Center describes itself as a public interest law firm dedicated to protecting and advancing the rights and well-being of children in jeopardy. Its clientele range from abused and neglected children to delinquent youth and children with special education needs.

The National Law Center on Homelessness & Poverty
1411 K Street N.W., Suite 1400
Washington, DC 20005
Phone: 202-638-2535
Fax: 202-628-2737
Web site: http://www.nlchp.org/

The National Law Center on Homelessness and Poverty serves as the legal arm of the movement to end homelessness. Using both legislative advocacy and direct litigation assistance, it works on a variety of issues, such as housing, education, and civil rights.

Examples of Law School Programs and Clinics

Youth and Education Law Clinic
Stanford Law School
Crown Quadrangle
559 Nathan Abbott Way

Stanford, CA 94305
Phone: 650-723-2465
Fax: 650-725-0253

The Youth and Education Law Clinic at Stanford provides representation in juvenile and education law cases to families in need. Realizing the connection between inadequate educational resources for low-income children and the risk for involvement with the juvenile justice system, the clinic works in areas ranging from school discipline to the special education needs of those incarcerated in the juvenile justice system.

Children's Education Law Clinic at Duke Law School

201 W. Main Street, Suite 202-D
Durham, NC 27701
Phone: 919-956-2580
Fax: 919-956-8179

The Children's Education Law Clinic is a community law office that provides free legal advice and representation in a variety of proceedings related to children and schools. The clinic focuses on special education and school discipline.

Children and Youth Advocacy Clinic

University of Washington School of Law
Clinical Law Program
William H. Gates Hall, Suite 265
Campus Box 353020
P.O. Box 85110
Seattle, WA 98145-1110
Web site: http://www.law.washington.edu/Clinics/Child.html

The Children and Youth Advocacy Clinic provides low-income families with a multidisciplinary approach that incorporates students from the school of law, medicine, and social work. It takes cases related to education law, health care, and immigration.

Examples of Organizations in an Urban Community (Pittsburgh)

Education Law Center of Pennsylvania

1315 Walnut Street, Suite 400
Philadelphia, PA 19107-4717
Phone: 412-391-5225
Web site: http://www.elc-pa.org/

The Education Law Center works in three major Pennsylvania cities to ensure that parents and children are informed of their educational rights. It also maintains a database of pro bono education attorneys.

Pennsylvania School Profiles
Web site: http://www.paprofiles.org/

The Pennsylvania Department of Education provides a listing of rankings of elementary and secondary schools within the state.

6
Health Care

Mary Anderson's experiences with the health care system begin in January 2000.[1] At that time, she was the mother of two children. Jim was eight years old and in the third grade. Lisa was four years old and in day care. Mary is divorced from the children's father and has not seen or heard from him in over three years. The family lives in a public housing complex in Chicago.

Mary successfully applied for public benefits under the Temporary Aid for Needy Families (TANF) program two years ago. She has participated on public works crews in fulfilling her TANF work requirements and has now entered an employment training program. She hopes to secure a paying job within the year and move out of the TANF program.

When Mary applied for TANF benefits, no one informed her that she could apply for child health coverage under the Medicaid program. The office administering the TANF program did not handle Medicaid applications or benefits. As a result, Mary and her children have been uninsured ever since she divorced her husband. Although she had the children properly vaccinated at public health clinics, she failed to take Jim and Lisa to a doctor or dentist for checkups.

In December 1999, Mary had to take Jim to a hospital emergency room when he sustained a minor injury playing soccer. Because she did not have insurance and could not pay the hospital bill, the hospital staff informed her that she could apply for Medicaid coverage for her children. They referred her to the appropriate office, and Mary completed and submitted the application in January 2000.

The state's Medicaid law required the Office of Medical Assistance to make a decision on all Medicaid applications within forty-five days.[2] The office regularly failed to meet this requirement. In March 2000, Mary received a request for employment verification and submitted the necessary information within two weeks. A week later, she received another request for employment verification. She did not respond to the second request and subsequently received a denial notice in April 2000 stating that she had failed to provide requested information. With the help of a legal services lawyer, Mary objected to the denial, and the Office of Medical Assistance approved her application for Jim and Lisa, stating that they were eligible retroactively from January 2000 through October 2000.[3]

While Mary waited for Medicaid approval, she failed to take Jim and Lisa to the doctor. Lisa suffered a serious ear infection during this period. Although she recovered, she was in great pain. She could not attend day care. As a result, Mary could not attend her job training program for a week and almost lost her seat in the program.

In July 2000, Lisa suffered another ear infection. When her fever was 102 degrees, Mary took her to an emergency medical clinic. A doctor examined Lisa quickly and wrote a prescription for an antibiotic. The clinic served indigent patients free of charge, and the staff did not require Mary to verify her Medicaid coverage.

Mary immediately went to a local pharmacy to fill the prescription. The pharmacist took Mary's Medicaid card and called the public Medicaid eligibility verification system. The system is accessible twenty-four hours per day, seven days a week. It is the primary method by which health care providers determine whether a person with a Medicaid card is currently covered. When a health care provider calls the system, he or she accesses a recorded message that indicates whether the patient or customer is eligible for Medicaid.

Unfortunately, the verification system is notorious for providing erroneous information. The system, when it is working, frequently reports individuals as currently eligible when they are not or falsely reports individuals as not covered. When the pharmacist called and entered Mary's information, the system reported that she was not covered. The pharmacist refused to fill the prescription.

Mary immediately contacted her legal services attorney, who contacted the Medicaid assistance office. The staff examined their records and adjusted the system to reflect Mary's eligibility. This process took a week. During this time, Lisa suffered with her infection. Fortunately, Mary was able to rely on a neighbor for child care and to continue her employment training program. Once Mary obtained the prescription medication, Lisa's infection diminished. She was fine.

When she received her Medicaid cards, Mary also received notice of the Early and Periodic Screening, Diagnostic and Treatment (EPSDT) program. This program requires states to offer certain medical services to persons under age twenty-one who are eligible for Medicaid. At a minimum, a state must offer screening services, including comprehensive health and developmental histories, comprehensive physical exams, immunizations, laboratory tests such as lead blood level assessments, and health education; vision services; dental services; hearing services; and other necessary health care to address conditions discovered by the screening services.[4] The purpose of the EPSDT program is to make sure children in poverty receive comprehensive, preventive health care services at an early age. Services are designed to provide health education, preventive care, and effective care for problems identified in checkups.[5]

Although the Medicaid intake staff was supposed to inform Mary about the EPSDT services available to her children, they did not do so. They mentioned the availability of services but did not explain them in any way. The written notice included with the Medicaid cards simply stated, "The EPDST program provides free health screening for children under the age of 21. These screenings are for regular health exams, immunizations, vision and hearing tests and dental care. You may get this check-up at the . . . public health clinic or from a private physician participating in our EPSDT program."[6]

Mary barely noticed the EPSDT flier. In addition, she did not fully understand this information and certainly did not understand how to get the services. As a result, Jim and Lisa did not receive EPSDT services such as vision and hearing tests, lead blood level assessments, and dental care.

The Medicaid staff did tell Mary that she would periodically need to apply for recertification in order to retain her family's benefits. They had to verify that Mary and her children continued to qualify for benefits. They told her that she would receive recertification forms about a month before her benefit period expired at the end of October 2000.

When Mary did not receive the form by October 15, she contacted the Medicaid office and requested the form. She received the form a week later, filled it out, and returned it immediately. Mary did not receive a notice of approval concerning the recertification until December 15, 2000. Thus, her family experienced a lapse in benefits from November 1 until December 15, 2000. During this period, Mary had to take Jim to the emergency room because he had a fever and was vomiting. Because he was not Medicaid eligible, Mary had to pay a deposit in order to secure treatment. She also had to pay for his prescription. These payments made it difficult to purchase adequate food and she was also unable to purchase a prescription medication for Lisa. Although Medicaid did eventually reimburse her for the expenses, the family suffered because of the lapse in coverage and an immediate reduction in financial resources.

In January 2001, Mary completed her job training program. As part of the program, she had interned as a private security guard. During the internship, she had consistently demonstrated a strong desire to learn, diligence, and competence. Her supervisor gave her very positive reviews, and the company decided to offer her a permanent position. Mary was thrilled, deciding to accept the job and begin working February 1, 2001. Her salary would place her at 120 percent of the federal government's poverty level for a family of three. This was significantly higher than her TANF benefits, and Mary thought it would significantly raise her standard of living.

Unfortunately, Mary's new employer did not offer health benefits to its employees. The cost was simply too high, and the employer could not afford the expense. Mary would still have to rely on public support for health coverage.

Mary was no longer eligible for Medicaid herself because of her income level. However, she could not afford private health insurance that would cost more than $500 per month. She decided to be uninsured and hope that she would not get sick or injured.

Fortunately, Lisa remained eligible for Medicaid. Children five years old or younger qualify if their family income is less than 133 percent of the federal poverty level.[7] Because Mary's salary was 120 percent of the poverty level, Lisa's Medicaid coverage was not interrupted.

In contrast, Jim lost his Medicaid coverage. Now age nine, once his family's income exceeded 100 percent of the poverty level, he was no longer eligible. Thus, Jim became one of the millions of uninsured children in the United States.

Mary was distraught about Jim's situation. He did tend to sustain injuries, and Mary frequently had to take him to the emergency room. She was afraid that she would not be able to pay the hospital bills and Jim would not receive adequate treatment. She almost decided not to accept her job offer because of this. However, she really wanted a job, and her TANF benefits clock was running out. Jim would just have to be careful and healthy.

Two months later, Mary was doing well in her job. She had a good partner that she worked with at the security desk of a downtown office building. Her partner also had young children. One day, they began talking about their children's health. Mary's partner had just taken her daughter for her annual checkup. Mary asked her how she afforded the cost of a doctor visit. She told Mary that everything was covered by the state insurance program.

Mary had never heard of this program, but she checked into it by visiting the state department of welfare office. A staff member told her about the State Children's Health Insurance Program (SCHIP) that provides health coverage to children in families that make less than 200 percent of the federal poverty level.[8] Mary realized that Jim qualified for this coverage, and she took an application form.

Mary filled out the form the next day. It was an easy process. The form did not require an extensive amount of information. More important, she did not have to complete an investigation or interview process. She simply submitted the form, and two weeks later she received Jim's SCHIP card. Mary breathed a tremendous sigh of relief when Jim qualified for health coverage. Although the SCHIP program benefits were less comprehensive than Medicaid, they would allow Jim to get regular checkups and any necessary care. Mary could not believe that she did not know about this program before. She now noticed all the posters and advertisements promoting SCHIP. They simply had not registered before. Now Lisa had Medicaid coverage and Jim had SCHIP coverage. Mary remained uninsured.

In November 2001, Lisa turned six years old. The Medicaid program had informed Mary that Lisa would no longer qualify for benefits. Children six years and older often do not qualify if their families have income over the federal poverty line. Because Mary's salary exceeded this level, Lisa no longer qualified for health benefits.

Mary was not concerned about this initially. She now knew about the SCHIP program and in October applied for coverage for Lisa. Unfortunately, the state had recently cut back the SCHIP program because of the funding difficulties it faced. The cutback meant there was a freeze on SCHIP coverage, and new applicants were placed on a waiting list. Thus, while her brother remained covered by SCHIP, Lisa could not get SCHIP coverage. On her sixth birthday, she became uninsured.

Mary could only hope that Lisa would move off the wait list quickly. She did not really understand how her older, less needy child qualified for coverage while Lisa, who suffered from asthma and allergies, was not covered. She was very anxious about this situation, concerned that she could not afford to obtain and fill prescriptions for Lisa.

In January 2002, Mary's employer informed her that they were very pleased with her performance. They proposed promoting her to a supervisory and training position. She would receive a raise that would bring her income to 210 percent of the federal poverty level. Although her children would no longer qualify for SCHIP coverage, Mary would be eligible for the employer's health plan. She would have to contribute $100 per month for full family coverage. In addition, the coverage would not be as comprehensive as SCHIP benefits. She would be limited to a specific HMO group and would have co-payments for all doctor visits ($10) and prescriptions ($20). After she considered all the financial implications, Mary decided to accept the promotion even though she realized she would not be that much better-off. At least Lisa would have health coverage.

In June 2002, Mary was enjoying her new duties at work. Everything was going well at home except Jim had pain in his knees. He had run track during the spring, and his knees swelled and had ached for the last three weeks. Mary decided that Jim needed to see a doctor. It was time for his annual checkup anyway. She called the HMO's appointments number and, after thirty minutes on hold, found out that the primary care physician assigned to her family had no openings for the next four weeks. The HMO scheduler was not sympathetic when Mary explained Jim's condition and would only set up an appointment for July. In addition, the appointment had to be in the middle of the workday and would require Mary to take a day off. Fortunately, the doctor could also examine Lisa on the same day.

Throughout June, Jim rested and put ice on his knees. When he finally saw his doctor, the physician noted the swelling. She thought it was a common condition for children who are growing quickly and that Jim should simply rest and ice the knees. Mary was not satisfied with the fifteen-minute examination and the doctor's advice. She asked for a referral to a sports medicine physician. The doctor refused, telling her to come back in the fall if Jim's knees did not improve. Frustrated at the lack of service she had become used to under Medicaid and SCHIP, Mary paid her $10 fee and left.

Fortunately, Jim's knees improved over the summer. However, in the early fall, Mary's employer experienced financial difficulties. The company notified Mary that they had to terminate her position. She was devastated. She knew that she could apply for unemployment benefits and look for another job, but she also knew that she would lose her employer's health coverage. Continuing her family under the federal Cobra program that her employer had explained to her in the process of terminating her position would cost more than $900 per month. Even coverage for only one child would cost more than $300 per month.[9] She just could not afford the coverage.

In late fall, Lisa came down with strep throat. Her fever was very high, and Mary knew that she had to take her to a doctor. All of the family's records were still with the primary care physician from her former employer's health plan. She called the physician's office, and the scheduler agreed to have Mary bring Lisa in for an examination.

Upon her arrival at the crowded waiting room, Mary checked Lisa in. The staff member at the desk asked for her HMO card. Mary explained that she was no longer covered by insurance. In a loud voice, the staff member then demanded payment of the $120 office visit fee before the doctor would see Lisa. Humiliated, Mary pulled out a credit card from her wallet. The staff member told her that they did not accept credit cards. They had learned that uninsured people like her often did not have valid cards or did not pay their bills. If she wanted Lisa to see the doctor, she would have to pay by check. Mary could feel everyone staring at her as she pulled out her checkbook and made the necessary payment. It was a long wait in the crowded room of onlookers. Mary was enraged that she was again one of the uninsured.

The doctor examined Lisa, took a culture from her throat, and gave Mary a prescription. Knowing that it would be difficult for her to pay for the prescription, Mary asked the doctor whether the prescription was really necessary. The doctor stared at her coldly and asked, "Do you want her to get better or not? If so, I suggest you get the medicine." The doctor turned and left the room shaking her head.

Mary went to a local pharmacy and asked how much the prescription would cost. The $55 charge, along with the cost of the doctor's visit, would just about wipe out her food budget. Unemployment benefits did not provide enough to take care of sick children and live an adequate life. Lisa and Jim simply could not get sick anymore.

Mary did apply for Medicaid benefits for Lisa and Jim because her unemployment benefits amounted to less than 100 percent of the federal poverty guideline. However, while her Medicaid application was pending, another security company offered Mary a job. She would have to start at the entry level. Her pay would provide 120 percent of the poverty level but would provide no health benefits. Mary felt she had to take the job in order to support her family and to feel useful and productive. But Mary knew that her salary would preclude her from qualifying for Medicaid. She started her job in January 2003 and informed the Medicaid office about the change in her situation.

While speaking with the Medicaid staff, Mary asked whether she could apply for SCHIP benefits for her children. The staff member told her that she would qualify because she made less than 200 percent of the poverty guideline. However, the state had frozen SCHIP benefits, refusing to allow any new applicants into the program even if they qualified. Mary asked whether Lisa and Jim could be put on a waiting list. The staff member told her that because the freeze would likely last a long time, they were not maintaining a waiting list. The state's financial situation was so bad that they did not want to give anyone false hope about SCHIP benefits. She suggested that Mary call the office once a month to see whether anything had changed, but she said it could be years before Lisa and Jim could get coverage.

Mary just hoped that Jim and Lisa would stay healthy now that they were eleven and seven years old. She had gotten them through the tough early childhood years, and maybe everything would be fine for a while. She did not plan to take them to a doctor for annual checkups. The perfunctory physicals offered at school would have to be sufficient. Hopefully, the school nurse would notice any significant health problems. Even better, no problems would arise at all.

This hopeful state lasted about six months. During the summer of 2003, Lisa began to experience difficulty breathing. It seemed to be the worst on extremely hot, humid days when there was a high level of ozone. A neighbor told Mary that Lisa probably had asthma and probably needed medication. Mary decided to ignore this diagnosis, have Lisa rest when she had a hard time breathing, and hope that her condition would improve on its own.

When school started in the fall, Lisa experienced allergies and symptoms of asthma. She was uncomfortable and had moments of panic when she could not breathe. In response, Mary let Lisa stay home from school. She did not feel that she could afford to take her to a doctor. Even if she could do so, she could not afford any necessary medication. As a result, Lisa simply missed one or two days of school a week. She fell behind in every subject, lost interest, and lost important connections with her classmates.

When the weather turned colder, Lisa's condition improved, and she attended school regularly. However, Jim began to experience a great deal of pain in his mouth. He had not seen a dentist in over a year and seemed to be suffering from significant tooth decay. Mary brought some over-the-counter mouth pain reliever and hoped this would get Jim through until she could afford a dentist appointment. The medicine did not help much.

The pain of his cavities distracted Jim during school. He could not sit still and concentrate on his work. His grades plunged. He also could not play basketball or even participate actively in gym class. Every move seemed to cause pain—even breathing in the cold winter air sent shudders through his body.

As spring came, Lisa's allergies and asthma returned. There was still no word on the SCHIP benefits becoming available. Every month Mary called and found out that there was still an enrollment freeze. Mary did try to save money every month for dental and medical appointments.

The complaints and suffering of Lisa and Jim finally became too much for Mary. She first took Jim to a dentist. The dentist chided her for not bringing Jim in sooner. The dental work cost her over $300, but Jim felt a lot better immediately. Mary also took Lisa to her doctor. She quickly diagnosed Lisa's asthma and prescribed medication. The doctor also recommended over-the-counter medication for Lisa's allergies. The appointment cost over $100, but the medication would be even more costly.

Mary did not know how she would afford it all and still be able to feed, clothe, and house her children. She decided not to pay her rent for a month and to ask for an extension. Her landlord was not sympathetic and threatened to evict the family. Nonetheless, Mary could not pay the rent, and she simply hoped the landlord would let her stay.

The stress of this situation was very high. Mary's thoughts always returned to her struggle for survival. Her job was all right. In fact, it was always a relief to get away from home. But it didn't pay enough. Every time she was with Jim and Lisa, she felt like a failure because she couldn't really take care of them very well. She yelled at them too much and ignored many of their needs and problems. Mary and her children were truly living on the edge of a financial and emotional breakdown. She was underpaid and they were uninsured. Each of them was unhappy and unhealthy, destined to muddle through and live out a lesser life for a significant period.

Health Insurance Coverage for Children

Lisa and Jim's situation is not unusual. Many American children do not have health insurance coverage. Despite significant increases in public investment in children's health programs, 12 percent of all children nationwide, a total of 9.2 million children, were uninsured in 2000.[10] Because there are serious negative consequences if children are uninsured, this situation constitutes a serious problem for American society.

The primary vehicle for providing children with health coverage is employer sponsored insurance plans. In 2000, 65 percent of American children had health coverage through employer plans.[11] Thus, in the first instance, a child's health coverage depends on whether his or her parent's employer offers an affordable health plan. This is consistent with the rhetoric of the private, autonomous family. In the first instance, the family should provide all the necessary support for its members, including health care for child members. The public should not have to provide this support. What this means in practical terms is that parents have an obligation to find employment that provides health coverage for family members. As several commentators have noted, in the United States, "allocation of health care resources has largely been left to personal choice and market forces."[12]

This does not mean that the United States spends less on health care than other nations. As a percentage of gross national product, the United States dedicates a relatively large share of resources to health care. However, the United States and South Africa are the only two industrialized countries that fail to provide citizens with universal access to health services. The United Kingdom, Canada,

France, Germany, and Australia provide universal access while devoting much less of their gross national products to health care.[13]

This situation reveals the power of the concept of the autonomous individual and family in this area of American life. Despite a willingness to invest immense resources, the allocation is left to personal resources and market forces. As a result, some have virtually unlimited access to health care, while others are largely denied access. For children, this means they are dependent on their family situation for access to health care. The public refuses to provide all children with access and relies on parents to secure employment that provides adequate health benefits or, failing that, to pursue limited benefits available through difficult, complex public bureaucracies and systems.[14]

In this environment, the allocation of health care resources takes on the characteristics of a zero sum game. Seemingly, no one can gain ground without someone else suffering. The nation as a whole is already dedicating a large amount of resources to health care, making absolute additions extremely difficult to achieve and sustain. Therefore, the allocation of more resources to a particular group such as low-income families and children requires a reduction in resources for other groups such as upper-middle-class families. For example, instituting a system of equal, universal care would hurt those who currently can afford higher-quality health care. The universal care system would grab most of the resources and provide many with less service. This is why those who oppose universal care draw up visions of long waiting lists for services and a denial of choice in doctors and other providers. They accentuate the losses to particular groups and regard the gains for other groups as unjust.[15] The end result is to lock in the current autonomy-based system. Any other system would supposedly require significantly more resources or result in substantial injustice.

Employer Sponsored Insurance Programs

The current system relies primarily on employer sponsored insurance programs. This is a firmly entrenched mechanism for providing health coverage. Health benefits are a major component of labor negotiations and a primary means for employers to compete for workers. The federal government favors and reinforces this system by offering employers and employees tax incentives to create and sustain health care programs.[16]

This system has worked fairly well for those fortunate enough to be employed in a position that offers health benefits. However, even for these individuals, the coverage may not be optimal. Employees increasingly must choose among plans with varying degrees of coverage and cost. As the extent of coverage increases, especially for preventive care and prescription drugs, the employee's contribution increases.[17] This makes some preferable forms of coverage unaffordable for many.

In addition to this variability in coverage, the employer sponsored system entails a large degree of instability and insecurity. Employers increasingly lay off or terminate employees and employees frequently change employers or change their status from full-time to part-time. These changes disrupt health coverage, placing stress on workers—health care coverage for themselves and their families depends on them keeping their job and their employer continuing to operate. There never truly is a state of autonomy or independence for those desiring health coverage because the vast majority of individuals cannot afford to pay the full cost on their own.[18]

Public Insurance Programs
Ironically, the situation in terms of health care coverage is better for some who do not have employer benefits. Those who successfully navigate complex public bureaucracies and qualify for public health care programs obtain access to a comprehensive package of benefits.[19] Two basic public programs that provide health coverage to children are in place. The first is Medicaid. This program is available to children whose families earn less than 100 percent of the federal poverty level (133 percent for children under age 6).[20] The second is the State Children's Health Insurance Program (SCHIP). This program's coverage varies from state to state, but generally it provides coverage to children whose families earn between 100 and 150 percent to 200 percent of the federal poverty level.[21]

Medicaid was enacted in 1965 with the purpose of providing health coverage to low-income Americans. It is a program that involves both the federal and state governments. The federal government provides matching funds to states for the services provided to Medicaid beneficiaries.[22] To receive the federal funds, the states must comply with federal guidelines on eligibility and extent of coverage. The states implement and administer the Medicaid program, making specific decisions on eligibility and benefits. While states must meet federal guidelines, they can decide to exceed the minimum federal requirements. States do have discretion to establish health care systems and to set payment rates for medical service providers.[23]

For families with children, eligibility for Medicaid was originally tied to eligibility for cash assistance through the AFDC program. Now eligibility is determined by family income levels, decoupling welfare and Medicaid coverage. In 1998, only 37 percent of children enrolled in Medicaid also received welfare support.[24]

Approximately 15 percent of American children are covered by Medicaid. Medicaid is an entitlement program. This means that any individual who meets the eligibility criteria is entitled to coverage. Most Medicaid enrollees do not pay premiums. Most covered children also do not have copayments or other cost-sharing requirements.[25]

Medicaid provides comprehensive services. The federal requirements include a list of basic health services that states must provide. One important component of coverage for children is the EPSDT program.[26] EPSDT entails a set of screening services and the treatment services necessary to address the results of screening. The program involves comprehensive checkups and treatment for any identified health problems.

Unfortunately, Medicaid does not provide coverage to many children who lack private insurance. Children in families that have income above the federal poverty level but do not have employer coverage or could not afford independent coverage are left uninsured by Medicaid. With the failure of comprehensive health reform in the 1990s, Congress in 1997 established SCHIP to address this situation.[27] The SCHIP approach is not a simple extension of Medicaid to those with higher incomes. It also is not a pure block grant program that would provide states with funds and unlimited flexibility to design health care programs for the targeted population.

Instead, SCHIP is a compromise approach to extend coverage to previously uninsured children. Unlike Medicaid, SCHIP is not an entitlement. States receive a capped amount of federal funds that they can use to match state expenditures (at a rate higher than Medicaid) to provide coverage to children. Once the state draws on federal funds up to the cap, the state must assume 100 percent of any additional expenditures.[28]

While states have more flexibility to design programs under SCHIP than under Medicaid, it is not unlimited. They have three options: States can use SCHIP funds to expand their Medicaid programs. They can create a separate child health program. Or they can use a combination of the first two approaches.[29]

States that choose to expand their Medicaid programs must follow all the Medicaid rules. They must offer full benefits and follow all cost sharing arrangements. Most important, such a state must enroll all eligible children and cannot cap or freeze enrollment. The state could always eliminate the SCHIP Medicaid expansion, but if the state offers it, the plan must comply fully. Thus, this option provides states with the least flexibility. Nineteen states have pursued this option, likely in order to take advantage of the already established Medicaid infrastructure and the security of Medicaid matching funds available in addition to the SCHIP block grant funds.[30]

States that choose to establish independent SCHIP programs have the authority to cap enrollments and control spending. They can create waiting lists, set time limits on coverage, and impose fees, copayments, or deductibles. These states can establish their own agencies to administer the program or even contract with private firms. They also have full authority to choose providers, develop service delivery systems, and monitor quality of care. Eighteen states have taken this option, likely because of the tremendous flexibility offered and the opportunity to allow families to avoid the stigma of poverty and dependency associated with Medicaid.[31]

The SCHIP initiative appears to be a limited success. The administrative experiment in federalism provided by the program has been a clear area of success. States have taken advantage of the flexibility provided by the federal block grant approach. State programs vary widely in terms of benefit packages, eligibility standards, outreach programs, cost sharing, and the use of private insurers. Each state appears to be actively exploring the best program design and mix for its particular situation. Hopefully, this program flexibility and tailoring will provide benefits to children who need public support for health coverage.[32]

Success is less clear in the areas of reducing the number of uninsured children and improving health care outcomes for children. As to uninsured children, SCHIP has served over two million children. SCHIP seems to have stemmed the increase in uninsured children whose families earn 100 to 200 percent of the federal poverty level and even to have resulted in a modest decline in uninsured children.[33] Yet the number of uninsured children remains high, with about nine million children lacking coverage. Ironically, a significant majority of uninsured children are eligible for either Medicaid or SCHIP.[34] Therefore, these programs can provide coverage to a significant number of low-income, uninsured children if they can reach and enroll them. Outreach efforts appear necessary. Like Mary, many parents may not be aware of public programs such as SCHIP. In 1999, parents of 27 percent of all uninsured eligible children said they had not heard of Medicaid or SCHIP, had not inquired because they thought their children were ineligible, or did not have enough information to apply.[35]

But outreach and education efforts do not guarantee enrollment. Premiums, fees, and copay requirements may dampen participation. Also, parents do not apply for coverage because of real or perceived administrative burdens such as obtaining transportation to program offices and the necessary documents. Even if parents do participate, their children may lose coverage inadvertently and unnecessarily through the periodic eligibility redetermination process. In addition, parents may decide that they do not want public coverage in order to avoid the stigma of public assistance. Although welfare benefits and public health benefits are no longer connected in terms of government procedures, parents may still believe there is a connection or that others will assume a connection. Thus, those who are opposed to welfare benefits may avoid Medicaid and SCHIP programs.[36]

States are trying to lower barriers to enrollment. Several have expanded eligibility for public programs such as SCHIP to parents. Research indicates that such expansions will stimulate participation. In addition, states are working to clarify the independence of Medicaid and SCHIP from welfare programs.[37] States are also simplifying the enrollment process. Most states now allow families to apply for both Medicaid and SCHIP on one form. They also do not count a family's assets (e.g., savings, vehicles), as was previously required, in determining eligibility. In addition, most states have eliminated the need for a face-to-face interview. Some states have even eliminated the need for applicants to provide corroborating evidence on income and other information, accessing data from other public systems instead. And some states presume that children are eligible, allowing them to enroll immediately while the full application process is completed.[38]

These efforts by states have resulted in increases in SCHIP enrollment, while Medicaid enrollments have decreased.[39] This trend was probably inevitable—a result of welfare reform that moved many parents into employment and raised some family incomes above the federal poverty line. It is also a result of more individuals becoming aware of SCHIP as it becomes more established.

One point to note about this trend is that SCHIP benefits are not as comprehensive as Medicaid. SCHIP covers doctor visits, hospital care, well-baby and well-child care, prescription drugs, and some personal care and behavioral services. However, SCHIP does not provide the full package of Medicaid diagnostic and treatment services. In addition, in contrast to Medicaid, SCHIP does not provide private nursing, orthodontia, and many personal care services. In the end, states' separate SCHIP programs offer lesser benefit packages than Medicaid. Even so, the SCHIP benefits are significant and most often exceed those offered through private insurance programs.[40]

The results of efforts to increase health coverage for children through public support and government programs have been mixed. Enrollment increases have been achieved. However, large numbers of children remain uninsured. Therefore, Mary's situation with two uninsured children is not unusual even though she is employed and has a salary in excess of the federal poverty level.

This situation demonstrates American society's rejection of universal health coverage even for children. The rhetoric of child well-being is regularly trumpeted by politicians and policymakers, but the results reveal this rhetoric to be rather empty. Although they create public programs to increase access and coverage, they fall far short of taking a comprehensive coverage approach.[41] Programs require active outreach efforts and promotion, with many children and families not receiving the message of support or the public services. Public systems seemingly provide services grudgingly. Society seemingly provides public health care benefits along with assigning a social stigma. The public constructs, refines, and sometimes simplifies a bureaucratic maze. This maze stands as a mysterious and high obstacle to many intended beneficiaries. In many ways, the goal does not seem to truly be to secure child well-being.

In fact, the goal appears to be to achieve and preserve a public presumption of individual and family autonomy. Under this presumption, the private family is supposed to provide health coverage for children. This explains the primary reliance on employer health plans. At least one parent should be employed in a position that provides family health coverage. Hopefully, children will grow up healthy, but if they experience illness, disease, or injury, they will receive health services through a private insurer plan provided by a parent's employer. This approach seems to work effectively for approximately 65 percent of American children.[42] The rest of families seemingly fail to live up to the ideal of the private, autonomous family.

This private family approach to health care is unlikely to change in the near future. Despite powerful pronouncements concerning child well-being, there appears to be no realistic prospect for comprehensive, universal health coverage for children and families. One initiative allows tax-free savings accounts for health care expenses.[43] But this plan offers far from universal coverage and actually reinforces reliance on private insurers and private families. A parent is supposed to be employed and make enough to take advantage of the tax benefit. At low incomes the power of this benefit has to be questioned. It is highly doubtful that this approach will result in a significant increase in health coverage for children in America.

Another approach is to provide government-funded health coverage for catastrophic medical conditions. This would free employer-funded insurance programs from responsibility for large individual claims and hopefully reduce the cost of coverage for employers.[44] Unfortunately, this approach would not help much to extend basic coverage. The preventive, early diagnostic services that are often very important for children would not be significantly expanded or enhanced. The individual and family autonomy narrative, although not often clearly and unabashedly articulated, would remain dominant. As a result, the public will leave many children who live within families that cannot live up to the ideal uninsured and unserved.

Securing and Using Public Health Benefits

With the practical rejection of comprehensive child well-being and universal coverage, families and children must learn to fully access the health coverage opportunities currently available. This requires a skilled and knowledgeable advocate at certain points in the process. However, basic knowledge of public health care program procedures and services can go a long way in securing access to good health care. In fact, most uninsured children would qualify for coverage under Medicaid or SCHIP.[45] Thus, if states provide adequate funding for these programs, the problem of uninsured children would largely be solved if parents knew about them and took active efforts to enroll their children.

For families with income below 100 percent of the federal poverty level, parents must realize that enrollment in Medicaid is not automatic. Even if they receive welfare benefits or food stamps, they are not automatically enrolled.[46] Increasingly, public systems do not communicate with each other and secure all possible services for those in poverty, even services as basic as health care. It is left to the individual recipient to secure and coordinate public services.

The first step is to learn about the benefits and services available. Many states have allowed and encouraged community-based organizations to assist in educating families about available benefits. Staff at family support centers, child care facilities, schools, churches, and human service providers may be able to help families learn of public health programs. A parent should be aware that many service providers can assist them in learning about the wide array of public services and benefits that they can access.

Staff at support organizations may also be able to assist in the Medicaid application process. Although federal law allows only official Medicaid program staff to determine eligibility, community service staff can perform initial processing tasks. Specifically, they can explain the rules and benefits of the program. They can also help families fill out necessary forms, collect the required documents, and submit an application. Parents should be aware of this available support and they should pursue it aggressively.[47]

Even though states have made application procedures simpler and community-based organizations provide helpful assistance, there are still problems. For example, many applicants submit incomplete applications. Applicants often fail to include required information or to sign the application. A report on California applications from July 2001 to June 2002 revealed that approximately 44 percent of applications were incomplete twenty days after submission. The report did indicate that applicants who receive assistance gain approval at a higher rate, with 79 percent approved as compared to 63 percent approved for those without assistance.[48] A parent seeking health benefits for his or her children is best advised to seek out assistance and to prepare the application with great care.

However, as Mary found, even a well-prepared application does not guarantee proper action by public officials and enrollment. The Medicaid office may not act on the application in a timely manner. There also may be errors in the review of eligibility information. When these types of problems arise, a parent needs to follow up with the public agency and not allow the application to be processed improperly or ignored.

Again, as Mary found, an advocate may be extremely helpful at crucial points in the process. Mary was fortunate to have access to a legal services attorney who was knowledgeable about the system and could make proper inquiries. A skilled advocate will know the individuals who have the power to make the right things happen. This knowledge is something the typical applicant for public benefits lacks. The system seemingly counts on this absence of knowledge to limit benefits.[49] This may partially account for the severe disconnect between a strong rhetoric of child well-being and the actual provision of public benefits and health services.

In a system that provides benefits grudgingly in actual practice, the best approach for a typical applicant is to find a skilled advocate who knows how to make the system work for a particular individual and family. These advocates can be either lawyers or laypersons. Legal services offices are often good places to start, although community service providers often have effective advocates on staff. Law school clinic programs that maintain low caseloads can also be very helpful. Closely supervised law students can learn a case inside and out and often perform effectively in securing public health benefits and services.

Once children are enrolled in Medicaid, parents need to make sure that they take advantage of all services. The EPSDT program provides a comprehensive set of screening services. A child's vision, dental, hearing, and general physical condition can be checked regularly by qualified medical professionals. The screening is like a comprehensive well-child doctor visit. If the screening results in a diagnosis of a treatable condition, the prescribed treatment is covered by the Medicaid program.[50]

Unfortunately, Medicaid-covered children often fail to participate in the EPSDT program in order to complete comprehensive health screenings. Parents need to become aware of the important benefits provided by the EPSDT program, and Medicaid generally, and then actively secure them for their children. Although this approach is largely based on family autonomy and responsibility rather than being a proactive public approach to secure child well-being, it reflects and addresses the pressing reality of the current public health benefit system in the United States. Parents need to be aware of this dominant approach and act accordingly for the benefit of their children.[51]

It should be noted that, once enrolled in Medicaid, families are not charged for services or required to pay premiums. Federal law prohibits virtually all charges. However, enrollment does not extend indefinitely. Families must renew coverage. The purpose of the renewal process is to verify continuing eligibility. The timing of the renewal process varies from state to state. Most states provide uninterrupted enrollment to children for twelve months, but some states require reapplication at one, three, or six months. Most states do allow reapplication by mail, without the need for a face-to-face meeting.[52]

The renewal process makes some sense, but it does expose families to an increased risk of bureaucratic error and an unwarranted termination of health coverage. For example, the Medicaid office can fail to send on time notices about the need to reapply. It can also neglect to process reapplications. Parents must be aware of the renewal requirement and follow up to make sure that their children are not inadvertently or mistakenly disenrolled. If problems do arise with the government process, they again need to access knowledgeable advocates to push their cases forward.

For families whose income exceeds the Medicaid eligibility criteria but does not exceed the rate set by state officials for SCHIP (usually 200 percent of the federal poverty level), SCHIP provides health coverage.[53] As with Medicaid, enrollment in SCHIP is not automatic. Despite outreach efforts, many eligible families and children do not know about SCHIP. Mary was in this situation until she learned about SCHIP from a coworker. As with Medicaid, community-based organizations can provide information on SCHIP and assist in the application process. However, because each state has more control over SCHIP eligibility criteria and procedures, the application process varies much more than for Medicaid. Parents trying to obtain coverage for their children must have help from those with experience in their particular state.

The benefits provided by SCHIP coverage are similar to those provided by Medicaid, but somewhat less comprehensive. The EPSDT program is not available, but SCHIP covers physician, hospital, and well-baby and well-child care, along with prescription drugs.[54] SCHIP often requires modest premiums and copayments, but the rates and fees vary widely from state to state. This cost sharing is allowed by federal law, but it cannot exceed 5 percent of a family's income.[55] A parent should investigate cost-sharing requirements thoroughly before enrolling and plan for these charges. Gaining health coverage is well worth the cost, but the charges need to fit within a family's financial plans.

As with Medicaid, SCHIP requires periodic renewal of eligibility, which exposes families to significant risk of disenrollment. Turnover is considerable as family circumstances change, and administrative procedures cause delays and errors. Some states have addressed these issues by providing twelve months of continuous eligibility once enrolled despite changing circumstances. However, the best approach is for parents to be fully aware of the particular renewal process and to have access to knowledgeable advocates when bureaucratic delays and errors occur.[56]

As for Mary and her children, Medicaid and SCHIP provide the opportunity for health coverage for most low-income families and children. More than 80 percent of uninsured children are eligible for some type of public health insurance. Over one-half of uninsured children are eligible for Medicaid, with another 25 percent eligible for SCHIP coverage.[57] If these families and children can be reached and convinced to apply for public health coverage, the number of uninsured children would decline significantly. Thus, one of the most important steps parents can take on behalf of their children is to seek out public health benefits.

But, as Mary's experience reveals, this step is not always enough. States facing fiscal constraints when the economy turns down are likely to limit SCHIP enrollment significantly. In fact, several states instituted enrollment freezes during the latest economic downturn.[58] Eligible children must wait to receive coverage, with families forced to gamble that they will not need expensive health insurance services while they wait.

Conclusion

The current reality of health coverage for children in the United States is rather bleak. Large gaps in coverage persist, with millions of children left uninsured. When public programs are made available, they require parents to actively apply and pursue benefits from a government bureaucracy that grudgingly provides coverage and benefits. This requirement is a very real barrier to achieving comprehensive coverage for children. All the efforts by government actors and community programs to reach out to parents and to encourage enrollment have simply not been effective in eliminating the lack of coverage for children.

Even when these efforts work, freezes in enrollment occur that preclude anything approaching comprehensive coverage. When states feel threatened financially, they sacrifice health coverage for children. This is true in a situation where many eligible families and children do not even seek public benefits. Therefore, it is highly unlikely that current programs could provide and sustain coverage for uninsured children if many more took advantage of public programs. In practical terms, states must limit the success of outreach programs. This practical reality may help explain the limited success to date of outreach programs.[59]

It should also be noted that public benefit programs provide grudging support to physicians and other health care providers. Payment rates are often low, regularly below those for elderly patients enrolled in Medicare. In addition, paperwork requirements are typically burdensome. As a result, some physicians are reluctant to have large numbers of Medicaid or SCHIP patients.[60]

This reluctance can translate into a lack of respect for individuals enrolled in Medicaid and SCHIP programs. Health care providers may be condescending, even rude, when dealing with these individuals and families.[61] Mary found this reaction in seeking care at her doctor's office. Such attitudes and behavior reinforce the social stigma felt by parents whose children depend on public health programs. Health care providers make them feel like second-class patients who are beneficiaries of grudging public charity. Because this is an uncomfortable status, many families forgo public health benefits rather than accept public charity.

Parents must overcome this negative reaction to public health programs so that they can pursue benefits for their children with the focus and drive that are required. The system is designed with the conception of the autonomous family at its base. This is the starting point for a public system that initially assumes family autonomy prevails throughout American society, and when this assumption fails for a particular family in relation to securing private health coverage, the system requires a significant degree of family autonomy in order to provide benefits. Currently, families must accept this conception and the burden it places on them. They must actively challenge the public system to live up to the rhetoric of child well-being. Fortunately, they do not have to carry this burden completely alone. There are knowledgeable, skilled, caring advocates available through community organizations, legal services offices, and law school clinics who can make the system respond to the claims of families and children.[62] This proactive approach is what is required, and parents must accept this challenge and seek out allies in order to secure important health coverage for their children and to have the public live up to its rhetoric of child well-being.

Of course, the long-term answer lies in American society living up fully to its rhetoric concerning child well-being. This would mean the provision of comprehensive universal health coverage for children. Under a universal public health program, there would be no eligibility criteria other than age. There would be no enrollment process and no need to engage in enrollment outreach programs. The primary public effort would be to educate families and children on the benefits of preventive health care. This program would encourage families to get comprehensive health services for their children free of charge. This is the way to truly achieve child health and well-being.

Unfortunately, the United States lacks the political will to provide universal health coverage for children. In contrast to the provision of universal coverage for adults, leading politicians openly discuss the desirability and feasibility of universal health coverage for children.[63] However, this discussion appears rather empty, at least for the immediate future. Until this discussion is taken seriously and lawmakers act, families must secure public health coverage largely through their own initiative. They must learn of the benefits, actively pursue them, and engage knowledgeable advocates at appropriate points. Despite the public's professed interest in child well-being, the concept of the autonomous, private family rules in this area. Families must realize this and accept the challenge to secure health coverage for their children.

Notes

1. The following story is based on multiple documented experiences of various families; see, for example, *Salazar v. D.C.*, 954 F. Supp. 278 (D.D.C. 1996).

2. See, for example, 42 C.F.R. § 435.911 (2005); D.C. Code § 4-205.26 (2005).

3. See *Salazar*, 954 F. Supp., 290.

4. 42 U.S.C. § 1396d(r) (2005).

5. *Salazar*, 954 F. Supp., 303.

6. *Salazar*, 317.

7. See Donna Cohen Ross and Laura Cox, "Out in the Cold: Enrollment Freezes in Six State Children's Health Insurance Programs Withhold Coverage from Eligible Children" (Washington, DC: Kaiser Commission on Medicaid and the Uninsured, 2003), 6.

8. See 42 U.S.C. § 1397aa (2005).

9. See John M. Broder, "Problem of Lost Health Benefits Is Reaching into the Middle Class," *New York Times*, November 25, 2002, A1.

10. See Carolyn V. Juarez, "Liberty, Justice, and Insurance for All: Reimagining the Employment-based Health Insurance System," *University of Michigan Journal of Law Reform* 37 (2004): 881, 888; Lisa Dubay et al., "Advancing toward Universal Coverage: Are States Able to Take the Lead?" *Journal of Health Care Law & Policy* 7 (2004): 1, 28; John Holahan et al., "Which Children Are Still Uninsured and Why," *The Future of Children* (Spring 2003): 55.

11. See Juarez, "Liberty, Justice, and Insurance," 884.

12. Loretta M. Kopelman and Michael G. Palumbo, "The U.S. Health Delivery System: Inefficient and Unfair to Children," *American Journal of Law & Medicine* 23 (1997): 319.

13. Kopelman and Palumbo, "The U.S. Health Delivery System," 319–20.

14. See Juarez, "Liberty, Justice, and Insurance," 884; Kopelman and Palumbo, "The U.S. Health Delivery System," 321; Ross and Cox, "Out in the Cold," 1.

15. See Juarez, "Liberty, Justice, and Insurance," 889–90 (discussing opposition to the Health Security Act of 1993).

16. Juarez, "Liberty, Justice, and Insurance," 884–86.

17. Juarez, "Liberty, Justice, and Insurance," 883.

18. Juarez, "Liberty, Justice, and Insurance," 883.

19. See Sara Rosenbaum et al., "Public Health Insurance Design for Children: The Evolution from Medicaid to SCHIP," *Suffolk Journal of Health & Biomedical Law* 1 (2004): 1, 11.

20. Rosenbaum et al., "Public Health Insurance Design," 9.

21. See Ross and Cox, "Out in the Cold," 1.

22. Cindy Mann et al., "Historical Overview of Children's Health Care Coverage," *The Future of Children* (Spring 2003): 33 (describing how the current federal match is approximately 57 percent of total costs).

23. Mann et al., "Historical Overview," 33.

24. Mann et al., "Historical Overview," 37.

25. Mann et al., "Historical Overview," 33–36.

26. Mann et al., "Historical Overview," 33; 42 U.S.C. § 1397d (2005).

27. Mann et al., "Historical Overview," 38; 42 U.S.C. § 1397aa (2005).

28. Mann et al., "Historical Overview," 38; 42 U.S.C. § 1397ee (2005).

29. 42 U.S.C. § 1397ee (2005).

30. Robert F. Rich and Cinthia L. Deye, "The State Children's Health Insurance Program: An Administrative Experiment in Federalism," *University of Illinois Law Review* (2004): 107, 121.

31. Rich and Deye, "The State Children's Health Insurance Program," 116, 121 (noting eighteen states have chosen to establish a separate SCHIP system; the remaining states have opted for a mixed system).

32. Rich and Deye, "The State Children's Health Insurance Program," 132.

33. Rich and Deye, "The State Children's Health Insurance Program," 131–32.

34. Holahan et al., "Which Children Are Still Uninsured," 64.

35. Holahan et al., "Which Children Are Still Uninsured," 69.

36. Holahan et al., "Which Children Are Still Uninsured," 67–70.

37. Holahan et al., "Which Children Are Still Uninsured," 67–68.

38. Donna Cohen Ross and Ian T. Hill, "Enrolling Eligible Children and Keeping Them Enrolled," *The Future of Children* (Spring 2003): 81, 83–84.

39. Rich and Deye, "The State Children's Health Insurance Program," 131; Mann et al., "Historical Overview," 44.

40. Kirsten Wysen et al., "How Public Health Insurance Programs for Children Work," *The Future of Children* (Spring 2003): 171, 178–80.

41. See George W. Bush, "Acceptance Speech at the Republican National Convention," September 2, 2004: "In a new term, we will lead an aggressive effort to enroll millions of children who are eligible but not signed up for the government's health insurance programs."

42. Holahan et al., "Which Children Are Still Uninsured," fig. 1.

43. Juarez, "Liberty, Justice, and Insurance," 905–7; Broder, "Problem of Lost Health Benefits," A18.

44. See Rosenbaum et al., "Public Health Insurance Design," 10 (discussing weak use of the Medicare Catastrophic Coverage Act of 1988); Broder, "Problem of Lost Health Benefits," A18.

45. Ross and Hill, "Enrolling Eligible Children," 82.

46. Ross and Hill, "Enrolling Eligible Children," 82.

47. Ross and Hill, "Enrolling Eligible Children," 86.

48. Ross and Hill, "Enrolling Eligible Children," 86.

49. See Ross and Cox, "Out in the Cold," 4.

50. Wysen et al., "How Public Health Insurance Programs," 175.

51. Wysen et al., "How Public Health Insurance Programs," 175.

52. See Wysen et al., "How Public Health Insurance Programs," 177–78.

53. 42 U.S.C. § 1397aa (2005).

54. Wysen et al., "How Public Health Insurance Programs," 179.

55. Wysen et al., "How Public Health Insurance Programs," 179.

56. Wysen et al., "How Public Health Insurance Programs," 178–88.

57. Holahan et al., "Which Children Are Still Uninsured," 65 (box 2).

58. Ross and Cox, "Out in the Cold," 1.

59. Holahan et al., "Which Children Are Still Uninsured," 70.

60. Mann et al., "Historical Overview," 46.

61. Mann et al., "Historical Overview," 46.

62. See the appendix to this chapter for a listing of examples of such services.

63. See Bush, "Acceptance Speech," 41; Edward Kennedy, "News Conference on Medicare," July 21, 2000: "The bottom line is that we have the resources to take this needed step and end the suffering and uncertainty that accompanies being uninsured."

Appendix to Chapter 6
Illustrative Service Organizations
That Address Health Care Issues

National

Insure Kids Now
Phone: 877-543-7669
Web site: http://www.insurekidsnow.gov

The U.S. Department of Health and Human Services manages this hotline and web portal that explains in detail the SCHIP and Medicare programs available in each state, as well as putting families in direct contact with the state insurance programs.

National Center for Children in Poverty
215 W. 125th Street, 3rd Floor
New York, NY 10027
Phone: 646-284-9600
Fax: 646-284-9623
E-mail: info@nccp.org
Web site: http://www.nccp.org

In conjunction with Columbia University's Mailman School of Public Health, the center provides research and data related to poverty and its effect on children. Its Web site provides detailed information that should help families in poverty navigate the health care system, as well as understand what effect any change in their location or lifestyle might have on their income or public support.

National Center for Youth Law
405 14th Street, 15th Floor
Oakland, CA 94612-2701
Phone: 510-835-8098
Fax: 916-551-2195
E-mail: info@youthlaw.org
Web site: http://www.youthlaw.org/

The National Center for Youth Law provides services to at-risk and low-income children, using the law to improve their lives. Its staff members focus on financial stability for low-income families, appropriate health care and mental health services, and transitions to adulthood for at-risk youth.

Examples of Law School Clinics and Programs

Civil Practice Clinic
University of Pittsburgh School of Law
P.O. Box 7226
Pittsburgh, PA 15213-0221
Phone: 412-648-1300
Web site: http://www.law.pitt.edu/academics/programs/clinic-family_
support.php

The Civil Practice Clinic at the University of Pittsburgh School of Law offers a focus on health law issues. Specifically, students and attorneys work on issues such as denial of benefits from Social Security and Medicare, as well as claims with employer-based health insurance.

Health Law Clinic at Milton A. Kramer Law Clinic Center
Case Western School of Law
11075 East Boulevard
Cleveland, Ohio 44106
Phone: 216-368-2766
Fax: 216-368-5137
E-mail: lawclinic@case.edu
Web site: http://law.cwru.edu/clinic/

The Health Law Clinic serves low-income residents of the Cleveland area in matters related to health benefits from the government or private health care providers.

Disability Law Clinic
University of Washington School of Law
Clinical Law Program

William H. Gates Hall, Suite 265
Campus Box 353020
P.O. Box 85110
Seattle, WA 98145-1110
E-mail: clinics@u.washington.edu
Web site: http://www.law.washington.edu/Clinics/Disability.html

The Disability Law Clinic works with low-income people suffering from disabilities in gaining benefits or compensation from Medicaid or Medicare, as well as finding community services and support and working to prevent institutionalization.

Examples of Organizations in an Urban Community (Pittsburgh)

Pennsylvania Community Providers Association
2400 Park Drive
Harrisburg, PA 17110
Phone: 717-657-7078
Fax: 717-657-3552
E-mail: mail@paproviders.org
Web site: http://www.paproviders.org

This organization promotes community-based services to persons dealing with mental illness, drug abuse, or other related issues. Besides acting as an umbrella organization for community groups, it also acts as a forum for the exchange of information and as a legislative advocacy group. If someone is suffering from health problems that require comprehensive assistance, the Pennsylvania Community Providers Association and organizations like it are good places to start the search for that assistance.

Community Human Services Corporation
374 Lawn Street
Pittsburgh, PA 15213
Phone: 412-621-4706
Fax: 412-621-7137

This group provides a variety of services to residents of Pittsburgh's South Oakland neighborhood as well as the greater Pittsburgh community. Its health program maintains a health station for physician appointments as well as providing outreach care at homeless shelters and soup kitchens around the city.

MercyCare Office at Mercy Hospital Health Center
1400 Locust Street
Pittsburgh, PA 15219
Phone: 412-232-5660

The MercyCare Office at Mercy Hospital assists low-income families with applying for Medicaid, SCHIP, and a private fund for qualified persons. The program also helps with enrollment outreach in the community's Catholic schools.

7

Unaccompanied Alien Children

Ann is a fifteen-year-old girl.[1] Ann is not her real name, but it is what everyone in the United States calls her. She doesn't like losing her name, but it is a minor irritant compared to the other conditions of her life in the United States. She thought she would arrive to a better life than the one she had in China. That is what her parents had told her and had hoped for her. So far, everything was worse, and now she was alone.

In China, she had lived with her parents and two older brothers in the countryside. They had worked side-by-side on a small farm. Because she was the third child in her family, Ann was a living violation of China's strict family-planning policy. As such, the Chinese government had denied her citizenship, refusing to enter her name in the official Household Registration Book. She also could not participate in the educational system or in the public health care system. She would never be able to hold a government job or secure a land allotment. She was a nonperson in her own country. Chinese officials had also fined her parents and sterilized her mother over the family's objection.

Despite all these adverse circumstances, Ann's parents recognized her energy and intelligence. They could not bear the injustice that life in China meant for her. Although they knew they would miss her dearly, they decided to find her passage to the United States and the chance for a real life. Ann traveled with a trucker to the southeast China coast. Once there, she contacted a shipper who some people in her community knew, gave him almost all the money she had, and boarded an aging ship for the voyage to the United States. All she had on the ship were the clothes she was wearing, one extra set of clothes and a coat. One hundred other refugees were on the ship.

The ship broke down near the island of Guam. The United States government seized the ship and detained everyone on board. U.S. officials charged Ann with trying to enter the United States without inspection.

After being held in a detention center on Guam for two weeks, Ann and five other children who were on the ship were transported by U.S. officials to Portland, Oregon. For the long flight, officials placed each of the children in handcuffs and leg chains. Ann did not understand the constraints. She had nowhere to go except to the United States. She certainly was not going to run away. The handcuffs and chains only scared her. She had no idea what awaited her, and no one would explain where she was going. It seemed like no one knew how to speak Chinese, and she did not understand English.

Upon arrival in Portland, police officers delivered the six Chinese children to the local juvenile detention center. Initially, the guards placed Ann in a holding cell for three days. They did not explain why they placed her in the cell or how long she would stay there. They also did not let her make phone calls or speak to an attorney. She really wanted to speak to her uncle who lived in New York. Her mother had written the phone number in Ann's diary. Her uncle was her best hope for a better life in the United States.

Ann and the five other Chinese children, who ranged in age from ten to seventeen, tried to settle into the cell. It was extremely damp and cold. The blankets were thin and dirty. Not enough cots were available, and Ann had to sleep on the floor. She was allowed to take a shower once every two days. The food was horribly overcooked, and there was not enough.

Ann was always hungry, cold, and afraid. She did not understand what was happening to her. The constant uncertainty about her situation was driving her crazy. She could not think straight. All she could do was cry.

After three days, the detention center staff transferred Ann to the main facility. This was a secure facility designed for the incarceration of juvenile offenders. The guards strip-searched Ann upon entry. They laughed at her frightened expression and made no attempt to comfort her. None of them spoke Chinese.

One male guard took Ann to her room. It was better than the holding cell, with two beds and a toilet and sink in the corner. Everything was open with no space for privacy. This did not really bother Ann. In fact, it reminded her of home.

The guard told Ann that she would spend most of her time in the room and then quickly introduced her to her roommate, Julie. Julie did not speak Chinese. She was American—a juvenile who had sold illegal drugs in Portland. The rest of the children in the facility, except for the six Chinese children, were juvenile offenders. Their offenses included rape, drug smuggling, carjacking, and assault. Although Ann had never committed an offense, the center staff treated her like any other offender.

The food in the cafeteria was better than in the holding cell. However, mealtime was chaos. There were always fights. The juvenile offenders did not understand the Chinese children and constantly taunted them. Sometimes this led to fighting. The guards used pepper spray to break up and restrain fighting children. On her second day in the cafeteria, Ann was near enough to a fight that the pepper spray affected her. Her eyes stung as never before. She panicked, fearing that she would go blind.

On her sixth day at the center, a staff member, using a Chinese-speaking translator, informed Ann that she could have a lawyer. Although the government would not pay for her lawyer, the staff member handed her a list of organizations that might provide her with free legal services. He did not offer her any assistance in contacting the legal service providers, and it was clear that the translator would not help Ann make the calls. Before taking her to a phone, the staff member handed Ann some papers and told her to sign them. Ann did so, not realizing that she was waiving her right to see a judge and that she was agreeing to voluntary departure back to China.[2]

Once Ann got to a phone, she pulled her mother's note out of her pocket. She dialed her uncle's number. The phone rang several times, and then a voice that sounded like her uncle spoke in English. Ann cried as she tried to speak to him. There was no response. It was his taped greeting. When she heard the tone, she calmed down and explained in Chinese where she was and that she needed his help. She shook with emotion as she hung up the phone. She saw no use in making more calls. No one would understand Chinese.

The staff member took Ann back to her room, told her to calm down, and closed the door. Ann's roommate ignored her. They could not understand each other and Julie had her own problems. At 6:00 P.M., they went to the TV room to watch the news for an hour. This was required every evening even if they did not understand English. The detention staff simply instructed them to watch quietly and to always ask permission before they left the room.

One of the other Chinese children was in Ann's wing and in her TV room group. Ann was excited to see him and they spoke softly in the back of the room. He told her that another of their group had already been sent back to China. He was afraid that he would be next.

A guard approached the two children and motioned for them to go out in the hall. He placed them in chains facing the wall without explanation. Ann guessed that they were being punished for talking. When the guard unchained her and marched her to her room, she noticed that all the sheets and blankets had been removed from her bed.

It was cold and damp in the room. Ann was used to sweaty heat, and she needed a blanket to sleep. She took one of Julie's blankets, and Julie objected. Ann could not understand Julie's harsh language, but she understood the punch in her stomach. She slapped Julie in the face, and the guards rushed in as both girls fell to the floor wrestling. A large male guard threw Ann against the wall and placed her in handcuffs. He then yelled at her and twisted her arm as he took her out of the room to the holding cell.

Two hours later, a guard took her to a large dormitory room. The four other remaining Chinese children were also there. Apparently, they were going to live together. Ann was glad to see them and be able to speak Chinese. The guard told the one child who understood some English that they would live together in the dorm and they would have no contact with the other children. They would eat their meals in this room and not leave without permission. If they left, they would likely get beat up because the other juveniles did not understand them and were just angry at the world. In addition, the guards would restrain them and place them in individual solitary confinement.

Ann thought that living in isolation with Chinese children had distinct advantages. She was almost ready to give up on life in the United States. It had been a horrible week, and it sure did not look like she would be released to a normal, better life. With the other Chinese children she felt safer, less depressed.

The next day, a guard called Ann out of the dormitory area. She followed the guard into a small room where she motioned for Ann to take off her clothes. Ann undressed, and the guard examined her body, touching her occasionally. The search was comprehensive and intrusive. It made Ann feel like she had done something wrong. She became quite distressed.

Finally, the guard handed Ann her clothes, and she put them back on. The guard then placed Ann in handcuffs. This really made Ann's heart race. The guard offered absolutely no explanation. Ann was certain she was being sent back to China. She was both relieved and full of fear.

The guard escorted Ann across the center's yard and had her enter the main administrative building. She took Ann into a small interview room that contained a table and two old chairs. The guard closed the door and left Ann alone with the handcuffs digging into her wrists. After what seemed like an endless half an hour, a man opened the door and began talking to Ann in English. He kept saying that he was the "district juvenile coordinator," but Ann did not understand what this meant. She gathered that he knew about her fight with Julie, and she recognized the word *help*. It seemed like he was trying to tell her that he would help her.

As Ann was escorted back to her room, she was very confused. She settled back into the room and started talking with the other children. The man who interviewed her had not met with any of them. Ann did not understand why he met with her. In her mind, it could only mean bad things.

During the next two days, two of the Chinese children were taken from the dormitory. They did not return. Ann thought they must be returning to China. She knew that she would be next. She lived in constant fear.

When the guard came for her, it was actually a relief. She could not sleep and just wanted to go home. She went into the small room again, undressed, and went through another humiliating strip search. She dressed and yielded to the handcuffs. She proceeded to the administrative building.

Ann entered the same interview room as before. A man was sitting at the table. He said hello to her in Chinese. He explained to her that he was part of a new program to provide guardian services to unaccompanied foreign children in the United States. He told her that as her guardian, he could help her decide what she wants to do and then try to help her get necessary support and services. He also told her how lucky she was to have a guardian because most children don't get one. The immigration official she met with had informed the guardian program about her because she might have a relative in the United States who would take her.

Ann was overjoyed to speak with someone who understood Chinese and who might understand the system in which she was trapped. However, she was still confused. She asked the guardian what he meant about finding out what she wants. The guardian explained that he could help her decide whether she wants to return to China or try to stay in the United States.

Ann was shocked at this response. She had essentially given up on the idea of staying. If this was possible, she wanted to stay. She described her life in China to the guardian and made it clear that she did not want to return. The guardian asked her a few questions about conditions in China and her uncle. He told her that she needed to speak with a lawyer to see whether she could make a claim for asylum. He assured her that he would help her talk with the lawyer, translating and making sure she could tell her story. He asked her to wait and then rose from the table and left the room.

Sitting alone, Ann felt relieved. For the first time since being in the United States, she was not filled with fear. She was actually hopeful. Her handcuffs did not hurt quite as much.

After about fifteen minutes, the guardian came back into the room. He was accompanied by a young woman. The guardian told her that Ms. Gonzalez would be her lawyer. The lawyer smiled and began asking her a series of questions about her life in China. The guardian translated as the lawyer explained to Ann that she would have to prove that she faced persecution in China because of her race, religion, nationality, membership in a particular social group, or political opinion.[3] Ann did not really understand this, but the lawyer felt that there was hope that the immigration authorities would find her to be a member of a persecuted social group—unwanted children who are denied citizenship by their own country.

Ms. Gonzalez explained how it would help if Ann's uncle would step forward and say that he would take her. This could lead to her immediate release from custody. It would certainly help as she pressed Ann's asylum claim because the hearing officer might be reluctant to grant asylum to a minor with no adult family member available to supervise her in the United States. She explained that U.S. officials rely largely on private families to care for alien children, and her uncle could help in this area. The availability of her uncle would

also help the lawyer argue that Ann had signed the voluntary departure form without knowledge. If Ann had a relative here and hoped
to stay, it would not make sense for her to agree to go back to a miserable situation in China.

Ann told Ms. Gonzalez about her telephone message to her uncle.
She had not heard back. However, the guards had not given her any
messages or access to a phone. Her uncle may have tried to call—she
did not know. She had not been able to call again despite asking for a
phone.

Ms. Gonzalez wrote down the phone number for Ann's uncle.
She said that she would have Ann's guardian call him. Ms. Gonzalez
stood up and handed Ann her card. Ann did not understand this. She
could not call her. The guardian recognized Ann's confusion and explained that they would be back in touch with her in order to prepare
for an asylum hearing.

Ann felt relieved as she returned to the dormitory. When she arrived, three Chinese children remained. They explained that another
had been taken out for a return trip to China. None of the other children had a guardian or a lawyer. Ann did not understand this predicament. She felt lucky but guilty.

After Ann did not hear from Ms. Gonzalez for two weeks, a
guard came to get her. Once again, the guard strip-searched her and
placed her in handcuffs for the walk over to the administrative building. The guard placed her in the interview room, and Ms. Gonzalez
and the guardian came in a few minutes later. Ms. Gonzalez apolo-
gized for not contacting her sooner, but she had many other clients
and had not been able to focus on this case until yesterday. She told
Ann that the guardian had spoken with her uncle and that he wanted
her to be with him in New York. He had tried to call her, but no one
would help him reach her. He could not afford to travel to Portland.
Ms. Gonzalez told Ann that her uncle's willingness to take custody
would really help with her asylum claim.

Ms. Gonzalez took a large stack of paper from her briefcase and
told Ann that they had to go through several complex forms prior to
their appearance before the immigration judge that afternoon. Ann
could not believe that she would be before a judge that very afternoon. She had no idea this could happen.

Ms. Gonzalez explained asylum proceedings to Ann. She told her
that immigration officials did not want to interview her. They would
simply rely on her signed voluntary departure form in trying to have

her deported. Therefore, Ann's chance for asylum rested entirely with the immigration judge.

Ms. Gonzalez and the guardian went through all the forms necessary for Ann's asylum claim. They accurately reflected the facts about her life in China and her uncle's situation in New York. His life sounded difficult but exciting to Ann. She really did want to live with him.

After reviewing the forms, Ms. Gonzalez described the hearing they were about to begin. She explained that the judge would treat Ann like an adult and that he was sometimes very brusque. She also told Ann that he would use legal terms without explanation, and Ann should let her respond as her lawyer. Ms. Gonzalez also warned that the immigration authority attorney would question her, sometimes harshly. She thought that this attorney would focus on the details of Ann's life in China and on her signed agreement for voluntary departure. Ms. Gonzalez told Ann not to be afraid, simply tell the truth, and explain how she did not understand the departure form she had signed.

Ms. Gonzalez motioned for the guard to enter the interview room. She rose and told Ann that it was time to go to the hearing. The judge required all asylum seekers to appear in restraints. The guard checked Ann's handcuffs and then led her to the hearing room. Ann felt humiliated as she walked through the hallway. Everyone stared at her.

When she entered the hearing room, the guard led her to a seat at a table. The judge wore a dark robe and sat behind a bench that was very high. Ann could just see his shoulders and head. He did not look at her. Ms. Gonzalez sat next to her, with her guardian on the other side. Two men in dark suits sat at another table in front of the judge.

The judge did not raise his head but addressed Ms. Gonzalez. "Your client is charged with entering the United States without inspection. The government contends that she knowingly signed a voluntary departure form, has since made fraudulent and frivolous statements about persecution in China, and should be deported immediately." Ann's guardian translated the judge's statements, but Ann did not understand phrases such as "without inspection," "voluntary departure," and "fraudulent and frivolous."

Ms. Gonzalez responded to the judge by telling Ann's story. Using a court interpreter, she asked Ann a series of questions about her life in China and her uncle. Ann had a hard time understanding the interpreter and kept her answers short and to the point. Ms. Gonzalez used the guardian to expand on Ann's testimony and provide more details.

When Ms. Gonzalez finished, one of the men at the other table questioned Ann. He confronted her with the voluntary departure form she had signed. Ann admitted that she had signed the form. He also asked a series of leading questions that, in the end, resulted in her agreeing that she loved and missed her parents and that she had enjoyed living with them. Ms. Gonzalez then asked questions that revealed that she had not understood the voluntary departure form, did not have a lawyer when she signed the form, had not been able to speak with her uncle, and wanted to remain in the United States. She also had Ann explain what life would be like for her as an adult in China.

The judge listened to all the testimony. He concluded that Ann did not understand the voluntary departure form and that she was now seeking asylum. He also found that Ann faced likely persecution if returned to China based on her membership in a group of unwanted individuals who are denied citizenship and other basic rights. The immigration authority attorneys indicated that they would not appeal the judge's findings and would support Ann in settling in the United States.

Ann waited for her guardian to translate the judge's statements, but she knew it was good news because of Ms. Gonzalez's reaction. She was going to be able to stay in the United States. She could not believe it.

The guardian explained that Ann would still have to live in confinement. The immigration authorities would have to complete an investigation of her uncle before they would release her. They were especially concerned about releasing Chinese children to adults because often smugglers would try to gain custody in this way. The "suitability assessment" could take months and would involve a significant amount of paperwork. But the guardian explained that if her uncle cooperates, the situation will work out.

The guard led Ann back to the dormitory. She settled back into the room with the other Chinese children carrying a sense of relief and hope, along with anxiety and guilt. She knew that the other children did not have attorneys and were likely to be sent back to China soon. She did not know when she would see her uncle and be able to go live with him. She was tired of life in a detention facility.

One big problem was school. Her parents and siblings had taught her new things every day. It was almost like being in school. But in the detention facility, Ann received very little in terms of educational services. She could not attend classes taught in English. The facility did not have a Chinese-speaking teacher or translator. The guards simply put some Chinese-language books in the dormitory and told the children to read. Ann could not wait to live with her uncle and enroll in a real school that would teach her English and other subjects.

As her time in the detention facility stretched on for several more months, Ann became extremely frustrated with the school situation and the lack of exercise. The guards barely allowed her to go outside and walk around. She had no word about her uncle and she had not heard from her guardian in the past two weeks. She desperately hoped to live with him soon. Otherwise, she thought she might go crazy. It may be better to be back in China, but she did not want to let herself think that way. She would just survive and wait.

Practices Surrounding Placement of Unaccompanied Alien Children

The number of unaccompanied alien children entering the United States has risen in recent years. In 1997, 2,375 children were detained by immigration authorities in U.S. facilities. In 2001, 5,385 children were detained upon entry.[4] These children present widely variable and complex life situations. Some are fleeing serious persecution, violence, and abuse. Others are being used by adults, smuggled into the United States in order to provide cheap labor. Still others are sent by parents or other caretakers in order to secure a better future in a country that appears to offer rich opportunities.[5]

Many of these children are detained in secure facilities designed for the incarceration of juvenile offenders. In fact, the number of children held in these facilities has been growing, with approximately 68 percent of unaccompanied children experiencing this placement in 2004 as compared to 35 percent in 1999.[6] This trend is strong despite the fact that these children are held for administrative reasons rather than for punishment of criminal behavior. It appears that U.S. officials use secure facilities because there is a severe shortage of nonsecure facilities such as shelters or foster homes. This placement practice violates both domestic policy and international law that authorizes the use of secure facilities only in cases in which the child poses a risk of flight or of violence.[7] However, as Ann's situation illustrates, this is the reality for many unaccompanied children.

Immigration authorities place children in detention pending immigration court proceedings. Prior to 2003, the now disbanded Immigration and Naturalization Service (INS) had responsibility for these children as they prosecuted the case against their presence in the United States.[8] This situation presented an inherent conflict. The INS had a primary law enforcement mission that often involved seeking the removal of unaccompanied alien children. The INS also had a secondary mission of providing appropriate placements and care for these children.[9]

This conflict between the primary law enforcement mission and the obligation to provide care for subject children resulted in practices that harmed affected children. As noted, the INS detained children in many instances when secure detention was not necessary. It also failed to provide children with access to guardian services and legal representation.[10] Because these children were its adversaries in asylum and deportation proceedings, the INS had little incentive to enhance children's capacity to oppose their positions and goals.

The only incentives would be to secure child well-being and family autonomy. These incentives would likely be fairly powerful when both principles support release of a child to a family member who is legally present in the United States. However, even in this situation, the INS was drawn strongly to its law enforcement mission. Using a list of priority among family members, INS officials would refuse to release a child to a particular relative if they believed that a more closely related person was illegally in the United States.[11] For example, the INS officials would not release a child to an uncle or grandparent if they suspected that a parent was illegally in the country. Through this practice, the INS would force the child to remain in a detention facility or the parent to come forward and face deportation proceedings. The INS was more than willing to sacrifice both child well-being and family autonomy in such a situation.

When the child had no relative who can provide care in the United States, the INS's incentives to release the child and to enhance his or her capacity to oppose deportation were even lower. Only the principle of child well-being would provide such an incentive. Accordingly, the INS consistently failed to recruit foster homes for unaccompanied children or even to place them in group shelter homes like those used within public child welfare systems.[12] Again, as Ann's experience indicates, the INS was satisfied to house children in juvenile detention facilities, often mixing unaccompanied alien children with delinquent children. Although this approach was in conflict with the principle of child well-being and with U.S. law and international law, the INS utilized it for many years.

Opportunities for Alien Children to Remain in the United States

The laws of the United States provide several avenues for unaccompanied alien children to resist deportation and remain in the country. First, children may establish that they meet the definition of "refugee" under U.S. law. The law defines a *refugee* as a person "who is unable or unwilling to return to his or her country of origin or last habitual residence because of persecution or a well-founded fear of persecution on account of race, religion, nationality, membership in a particular social group, or political opinion."[13] Just like adults, children must prove that they were persecuted or that they have a well-founded fear of future persecution on account of one of the five enumerated grounds. The persecution must be at the hands of the government or an agent whom the government is unable or unwilling to control. These required elements are often difficult to establish to the satisfaction of an immigration judge presiding over a removal proceeding. The facts concerning conditions for children in foreign countries are usually complex, and many judges are not sensitive to how certain conditions constitute persecution for children even if not for adults (e.g., children left to live in the street, children drafted into the army).[14]

In addition to seeking asylum in the United States as a refugee, unaccompanied children who would be at risk in their home countries may be able to pursue special immigrant juvenile (SIJ) status.[15] Children seeking SIJ status must apply to a juvenile court in the United States for placement in long-term foster care. The juvenile court must determine whether the specific applicant child has been abused, abandoned, or neglected and that it would not serve the child's best interests to return to his or her home country. Thus, this avenue of relief is open to children who have experienced domestic violence or suffered abuses as street children. If the juvenile court makes the necessary finding, the child can present an SIJ status application to U.S. immigration authorities. If the authorities accept the application, they will grant the child lawful permanent residence in long-term foster care in the United States.

The SIJ status procedure seems to offer unaccompanied children an opportunity to avoid the difficult asylum process and to access juvenile courts that have experience and expertise in dealing with children's needs. However, this procedure is not freely open to all affected children. Before children can access a juvenile court, they must obtain the express consent of immigration officials.[16] These officials have no experience or expertise in dealing with children. Yet they must determine whether access to a juvenile court would serve the best interests of a particular child.

In exercising the authority of their initial screening role in the SIJ status process, immigration officials often hinder or prevent children from seeking this form of relief. They deny children access to juvenile court or they delay decisions in these matters. The decisions and delays often seem arbitrary. Immigration officials view children's claims of abuse with a high degree of skepticism. Although a determination of the veracity of a child's claims of abuse should appropriately rest with the juvenile court, immigration officials regularly make this determination in order to deny children access to juvenile court. This is a dramatic example of the negative impact of placing decisions concerning child well-being in the hands of government officials who view their primary mission as one of law enforcement and deportation. The result is the subversion of a well-intended legal process.[17]

U.S. law also provides relief for unaccompanied children who are the victims of child smuggling and trafficking and/or child abuse. The Victims of Trafficking and Violence Protection Act protects victims of trafficking and of domestic abuse.[18] Victims of severe forms of trafficking can often obtain visas to remain in the United States if they can establish that they would suffer unusual or severe harm as a result of removal from the United States. Victims of criminal acts that constitute and inflict substantial physical or mental abuse may also be eligible for visas if they help in the criminal investigations. This avenue of relief is relatively new, somewhat narrow, and possibly underused.

The Definition of Refugee Status for Children

For practical reasons, the 1980 Refugee Act's definition of refugee status provides the primary avenue of relief for unaccompanied children in the United States. This U.S. law is rooted in international law and standards. The 1951 United Nations (UN) Convention relating to the Status of Refugees provides that no individual should be returned to a country where he or she faces a significant risk of human rights abuses.[19] It focuses nations on humanitarian principles in the development of laws and procedures for refugees. The convention also provides that states should not penalize refugees and encourages a presumption against detention unless necessary for an enumerated reason. Even then, detention should last only as long as it is necessary. Congress's passage of the 1980 Refugee Act brought the United States into formal conformity with the Refugee Convention and, for the first time, provided a comprehensive statutory framework for the admission of refugees into the United States.[20]

The basic international and U.S. refugee provisions are the same for adults and children. No distinctions are drawn. However, international law now includes the 1989 Convention on the Rights of the Child (CRC).[21] The CRC is the most widely ratified human rights treaty in history, with more than 190 countries embracing its provisions. The United States has not ratified the CRC, but it has signed it and is obligated to not undermine the purposes of the CRC. In addition, the United States has acknowledged the useful guidance provided by the CRC in developing policies for child asylum seekers.[22]

The CRC is the first international treaty to expressly address children's rights. The CRC requires states to provide protection and humanitarian assistance. All social welfare organizations and government bodies must invoke the best interests of the child as the primary consideration when dealing with children. The CRC applies to all children within a particular state, regardless of status. Thus, unaccompanied children are to be accorded the same protection as any other child permanently or temporarily deprived of his or her family environment for any reason.[23]

Despite the failure of international and United States law to expressly treat children differently from adults in determining refugee status, some progress has been made in this area. Influenced by the CRC, the UN's High Commissioner for Refugees formulated a set of guidelines for cases involving children.[24] The guidelines recognize that officials should approach child asylum claims in a manner tailored to the needs of children specifically, rather than in a manner suitable to adults.

The guidelines provide that government officials should assess a child's degree of maturity. If they find that the child is mature enough to comprehend and express a well-founded fear of persecution, immigration officials can handle the case with the normal adult approach. However, if the child lacks this capacity, officials must examine objective factors vigorously and thoroughly in order to make an appropriate determination of refugee status. They should actively examine a particular child's social or ethnic group membership, the political situation in the child's home country, and the circumstances of the child's family. They should also make sure that children have adequate representatives in the role of guardians *ad litem*. In addition, officials should conduct interviews with a high degree of sensitivity, giving children the benefit of the doubt if credibility is at issue.[25]

Growing out of these trends in international law, U.S. immigration officials have issued guidelines providing asylum officers with training and guidance related to child-sensitive interview procedures.[26] The guidelines embrace the CRC's best interests approach for determining appropriate interview procedures for child asylum seekers. However, they do not adopt the best interests approach for determining substantive eligibility for refugee status. The adult standards remain in full force in this latter area. The goal of the guidelines is simply to create a child-friendly asylum interview environment.[27]

The guidelines provide suggestions for developing rapport with child interviewees. They also suggest specific techniques to verify that a particular child understands the process. They direct asylum officers to tailor questions to the child's age, level of language skills, and stage of development. While the child still carries the burden of proof in establishing refugee status, the asylum officer must actively assist in gathering and considering objective evidence that allows for a full evaluation of the child's claim. In this area, the guidelines clearly depart from the standard approach that treats children like adults.[28]

The guidelines point out the important role that a child's guardian can play in the asylum process. The guardian is a trusted support person who can assist asylum officials in treating the particular child fairly and in reaching an appropriate result. She or he can actively bridge the gap between the child's culture and the asylum interview process. Despite the guidelines' endorsement of the guardian role, they do not require the government to provide each child with a guardian.[29] This failure is compounded by the fact that the guidelines do not guarantee legal representation for children, with less than half of the children in the custody of immigration officials having representation.[30] The result is many children left to fend for themselves within a foreign and complex system.

The U.S. guidelines are nonbinding. In addition, they are only used for children who make affirmative claims for asylum.[31] Affirmative applications for asylum involve children who are already in the United States and who present themselves voluntarily to the immigration authorities and request asylum. In these cases, asylum officers conduct an initial nonadversarial adjudication of the particular child's claim aided by the guidelines. In contrast, the guidelines do not apply to children who have been taken into custody by immigration officials and compelled to participate in removal proceedings. Thus, the guidelines would not apply to children in Ann's situation. These children must present their cases in immigration court proceedings before immigration judges who are not required to follow the guidelines in conducting hearings or in making decisions.[32] Some hope that the existence of the guidelines and their use in some settings will sensitize the entire system to the particular needs of children, but there is no guarantee, or even mandate, that this occur within the current U.S. process.

Obtaining Refugee Status and Asylum

Children in all asylum proceedings require competent legal representation and the benefit of the doubt concerning their credibility and the evidence related to their asylum claims. The elements of proof required to gain asylum are complex. The asylum seeker must establish that he or she suffers persecution in his or her country of origin. U.S. officials have defined *persecution* as a threat to the life or freedom of, or the infliction of suffering or harm on, those who differ in a way regarded as offensive.[33] Examples include government-imposed restrictions that are discriminatory, prosecution based on group membership or political opinion, and harmful economic measures directed at specific groups. Persecution can be at the hands of government actors or at the hands of nongovernmental actors who the government is unwilling or unable to control. This last element is especially difficult to prove for children citing mistreatment within the family home as persecution.[34]

The asylum seeker needs to establish that he or she has a well-founded fear of persecution individually. Immigration officials examine both subjective and objective evidence to determine whether a well-founded fear exists.[35] The asylum seeker must be able to articulate his or her feelings of fear and convince the judge that these are true feelings. Such an articulation of inner thoughts is especially difficult for children who may not be fully aware of their feelings or may not be able to describe them fully. The evidence concerning subjective feelings of fear must be supported by objective evidence of the situation in the asylum seeker's country of origin. Evidence of past persecution of the asylum seeker or of similar individuals is the best type of objective evidence. Again, children may have special difficulty in this area. Their capacity to guide investigations concerning distant lands and past events is likely limited in comparison to an adult. Children face a significant challenge in articulating their fear of persecution and providing proof that their fear is well founded.

Asylum seekers must also prove that they are targeted for persecution on account of a particular, enumerated factor. The statute enumerates five possible factors: race, religion, nationality, social group, or political opinions.[36] The asylum seeker must prove that the persecutors were actually motivated by one of the statutory factors. In other words, it must be established that the persecutors actually intend to harm the asylum seeker because of his or her race, religion, nationality, social group, or political opinion. Proof of such motivation and intent is extremely difficult to present, especially when compounded by language differences and by significant distances between the site of the feared persecution and the site of the evidentiary hearing.

To establish persecution on account of race or nationality, the asylum seeker must establish that he or she is a member of a persecuted race or nationality. Violence among racial and ethnic groups is not adequate to establish persecution on account of race. The government must be shown to tolerate or be unable to stop the racial or ethnic violence. In addition, the asylum seeker must show more than mere membership in the racial group or nationality. He or she must produce specific facts that establish an actual risk of discrimination and persecution to him or her individually.[37]

Similarly, an applicant for asylum trying to establish persecution on account of religion must prove more than membership in a particular religious community. The applicant must establish that the government causes or tolerates serious discrimination on persons like the applicant because they practice their religion or belong to a particular religious community.[38]

An applicant trying to establish persecution on account of inclusion in a social group must prove membership in an identifiable group. Group identification may be based on common habits, social status, immutable characteristics, lifestyles, cultures, or political views. However, the existence of shared characteristics alone is not enough. The applicant must establish that persecution is occurring because of the group's identifying characteristics that are possessed by the applicant.[39]

Finally, an applicant attempting to prove persecution on account of political opinion must establish that he or she is perceived to hold opinions not tolerated by the authorities because these opinions are critical of their policies or methods. The perceptions of the persecutor are important. The applicant must present evidence of the persecutor's view of his or her opinions and the resulting likelihood of persecution.[40]

In the end, each of the classifications recognized by U.S. asylum law are difficult to establish for an individual asylum seeker, especially for children. They involve complex evidence and matters of proof. Even if officials deem children to constitute a broad yet distinct social group, proving persecution on account of this group status would often be very difficult. An individual child would have to present evidence that he or she is targeted for persecution because of his or her status as a child.[41] With many children likely not being targets of persecution, the group status will not get the child asylum seeker very far. She or he will likely have to prove membership in a more specifically targeted social group, racial group, religious group, or nationality. With language difficulties being compounded by a lack of maturity, it may be virtually impossible for child asylum seekers to sustain the burden of proof required under U.S. asylum law.[42]

This difficulty would be true under the best of conditions. Unfortunately, as Ann's story illustrates, the U.S. approach to dealing with unaccompanied minors hardly presents the best of conditions. The harsh realities of this approach have been documented in numerous reports and in court decisions. In fact, several judicial opinions provide a telling glimpse into the U.S. asylum system and its treatment of children.

In the *Perez-Funez* class action litigation, Judge Edward Rafeedie of the United States District Court for the Central District of California described the process confronted by unaccompanied alien children in the early 1980s.[43] The plaintiffs challenged immigration officials' practice of procuring voluntary departure consent forms. (*Voluntary departure* is a procedure by which a qualifying alien may consent to summary removal from the United States. The alien must sign a voluntary departure form, waiving the right to a deportation hearing and all alternative forms of relief.)[44] As the judge stated, "The principal allegation is that INS policy and practice coerces class members into unknowingly and involuntarily selecting voluntary departure, thereby waiving their rights to a deportation hearing or any other form of relief."[45]

The lead plaintiff presented a case typical for the plaintiff class. Perez-Funez was sixteen years old when immigration officers arrested him near the Mexican border in California. The officers allegedly presented him with a voluntary departure consent form without advising him of his rights in any meaningful way. Although Perez-Funez claimed that he did not want to return to his home country of El Salvador, he signed the form in order to avoid detention. An immigration officer had told him that if he did not sign the form, he might be in detention for a long time. Officials quickly took him to the Los Angeles airport for a flight to El Salvador when an attorney intervened to keep him in the United States. Perez-Funez withdrew his consent for voluntary departure. However, after the attorney left, the immigration officer told him that he would not be able to afford bail. Perez-Funez again signed the voluntary departure form.[46]

The court addressed the plaintiffs' assertion that government officials coerce class members into choosing voluntary departure and waiving their rights, regardless of whether this course of action serves the child's best interests. The court began its analysis by noting that unaccompanied alien children possess substantial constitutional and statutory rights.[47] Foremost is the right of every alien to a deportation hearing. The court then examined whether the waiver of this significant right was effective in this context. To be effective, the alien individual must fully understand the right he or she has to a hearing and must voluntarily intend to relinquish this right.

In making specific findings surrounding the waivers in this case, the court rejected the plaintiffs' claims that immigration officials had mistreated them physically and abused them verbally. However, the court also found that unaccompanied minors do not understand their rights when immigration officials confront them with the voluntary departure form.[48] These children are in a stressful situation, often separated from their families and faced with a foreign culture. The court found that children in this situation cannot make a knowing and voluntary choice. Even the immigration officials conceded that the children did not understand the technical legal language in the forms and did not know what to do. The children's tendency is simply to defer to the authority before them and waive their rights without understanding what they are doing.

The court went on to note the details of the setting in which government actors force children to make critical decisions. "The interrogators are foreign and authoritarian. The environment is new and the culture completely different. The law is complex. The children generally are questioned separately."[49] The court concluded, "In short, it is obvious to the Court that the situation faced by unaccompanied minor aliens is inherently coercive."[50]

After making these findings, the court reiterated the important interests at stake for unaccompanied minors in the waiver context and the high risk of error in obtaining "voluntary" consent for departure from affected children. It then ordered immigration officials to improve the procedures surrounding the procurement of consent. First, the court ordered government officials to devise the simplest and most accurate written advisal possible.[51] Although a simplified form alone would not adequately guard children's interests, it would be helpful. Second, it ordered that the government give affected children early access to telephones and an updated list of organizations that provide free legal services.[52]

In entering this latter order, the court found that immigration officials are in an adversarial role in relation to unaccompanied minors. They are not in a position to help children understand and appreciate their rights. Thus, contact with a third party is necessary, and consultation with legal counsel would afford the best insurance against a deprivation of rights. Although the court recognized that unaccompanied minors do not have a right to publicly paid counsel, access to free legal advice is one effective way to remove these children from an overly coercive environment. The court found that in the absence of such communication, the great majority of these children will commit an unknowing and involuntary waiver. In the end, the court relied on this telephone access to protect children's interests and ordered immigration officials to stop presenting consent forms before they allow such access, begin updating lists of legal service providers, and verify that children have communicated with an appropriate individual or organization.[53]

Despite the success of the class action litigation in *Perez-Funez*, U.S. immigration officials do not regularly provide unaccompanied children with early phone access. They also regularly fail to provide updated lists of legal service providers.[54] Ann's experience reflects this reality. Whether these officials push children to accept voluntary departure or not, it is clear that they have an adversarial relationship to the children and that they do not act to secure the children's best interests. This failure to pursue children's best interests manifests itself throughout the system and appears to have the approval of the U.S. Supreme Court.

In the case of *Reno v. Jenny Lisette Flores et al.*, a class of plaintiffs consisting of unaccompanied minors claimed that the Constitution and immigration laws required their release from detention to "responsible adults."[55] They challenged an immigration authority regulation that limited their release, in order of preference, to a parent, a legal guardian, or an adult relative who is not presently in detention (e.g., brother, sister, aunt, uncle, grandparent).[56] If no appropriate person was available to allow the juvenile's release, immigration officials would place the child in a facility that meets state licensing requirements for shelter care, foster care, group care, and related services to dependent children. The plaintiffs claimed that the regulation violated their due process rights by not including "other responsible adult party" on the list allowing their release.[57]

The Supreme Court upheld the regulation by first finding that it was within the attorney general's power under U.S. immigration statutes. It then turned to the plaintiffs' substantive due process claim. The Court defined the right at issue as "the alleged right of a child who has no available parent, close relative, or legal guardian, and for whom the government is responsible, to be placed in the custody of a willing-and-able private custodian rather than of a government-operated or government selected child-care institution."[58] The Court rejected the plaintiffs' claim and held that where the conditions of governmental custody are decent and humane, such custody does not violate the Constitution. The government's approach in this area is rationally related to securing the child's welfare and is not punitive.[59]

Interestingly, the Court expressly rejects the best interests of the child standard as a constitutional requirement. "It seems to us, however, that if institutional custody (despite the availability of responsible private custodians) is not unconstitutional in itself, it does not become so simply because it is shown to be less desirable than some other arrangement for the particular child."[60] All that is required is a minimally adequate level of care, certainly not the best level of care.

As Ann's case indicates, the level of care provided to unaccompanied minors in detention approaches, if it doesn't fall below, the floor of minimally adequate care. However, the Court assumes that the minimally adequate level of care is provided by the government, citing a consent decree between the plaintiffs and the government concerning the conditions of detention.[61] This assumption appears faulty.

The U.S. government, in connection with a separate class action case filed in 1985 (*Flores et al. v. Janet Reno*), entered a consent decree in 1997. The *Flores* agreement is designed to ensure that immigration authorities treat children in their custody with "dignity, respect and special concern for their vulnerability as minors."[62] Under the agreement, immigration authorities are to release children from detention promptly; if necessary, place children in the least restrictive setting appropriate for their age and needs; and implement standards of care and treatment that include access to legal representation, telephones, health care, education, recreation, and religious services. The agreement called for immigration officials to incorporate these standards into an administrative regulation, but they have failed to do this.[63]

In addition, immigration officials have failed to fully implement the substantive provisions of the agreement. Although children's treatment improved to some degree, the U.S. Office of the Inspector General noted continued deficiencies in the handling of juveniles.[64] A number of studies have revealed that unaccompanied alien children are readily detained and not released promptly. These children also are not held in the least restrictive setting possible. Rather, they often are held in detention facilities that house juvenile offenders. In addition, these children do not have ready access to telephones or to free legal services. Many do not have legal representation in the complex asylum process. Finally, these children frequently do not receive adequate education, recreation, and other services.[65]

Some members of Congress have proposed legislation to address this situation. If adopted, the legislation would provide children with legal representation and guardians *ad litem*, along with other important services.[66] This federal legislation raises hope for unaccompanied alien children to escape current burdensome conditions and unfair treatment. However, Congress has not adopted this proposal during the past two years, and it is unclear whether it ever will.

Even if the proposed legislation is enacted, it may be avoided, ignored, and/or subverted as federal guidelines and consent decrees have been in the past. This outcome is likely even though, as noted earlier, the adversarial INS has been abolished and replaced by the more child-friendly Office of Refugee Resettlement. This office has inherited the dysfunctional INS system for juvenile placement, and it does not command adequate resources to make necessary changes.[67]

Conclusion

The rhetoric of child well-being is very weak in the context of unaccompanied alien children. As the Supreme Court seems to have indicated, these children are entitled only to the barest minimum in terms of placement services and care.[68] Even this low standard will not be monitored closely by the courts or administrators. Standing alone, the concern for child well-being provides very little protection or hope for unaccompanied children.

The best hope for these children is to align the more powerful rhetoric of family autonomy with the concern for child well-being. Immigration officials appear sympathetic to alien children who can identify a family member who will take custody of and provide care for them.[69] They seemingly feel that they are establishing or reestablishing a family association that they can trust. Although, as Ann's story indicates, officials may move slowly to this type of resolution of an alien child's situation, they will pursue it, ultimately saving the child from exclusion, deportation, or long-term detention.

In the absence of identifiable family members, unaccompanied children absolutely need access to strong advocates. Knowledgeable and zealous advocates may be able to push a particular child's case so that a least restrictive placement can be secured and appropriate services can be provided. Unaccompanied children need to know their right to telephone access and to lists of legal service providers. And legal service providers must be ready to provide well-trained, zealous advocates for these children. Only in this way can unaccompanied children without other family members in the United States overcome the extremely weak concern for their welfare that permeates an underfunded immigration system and characterizes undertrained immigration officials. Unaccompanied alien children have opportunities to avoid either quick deportation or long-term detention, but it will be a battle every time, and they will always need an active ally at their side. Within the current system, securing this ally should be the primary goal for those interested in assuring the well-being of unaccompanied alien children.

Notes

1. This story is based on Julie Sullivan, "Chinese Girl Waits in Portland Jail for Months Despite Getting Asylum," *The Oregonian*, December 10, 1999, A1.

2. See *Perez-Funez v. Director of INS*, 619 F. Supp. 656, 658 (C.D. Cal. 1985) (discussing INS form I-274 and its use with minors).

3. See 8 U.S.C. § 1101(a)(42)(A) (2005).

4. Amnesty International, "United States of America: Unaccompanied Children in Immigration Detention," June 18, 2003, 1, http://www.amnestyusa.org/refugee/pdfs/children_detention.pdf.

5. Amnesty International, "United States of America," 1.

6. Margaret Graham Tebo, "Children without a Country," *A.B.A. Journal* (March 2004): 39, 42.

7. Tebo, "Children without a Country," 42.

8. Amnesty International, "United States of America," 6.

9. Amnesty International, "United States of America," 6.

10. Amnesty International, "United States of America," 46–54.

11. Amnesty International, "United States of America," 41–42.

12. Amnesty International, "United States of America," 16.

13. 8 U.S.C. § 1101(a)(42)(A) (2005).

14. Amnesty International, "United States of America," 11–12.

15. 8 U.S.C. § 1101(a)(27)(J)(iii) (2005); Amnesty International, "United States of America," 12–13.

16. 8 U.S.C. § 1101(a)(27)(J)(iii)(I) (2005); Amnesty International, "United States of America," 13.

17. Amnesty International, "United States of America," 13.

18. 22 U.S.C. § 7105(b) (2005); Amnesty International, "United States of America," 13–14.

19. U.N. Convention Relating to the Status of Refugees, July 28, 1951, http://www.unhchr.ch/html/menu3/b/o_c_ref.htm.

20. 8 U.S.C. § 1101(a)(42)(A) (2005); Rachel Bien, "Nothing to Declare but Their Childhood: Reforming U.S. Asylum Law to Protect the Rights of Children," *Journal of Law & Policy* 12 (2004): 797, 803–4.

21. U.N. Convention on the Rights of the Child, Nov. 20, 1989, available at http://www. ohchr.org/english/law/crc.htm.

22. See Bien, "Nothing to Declare," 811–12.

23. U.N. Convention on the Rights of the Child, Art. XXII, § 2; Danuta Villarreal, "To Protect the Defenseless: The Need for Child-Specific Substantive Standards for Unaccompanied Minor Asylum Seekers," *Houston Journal of International Law* (2004): 26.

24. U.N. High Commissioner on Refugees, *Refugee Children: Guidelines on Protection and Care* (Geneva: Office of the United Nations High

Commissioner on Refugees, 1994); Villarreal, "To Protect the Defenseless," 759–61.

25. U.N. High Commissioner on Refugees, *Refugee Children*, 101; Villarreal, "To Protect the Defenseless," 760–61.

26. INS, "Guidelines for Children's Asylum Claims," December 10, 1998, http://uscis.gov/graphics/lawsregs/handbook/10a percent20chldrn Gdlns.pdf.

27. INS, "Guidelines"; Villareal, "To Protect the Defenseless," 762; Bien, "Nothing to Declare," 820–21.

28. Bien, "Nothing to Declare," 820–21.

29. Bien, "Nothing to Declare," 821–22.

30. Office of the Inspector General, "Unaccompanied Juveniles in INS Custody," Report No. I2001009, September 28, 2001.

31. Office of the Inspector General, "Unaccompanied Juveniles in INS Custody."

32. Office of the Inspector General, "Unaccompanied Juveniles in INS Custody."

33. Villareal, "To Protect the Defenseless," 751, n. 39; *In re Sanchez and Escobar*, 19 I. & N. Dec. 276, 284 (BIA 1985).

34. Villareal, "To Protect the Defenseless," 766.

35. Villareal, "To Protect the Defenseless," 762.

36. 8 U.S.C. § 1101(a)(42)(A) (2005).

37. See, e.g., *In re R*, 20 I. & N. Dec. 621, 626-27 (BIA 1992); Villarreal, "To Protect the Defenseless," 752–53.

38. Villareal, "To Protect the Defenseless," 753.

39. Villareal, "To Protect the Defenseless," 754, 770.

40. Villareal, "To Protect the Defenseless," 755, 769.

41. Villareal, "To Protect the Defenseless," 771–72.

42. Bien, "Nothing to Declare," 828.

43. *Perez-Funez*, 619 F. Supp., 656.

44. *Perez-Funez*, 658.

45. *Perez-Funez*, 656.

46. *Perez-Funez*, 657–58.

47. *Perez-Funez*, 659.

48. *Perez-Funez*, 661.

49. *Perez-Funez*, 662.

50. *Perez-Funez*, 662.

51. *Perez-Funez*, 664.

52. *Perez-Funez*, 665–66.

53. *Perez-Funez*, 664–66.

54. See Amnesty International, "United States of America," 20; Devon A. Corneal, "On the Way to Grandmother's House: Is U.S. Immigration Policy

More Dangerous Than the Big Bad Wolf for Unaccompanied Juvenile Aliens?" *Penn State Law Review* 109 (2004): 609, 630.

55. *Reno v. Flores*, 507 U.S. 292 (1993).

56. *Reno v. Flores*, 296; 8 C.F.R. § 242.24 (1992).

57. *Reno v. Flores*, 507 U.S. 292.

58. *Reno v. Flores*, 302.

59. *Reno v. Flores*, 315.

60. *Reno v. Flores*, 303.

61. *Reno v. Flores*, 301.

62. *Stipulated Settlement Agreement, Flores v. Reno*, Case No. CV85-4544-RJK (C.D. Cal. 1996).

63. *Stipulated Settlement Agreement*; Amnesty International, "United States of America," 7.

64. Office of Inspector General, "Unaccompanied Juveniles in INS Custody."

65. Office of Inspector General, "Unaccompanied Juveniles in INS Custody."

66. See Unaccompanied Alien Child Protection Act, S. 121, 107th Cong. § 101 (2001).

67. Bien, "Nothing to Declare," 818.

68. *Reno v. Flores,* 303.

69. See, for example, Sullivan, "Chinese Girl Waits," A1.

Appendix to Chapter 7
Illustrative Service Organizations That Address Unaccompanied Alien Children

National

International Rescue Committee
122 East 42nd Street
New York, NY 10168
Phone: 212-551-3000
E-mail: info@theirc.org
Web site: http://www.theirc.org/resettlement/

The International Rescue Committee, through a partnership with the State Department, settled 9,519 refugees in 1998. It provides financial support to cover initial costs of resettlement. This service, however, is available only for persons already designated as refugees by the U.S. State Department.

Lutheran Immigration and Refugee Service
700 Light Street

Baltimore, MD 21230
Phone: 410-230-2700
Fax: 410-230-2890
E-mail: lirs@lirs.org
Web site: http://www.lirs.org

The Lutheran Immigration and Refugee Service dedicates a large portion of
its mission to helping unaccompanied alien children. Specifically, it is a primary agency authorized to find foster care placements for unaccompanied
alien children. It also provides education and outreach related to trafficked
children.

American Immigration Lawyers Association—Immigration Lawyer Referral Service

Phone: 800-954-0254
Web site: ilrs@aila.org

The American Immigration Lawyers Association, a professional organization of immigration attorneys, offers this referral service for immigration attorneys. This organization is not purely pro bono, however.

National Immigration Law Center

3435 Wilshire Blvd., Suite 2850
Los Angeles, CA 90010
Phone: 213-639-3900
Fax: 213-639-3911
E-mail: info@nilc.org
Web site: http://www.nilc.org

The National Immigration Law Center is a public advocacy organization
that conducts research and impact litigation to ensure the protection of
rights for immigrants in the United States. Its Web site contains information
on immigration policy as well as links to community organizations.

American Civil Liberties Union (ACLU) Immigrant Rights Project

125 Broad Street
New York, NY 10004-2400
Phone: 212-549-2660
Fax: 212-549-2654
E-mail: Immrights@aclu.org
Web site: http://www.aclu.org/ImmigrantsRights/ImmigrantsRights.
    cfm?ID=9928&c=22

The ACLU's Immigrant Rights Project provides legal support to local advocacy groups throughout the country as well as litigating cases in the fed-

eral courts. The project has full-time lawyers and coordinates with pro bono attorneys from the private sector.

Examples of Law School Clinics and Programs

Harvard Law School Immigration Clinic
Harvard Law School
Cambridge, MA 02138
Phone: 617-495-3100
Web site: http://www.law.harvard.edu/academics/clinical/irc/

Harvard students enrolled in the Immigration Clinic assist aliens subject to deportation proceedings as well as developing amicus briefs for political asylum claims around the country.

University of Minnesota Immigration Law Clinic
University of Minnesota Law School
Walter F. Mondale Hall
229 19th Avenue South
Minneapolis, MN 55455
Phone: 612-625-5515
Fax: 612-624-5571
Web site: http://www.law.umn.edu/clinics/immigration_clinic.html

The University of Minnesota Immigration Law Clinic works in the unique immigrant environment of Minneapolis, where large numbers of Hmong and Somali refugees have settled. Students represent low-income aliens and refugees in a variety of proceedings.

University of Colorado School of Law Immigration Clinic
University of Colorado School of Law
Legal Aid and Defender Program
404 UCB, Fleming Law Building
Boulder, CO 80309-0404
Phone: 303-492-2637
Web site: http://www.colorado.edu/law/clinics/immigration/

The Immigration Clinic at the University of Colorado helps unaccompanied alien children navigate the legal proceedings in front of them. It obtains its cases through referrals from appointed guardians.

Examples of Organizations in an
Urban Community (Pittsburgh)

Jewish Family and Children's Services of Pittsburgh
5743 Bartlett Street
Pittsburgh, PA 15217
Phone: 412-422-7200
Fax: 412-422-9540
Web site: http://www.jfcspgh.org/refugee.asp

This organization has provided support for refugees and immigrants granted asylum for over fifty years. The comprehensive program not only plans legal strategies for persons in need but also enrolls them in vocational training and provides the necessary community support for successful integration.

Catholic Charities of Pittsburgh Refugee Services
212 Ninth Street
Pittsburgh, PA 15222
Phone: 412-456-6977
Fax: 412-456-6180
Web site: http://www.ccpgh.org/Website/refugee.htm

Catholic Charities of Pittsburgh provides language and vocational training for persons forced to leave their homeland to avoid persecution. Also, it helps find housing for refugees and persons granted asylum.

8

Conclusion

The various laws affecting children in their everyday lives have been shaped by public discussions of the family and of child well-being. The metanarrative of the private, autonomous family is very powerful within American society. It gives rise to a conception of the acceptable, desired family association. The public charges this association with responsibility for its child members. The adult members (parents) provide the financial resources necessary to secure the well-being of their children. At the least, they provide minimally adequate care and secure basic education and health care services.

Mainstream laws that affect children operate on the assumption that they live within a family association that fits the autonomous ideal. The children for whom this assumption is not true are often legal outcasts. Alternative social narratives and laws apply to them as the public responds to their situation.

The primary metanarrative that affects these "outcast" children is one of child well-being. The public talks about stepping in to save these children from inadequate family associations. This form of public action can be very intrusive. Ironically, it can also be largely inadequate. The public becomes involved in some of the most important and intimate areas of children's lives, but it often fails to provide the resources and services necessary to secure basic well-being. The law is, at least in part, responsible for this situation, but it may offer relief, too.

The intrusiveness arises primarily from the often articulated public goal of securing children's best interests. This is an ambitious goal if it is interpreted to mean that the public must work to secure the best outcome possible for each child. This interpretation sounds and feels good to many and is frequently embraced. Public discussions of children and families are often focused on this goal. In addition, many legal decisions turn on an assessment of a particular child's best interests.[1]

The resulting intrusion into children's lives and their family associations occurs at two levels. First, the best interests standard calls for a process of assessment. This can occur only through questioning and investigation. If done properly, it entails the exposure of extensive details of a child's life and living conditions. Public actors examine the behavior of the child's parents. They observe the child's home. They observe the child's school and play. They even elicit the child's thoughts and weigh his or her psychological health. This is a highly intrusive, often threatening, anxiety-producing process for the child and his or her family.[2]

Second, the best interests standard involves substantive assessment and judgment. The public determines whether a child's situation meets the standard. For example, this could mean that neighbors and acquaintances view a young mother as failing if she does not breast-feed her baby. The sanctions for such a perceived failure are not formal legal measures but instead informal social mechanisms. The young mother will suffer whispered indictments, disapproving looks, and possible ostracism.[3] This public assessment could also mean similar social sanctions imposed on a father who employs corporal punishment in disciplining his young children. This father may also face formal legal sanction, with government actors seeking court jurisdiction over the child and possible removal of the child from the father's custody.[4]

There are many ways in which the public can monitor and second-guess parenting approaches and decisions, along with other aspects of a child's life, by employing the best interests of the child standard. In essence, this standard provides an effective means for one group of adults to police the actions of other adults in regard to children's well-being. It forms the backdrop for disputes among adults over control of children's lives.

A real tension exists between the two metanarratives. The metanarrative of the autonomous family argues primarily for leaving family associations alone. In contrast, that of child well-being primarily supports monitoring of and intrusion in family associations. This metanarrative also justifies public support of family associations so that these associations can secure child well-being, but this support itself often gives rise to public monitoring, regulation, and intrusion. In other words, public support often comes with significant strings attached.

This tension between the two metanarratives allows participants in public discussions to selectively choose their approach to families in different situations. For what many view as the normal, nuclear family, the narrative of family autonomy most often dominates public discussions. In these discussions, participants usually perceive the family as being self-sufficient, not requiring any public support. This family is valued and held up as the desirable model. It is respected and can actually receive public support without stigma.[5]

For what many view as a deviant or dysfunctional family, the narrative of child well-being most often plays a large and powerful role in public discussions. In these discussions, participants often perceive the family as having failed in some sense. Maybe the family is headed by a single adult who cannot alone provide child care or adequate financial resources. Or maybe the family is unable to secure health care coverage for children. This family is not viewed as autonomous in the traditional sense. It is obviously and notoriously dependent on others.[6]

For issues and laws that primarily affect what many view as normal, autonomous families, discussants may express an approach of respect and advocate support without limits. This approach may lead to subsidies to families without strings attached. For example, public discussions may lead government to provide tax deductions for single-family home ownership or for dependent children. Government actors simply provide these forms of public support without public intrusion in the family. The model of the autonomous family seems to provide the basis for the public discussion and to justify the resulting approach.

In contrast, for issues and laws that primarily affect only families that many view as deviant, discussants may express an approach of disrespect and control. Many view the public as having a license to intrude in these families, lending support only in conjunction with examination, regulation, and control. For example, public discussions may lead government to provide welfare payments to families experiencing poverty along with close examination of these families' members and structures. Government actors provide public support to deviant families with strings attached that often expose these families to public scrutiny. This is done primarily to secure child well-being. The public does not trust these families to use public resources in order to properly raise children on their own.

The nature of public discussions of the family, with the tension of the two primary metanarratives in the background, has a significant impact on the everyday lives of children in poverty. For these children, adults often focus their rhetoric on securing child well-being. However, the values and desirability of the autonomous family remain as powerful influences on the discussions and, more important, on the product of those discussions—the laws, policies, and practices that affect children.

The public appears to have one of two general reactions to children in poverty. Which reaction becomes operational in a specific situation depends on the perceived scope of the remedial program and the relative sympathy evoked by children and families in the specific type of situation. Some situations appear to call for a limited remedial program because there are not vast numbers of affected children. In these situations, the public is likely to be supportive of initiatives that secure child well-being and that assign less responsibility to autonomous families. Addressing the situation appears realistic, manageable, and affordable. In addition, some situations involve sympathetic categories of victims that could include both children and their families. In these cases, the public is also likely to be supportive of initiatives that secure child well-being and that assign less responsibility to autonomous families. Addressing these situations appears desirable and just.

An example of this first type of situation is child abuse and neglect cases.[7] A relatively small percentage of children suffer serious abuse or neglect at the hands of their adult caretakers. It is certainly not a universal experience. Therefore, it appears to be a problem that the public can address without drawing too heavily on public resources. In other words, addressing these situations appears affordable. It also appears necessary and just. Abused and neglected children are in great need and are very sympathetic, at least when their lives are initially disrupted by violence. Addressing their situation is viewed not only as affordable but also as highly desirable in a just society.

A second example is provided by children living in poverty generally.[8] This situation is less confined than the abuse and neglect situation, but it is still not universal. Not every child lives in poverty, with the current official rate of children living in poverty in the United States standing at less than 20 percent. Therefore, the public is likely to believe that they can afford to address this situation. In addition, children suffering in conditions of poverty elicit sympathy. The public does not view them as being responsible or at fault for their situation. Although many members of the public may balk at, or object to, providing support to the parents of these children, they do want to support the children. The situation may not present as affordable or as sympathetic as the abuse and neglect situation, but it does evoke a public response of support. Such support is widely viewed as desirable and just.

A third and final example is provided by children involved in the delinquency system.[9] Because most children do not become involved in delinquency proceedings, the situation is again confined. Therefore, the public is likely to view this as a problem that society can address affordably. In addition, the cost to many would be high if the public fails to address this problem. Members of the public stand to be victims of child offenders and this alters the cost/benefit analysis in favor of public response and support. Also, child offenders are somewhat sympathetic. They have allegedly broken the law, but they are still individuals who are not fully developed and need support to recover and become competent adults. Although they are not blameless victims, they do evoke some sympathy, and the public often views the provision of support as justifiable and desirable.

For these types of situations, the public most often employs the rhetoric of child well-being. The response is one of support for children, if not for their family associations. Most participants in the public discussion appear to be truly motivated to pursue and secure child well-being. However, as the challenges emerge, the rhetoric of child well-being appears to fade. It does not seem to have the power necessary for sustained effort.

For example, in the child abuse and neglect situation, it is often difficult to safely maintain children within their original families. The public must dedicate substantial resources in attempts to preserve these families, and public actors must make sustained efforts. These efforts involve much more than securing child safety as an initial response to incidents of abuse and neglect. The public often cannot sustain the necessary effort, with the result that government actors remove many abused and neglected children from their original family associations.

Once removed from their original families, many of these children languish in temporary foster care placements. Public actors often forsake child well-being as these children experience frequent moves and other disruptions. In many cases, children cannot form appropriate bonds. Their situation is a state of impermanence. The public largely ignores their long-term well-being—on one hand, failing to return them to rehabilitated original families and, on the other hand, failing to secure an alternative permanent placement through adoption or permanent guardianship. The result is serious developmental harm to affected children.[10] The rhetoric of child well-being obviously does not adequately sustain the public in its effort to secure permanent placements for child victims.

The provision of welfare payments provides another example of the weakness of an initial expression of public concern for child well-being. The public professes its commitment to support children in poverty, but it provides very meager support in the end. Welfare payments barely provide enough support to allow children and families to survive, let alone escape poverty or thrive. And this support comes with significant strings attached. The public subjects affected children and families to regulation and control. One aspect of this control is severe time constraints on benefits. A parent receives only a limited number of years of benefits, a period that does not even approach a full term of childhood. The public forces parents to secure paid employment and achieve financial autonomy no matter the consequences for child well-being. In the end, the public's strong expression of concern for child well-being yields little support—support that likely terminates well before many children develop fully and reach maturity.[11]

This pattern of public behavior is also evident in the juvenile delinquency system. At least historically, the public's initial reaction to juvenile offenders has included a strong concern for child well-being. The juvenile court movement has been propelled by concepts of treatment and rehabilitation. The presumption is that youth can be saved and that society should afford them this opportunity.

Recently, however, this presumption has weakened. The public has come to view juvenile offenders as extremely dangerous predators. Although crime statistics do not justify this perception, it has led to an abandonment of special rehabilitative approaches for youth. More and more juvenile offenders are now treated as adults within the criminal justice system. While they do possess more formal legal rights, they also face adult punishment. The public is no longer, if it ever truly was, dedicated to saving these children. Their well-being is a secondary concern, with the public primarily focused on punishing them and deterring others. The public's historical initial reaction to juvenile offenders has been overwhelmed by a new type of initial reaction. Concerns with child well-being have largely faded from the scene of the juvenile justice system.[12]

The second general reaction of the public to children in poverty arises in situations that appear to call for a vast, resource-intensive response. In these situations, the public is unlikely to express strong support for child well-being even initially. It is more likely to emphasize from the outset concepts of family autonomy and self-reliance. The focus in these situations appears to shift from concern and sympathy for children to disappointment with and abandonment of adults whom the public views as responsible to provide care for children. The public seems to shrink from actively addressing these situations, considering the provision of comprehensive public support as undesirable and unaffordable. In essence, addressing these situations through public means and resources appears overwhelming and unrealistic.

An example of this second type of situation is provided by public education.[13] The concept of a rigorous, high-quality education for every child is a vision shared by many. But in public discussions, participants largely take for granted the vast differences in educational quality among school districts. They seem to view the provision of inadequate public education services in poor districts as a relatively permanent condition. The public will to change this condition is not regularly and strongly articulated. The problems of public schools appear insurmountable and the public is largely unwilling to commit the substantial resources and make the significant sacrifices necessary to secure high-quality education for all children.

This is apparent in the public debate concerning the well-intentioned, if flawed, federal educational initiative to leave no child behind. The federal government has failed to fully fund this initiative, and the states are objecting to the resource requirements imposed by the law.[14] The public discussion centers on the inability to fund education services. In this area, the rhetoric of child well-being is tempered, if not silent, and the rhetoric of family autonomy, educational choice, and local control is predominant.

A second example is coverage for health care expenses.[15] This issue presents a huge challenge for the public generally, but one that is especially acute for children. Children are in a phase of life that demands comprehensive, preventive health care services. Their development frequently depends on it. However, the costs for these services are substantial both for the individual receiving treatment and for society as a whole. In addition, these costs are growing at what seems to be an exponential rate. As a result, providing universal coverage for children's health care services would require substantial public resources. The reaction in the United States has been to rely primarily on private coverage provided by parents' employers. For families for which this is not possible, the public grudgingly provides some support but leaves many children uncovered. Increasingly, the rhetoric of child well-being is emerging in public discussions, but there remains a reluctance to truly embrace this rhetoric. The public still appears more comfortable with the rhetoric of family autonomy and responsibility in this area.

A third example is the treatment of unaccompanied alien children.[16] In fact, this is probably the most dramatic and stark example of this second type of public reaction. The American public largely rejects these children from the outset, with little expressed concern for child well-being. The public seems to fear a flood of immigrant children who will demand massive social, health, and educational services. The public discussion is dominated by these concerns and the "illegality" of the children's presence in the United States.

The result is that if the unaccompanied child has a relative who is legally present in the country and who will care for the child, the public authorities may be disposed to assist the child in remaining in the United States. In this situation, the rhetoric of the autonomous, self-supporting family carries the day and in a sense rescues the child. In contrast, if the child has no such relatives, the public authorities are likely to either quickly deport the child or incarcerate the child for an extended period. The rhetoric of child well-being never really becomes operational in this context; if it does, it is very weak. This rhetoric certainly does not have the power to spare the child from harmful consequences.

Both types of general public reaction to children in poverty reveal a common theme. Whether embraced initially or kept in a secondary role from the outset, the rhetoric of child well-being is relatively weak. As a result, children in families that do not fully meet the ideal of the autonomous, private family are in jeopardy. The public leaves them to the mercy of governmental bodies and actors who implement a commitment to child well-being. Unfortunately, the public shrinks from a strong, sustained commitment in this area.

Ironically, the public as a whole may shrink from the necessary commitment to secure child well-being for all children because many members of the public embrace a highly ambitious vision of child well-being. The public discussion is often characterized by the rhetoric surrounding the concept of children's best interests. This concept is frequently taken to mean much more than simply securing basic support for children such as minimally adequate food, housing, and education services. It seemingly calls for society to secure the best possible environment for development for each individual child.[17] But in a contingent, unpredictable world, it is impossible to define and identify the best possible environment for each child. Development depends on a complex combination of individual genetic attributes and environmental factors.[18] Even if we could agree as a society on a definition of "best possible developmental goals," we would be unable to determine the optimal environment for each child to realize these goals.[19] The complexity of such an endeavor is beyond our comprehension and is likely to remain so in the foreseeable future.

But achieving this optimal developmental environment is not only politically and technologically questionable but also highly unlikely in light of available resources. To truly provide the best developmental environment for each child, the public would have to devote tremendous resources. It would have to provide each child with high-quality adult caretakers, food, housing, education, health care, recreational experiences, peer interactions, and more. In essence, adults would have to enslave and sacrifice themselves in order to maximize children's well-being.[20]

The public's failure to fully realize the extremely high cost of its desire to secure the best interests of each child does damage. As each child is held up as precious—a public good that must be protected and actively nurtured in a publicly defined manner—the public response to children's situations becomes warped in several ways. This view of childhood invites the public to identify too many situations as involving inadequate care for children. It invites biases against parents experiencing poverty, single parents, illegal aliens, schools with a large number of minority students, and low-income communities. The public is quick to impose its biased views, constructing a vision for child well-being and implementing a strategy of child rescue rather than one of family support and respect.[21]

Once the rescue operation is launched, the public's stated goal is often a high-performing family, school, and community environment.

But the public frequently expects parents, schools, and local communities to respond largely on their own. The public provides only sketchy, marginal services, and when they do not work, the public takes parents, schools, and communities to task for failing to provide a high-quality environment for child development. This situation leads to the public's frustration with the attempted rescue operations and to the eventual abandonment of affected children to inadequate environments. Interestingly, abandonment can occur even before rescue is attempted because the public anticipates the frustration of an inadequate response and avoids it.

The public child welfare system illustrates the harmful impact of seeking the best environment possible for every child. This goal results in the construction of a relatively low hurdle to public intervention in families and in children's lives. Children who appear to suffer within family situations that are minimally adequate, but not optimal, are at risk for removal from their parents' custody. The easy course of action in such a situation is one of child rescue. The public believes that government actors can step in and place children in better environments.[22]

However, the rescue effort often goes astray. Removal from marginal parents certainly does not guarantee an optimal environment for a child and frequently worsens a particular child's situation. Placement in foster care may deliver a child to another marginal home that lacks the established family relationships necessary for healthy development. And relatively strict requirements for adoptive homes or other permanent placements often keep a child in a temporary foster care placement for an extended period. In the end, the public's attempt to secure the best interests of every child results in developmentally harmful long-term placements in foster care. The low hurdle to entry, combined with the high hurdle to exit, can work to trap children in damaging environments—environments that may be significantly worse than their original marginal, yet minimally adequate, homes.[23]

Because the public's initial concerns and expectations for children's environments are unrealistically high, laws, policies, and practices founded on these concerns and expectations can unnecessarily harm children. This is an area in which the best may truly be the enemy of the good, or at least the acceptable. Certainly, the current situation of children trapped in temporary foster care placements for extended periods is unacceptable. So are situations of children in poverty without welfare program support, juvenile offenders in the adult justice system and in adult prisons, children in neglected public schools, children without health coverage, and children seeking sanctuary who are either quickly deported or effectively incarcerated.

The Minimal Adequacy Approach

The question is whether we can do better if we lower our concerns and expectations for children's environments to a more realistic, attainable level. For instance, the public may contribute more to overall child well-being by only attempting to ensure that each child has a minimally adequate environment for development. By setting this more modest goal, the public could target resources to areas of true need and, most important, make a compelling case for adequate resources.[24] For example, ensuring each child a minimally adequate education may be more feasible than trying to provide a high-quality education for every child. The public would have to define the term *minimally adequate*, but at the least it would include adequate facilities and teachers. The public would then make every effort to raise and target the resources necessary to make sure that each child had access to this basic level of educational service. Such an express modification may make public education goals attainable, along with introducing a degree of equality and an enhancement of child well-being beyond that currently being achieved.

More specifically, this approach of minimal adequacy would have significant implications for each area of children's everyday lives previously discussed in this book. In the area of public child welfare systems and foster care placements, this approach would likely result in increased support for children's original families even if they are marginal at times. The public would no longer view these families as inadequate if they could not meet the public's definition of an optimal developmental environment. As long as they provide, or could provide with some public assistance, a minimally adequate environment for child development, the public would not view these family associations as seriously deficient or deviant. These families would deserve tolerance, respect, and assistance.[25]

With this change in expectations and goals, the public would likely increase services to families in crisis or experiencing parenting difficulties. Through the dedication of modest public resources, families would be able to remain intact, provide minimally adequate environments for children, and avoid the harm of foster care placements. In addition, the public would be more likely to realize the value of proactive assistance to families that have not yet experienced problems or crises but are at risk of falling below the floor of minimal adequacy. Rather than trying to transform these families into associations that provide optimal developmental environments, the public would avoid substantial expense and frustration by focusing on the realistic goal of securing minimally adequate family environments.

If a foster care placement is necessary to provide a child with a minimally adequate environment, the public would not view such a placement as a step on the path to securing an optimal developmental environment. Foster care would simply constitute a temporary salvage operation with a modest goal of quickly securing a minimally adequate permanent home for the affected child. Under this approach, proposed adoptive homes would not have to meet some ideal form or standard of performance. Therefore, more homes would be candidates for adoptive placements. In addition, open adoption arrangements that provided a child's original parents with access and communication would likely be more acceptable because they would not render the adoptive home less than minimally adequate. In fact, legally informal open guardianship arrangements would likely be more acceptable.

The public would likely respect these diverse, flexible family associations because, unlike harmful lengthy temporary foster care placements, these associations would provide an affected child with a minimally adequate environment. Whether the new permanent home conformed to the nuclear family ideal or something quite different, the public could provide support in order to assure minimal adequacy. The families receiving support without an expectation of some ideal form or label of deviancy would include single-parent families, gay parent families, low-income-parent families, mixed-race families, large extended families, and many others.

In summary, the minimal adequacy approach, in contrast to the best interests approach, would likely reduce the pressure on, and justification for, the public to intervene in children's lives and disrupt their family associations. If the public did intervene in order to ensure a minimally adequate environment, the intervention would likely be more supportive and less severe. It would likely be for a shorter period—only as long as necessary to secure a new permanent placement that would provide a minimally adequate environment. The result would be quick, less disruptive interventions with realistic goals.

In the area of public welfare for families and children, the minimal adequacy approach would likely result in the public identifying children at risk for falling below a minimal floor of financial support. The public would target support to make sure that each child is guaranteed adequate food, housing, and other basic conditions and services for basic development within modern American society. Relatedly, the public would provide these resources without conditions on parents that entail intrusive regulation and control.[26] Each family would deserve these resources without condition other than that the family provide a minimally adequate environment for development. For example, a parent would not be required to work in paid employment in order to receive financial support for a child. As much as the public may believe that it is best for children to have parents who are employed, the public would not impose this view on recipients of public support. Unemployed parents can provide minimally adequate environments, and the public would provide support to secure only this level of care, nothing more.

This approach would also reduce the public's intrusion through accepted definitions of proper family form and behavior. For example, a parent could provide a minimally adequate environment with an unmarried partner in the family home. Although the public may view this situation as less than optimal, it would not lead to a loss of public support directed at ensuring a minimally adequate environment. Thus, this approach would reduce the negative consequences of inappropriate public biases for children and their diverse family associations.

In the area of delinquency, the public increasingly processes juvenile offenders in the adult system. This system affords children formal legal rights equivalent to those of adult offenders. In this sense, children receive the full protections available in the criminal justice system. These protections may help secure children's best interests as they are exposed to adult punishment.

But the resources allocated to protect individual rights within the criminal justice system often fall short of the level necessary to secure these rights properly and fully. Therefore, treating juvenile offenders as adults often exposes affected children to adult punishment without adequate legal assistance and other protections. An approach that only provides juveniles with a minimal level of legal protections may be more effective. It may revive the concept of a therapeutic juvenile justice system.[27] The public would not view children as adult offenders appropriately subject to adult procedures and adult punishment, but as youths in need of rehabilitation. The public would process these children through a less legalistic, less adversarial system that would not provide them with the best form of criminal justice, but it would provide minimally adequate legal protections that would allow for creative preventive and rehabilitative approaches that would benefit both children and their families.

When one turns to education, one witnesses an unrestrained best interests approach for children in affluent areas. At times, it appears that the public will spare no expense in relation to children's education. (This point is especially apparent in the area of athletics, where multimillion-dollar investments in facilities and operations are now commonplace.[28]) This public attitude that children in certain geographic areas are highly valued and must have huge public resources for education affects children in less affluent areas. The resulting concepts of local control and systems of local taxation ensure the best education for affluent children, while at the same time abandoning poor children to educational systems that do not provide minimally adequate experiences and opportunities.

Many participants in the public discussion of education seem to view this area as a zero sum game. Poor districts can only benefit by taking resources from rich districts. Thus, many view proposals for a fairer allocation of resources as a significant threat.[29] If society tries to provide optimal educational resources for all children, it will be too costly, and many children's education will be diminished. Parents in more affluent districts fight all out to prevent this diminishment. Because of the emotion and political power, if not the justice, of their appeal, nothing changes—local control is maintained, local resources are retained, inequities prevail, and poor children receive less than minimally adequate educational services.

A worthwhile strategy may be to seek to secure minimally adequate educational experiences for all children. Rather than pressuring affluent districts to underwrite poor districts in order to achieve optimal or even equal educational experiences, it may be more realistic to seek public support for minimally adequate schools in poor districts. This strategy would be less threatening, and although it may not yield equal athletic facilities or even teacher qualifications, it is more likely to result in adequate school buildings and adequate teachers. Residents in the poorer districts who participate in implementing this strategy would initially focus on establishing a basic floor of adequate educational services for their children. Subsequently, they could work to raise their schools above the floor. In this way, they may spare their children from the largely inadequate educational experiences that are currently prevalent in poor districts.

In the health care area, the problem of seeking the best care for everyone is pervasive. It has led to a cost explosion that is threatening and appears unsustainable.[30] New technologies designed to provide the best possible care are very costly and are increasingly viewed as necessary. The result has been extremely high quality care for some—those who can afford the cost of such care, or at least health insurance to cover the costs. The result has also been no care or time-pressured emergency care for those who cannot afford the cost.

The public shrinks from the huge costs of providing universal coverage for children in this latter group. The public is unwilling to commit the significant resources to provide high-quality comprehensive coverage for every child. Once again, a more modest approach may be beneficial. A defined list of health services that ensure a minimally adequate level of care may be viewed as affordable even at the level of cost necessary for universal coverage. The development and popularity of SCHIP programs indicate that such an approach may be successful. If states are not required to provide a full range of Medicaid services, they may be willing to provide minimally adequate services to all uninsured children.

When one turns to the situation of unaccompanied alien children, the public has a vision of what is best—placement with an established family member legally present in the United States. Unfortunately, this best situation is not a possibility for many of these children. The public does not have an alternative vision in this situation. Affected children are either returned to their original country or warehoused in public facilities for extended periods. No real attempt is made to secure the best interests of these children.

Government officials who deal with unaccompanied alien children do not appear to understand the concept of children's best interests.[31] The resulting treatment of these children amounts to harmful neglect, even abuse. The conditions for these children falls below the level of minimally adequate care.

The concept of minimal adequacy may provide an opportunity to improve the situation for these children and, specifically, an opportunity to educate officials on the basic conditions necessary for adequate care. Rather than some ambiguous goal that appears unrealistic—to secure all children's best interests—the public could embrace a concrete, understandable, and likely achievable goal of providing minimally adequate conditions for affected children. This would constitute a realistic alternative to the desired best outcome (placement with a family member), allowing for the placement of these children with willing, unrelated adult caretakers. The public would charge these adults with providing at least minimally adequate care in a noninstitutional setting that would provide a base for alien children to actively pursue their claims for asylum.

Minimal Adequacy and Family Preservation

A story from the public child welfare system brings to life the practical impact of the minimal adequacy approach.[32] Jean was a single mother with two children. Amy was six years old and Tammy was four. Jean had been employed for short periods during the past two years, but she could not seem to keep a job for more than a month. Her attitude at work was lethargic at best and it was always difficult to arrange for child care. She largely maintained her family through welfare benefits.

Jean also had a problem with housing. She hated cleaning her house, and it was filthy. Several volunteers from the local family support center had helped Jean with the cleaning, teaching her skills that hopefully she could use on her own. Unfortunately, Jean never seemed to be motivated to clean. In addition, Jean was often behind on her rent payments, and the landlord regularly threatened to evict her.

Despite these problems, Amy and Tammy were very attached to Jean. Jean made sure they were well fed and supervised. She regularly engaged them in conversation and play. The condition of the house presented some fairly significant health risks, but the children had not experienced serious illness or injury.

Because neighbor children would play with Amy and Tammy at Jean's house, some neighbor parents became concerned with the filthy house. They contacted government officials, who sent a child welfare agency caseworker to investigate. Jean welcomed the caseworker into her home. The caseworker was appalled at the filthy conditions, refused to sit on the food-stained sofa, and asked Jean numerous questions. She was especially concerned that Jean may have a serious substance abuse problem.

However, the caseworker learned that Jean suffered from several mental disabilities. Slowly and carefully the caseworker elicited Jean's story. Jean spent a good deal of time with her children and never left them alone overnight. This was a strong sign that Jean did not have a serious substance abuse problem. Jean provided the children with adequate food, but she just seemed unable to maintain an acceptably clean home. The caseworker spoke with Amy and Tammy in a separate room from Jean. They were fairly dirty, but they were spirited and happy. They explained their mother's care in a way that was entirely consistent with Jean's description.

The caseworker left Jean's home with serious concerns for the children's safety and well-being. However, she did not immediately seek to rescue Amy and Tammy from the care of their mother. She knew that many of her fellow caseworkers would have called the police following their visit and had them remove the girls. They would think that foster care placements would provide a clean, organized setting that would be better for each child's development.

The caseworker disagreed with this view of foster care. She had seen too many children become trapped and miserable for extended periods in clean, organized foster homes—children who suffered significant developmental harm. Jean seemed to be providing at least minimally adequate care for Amy and Tammy. In fact, even the neighbors who complained about the conditions of the house remarked on the constant attention Jean paid to her girls and how the children were always pleasant and happy. The situation was certainly not best or optimal, but it seemed acceptable.

The caseworker also noted the close bond among Jean and her children. They were all very comfortable with each other. It seemed like a family situation worth trying to preserve and possibly improve.

This effort would require public resources. It could be as simple as providing Jean with a housekeeper every week. However, the caseworker realized that these cases are hardly ever as simple as they appear on the surface. There had to be a reason for Jean's behavior. Individual and family counseling may help Jean, and the caseworker would offer it to her on a voluntary basis. The caseworker did not feel it was appropriate to compel Jean to participate in such services. After all, the home situation was minimally adequate. But maybe Jean would want to try to improve her family's situation, possibly raising the children's environment above the level of minimal adequacy.

The public resources required for this family preservation effort would likely be much less than those required for foster care placements for the girls. This is one aspect of the minimal adequacy approach that provides public benefits in comparison to the child saving approach. In addition, the public would likely secure significant developmental benefits for the girls using a family preservation approach. They would be able to maintain their strong attachment to their mother and to avoid the harmful disruption of removal and relocation. Although they would not experience an optimal home environment, they likely would enjoy a relationship with their mother that would be superior to anything the state could offer through the foster care system.

Despite the public benefits, the current child welfare system is not designed to secure family preservation. Significant financial and political incentives lead to the overuse of foster care.[33] This is why children living within minimally adequate family associations need a sensitive, zealous advocate in order to secure necessary support for the maintenance of their families. For Amy and Tammy, the caseworker served this role. The girls were lucky: They benefited from a professional who was attuned to the realistic possibilities for children in their situation. This professional knew that she was engaged in a salvage operation where the best was not possible, but minimal adequacy could be achieved without exposing the girls to a significant risk of harm.

Minimal Adequacy and Foster Care

The minimal adequacy approach can also be beneficial in the effort to have children exit foster care in a timely manner. Consider the situation of Andy, a six-year-old African American boy who has lived in a foster home for the past two years.[34] Andy's mother suffers from severe mental disabilities. She visits Andy sporadically, with the last visit having occurred over six months ago. Despite the public agency's efforts, it has no realistic prospect of Andy returning to his mother's custody.

Andy's foster parents have provided him with good, basic care. However, they intend to serve only as temporary foster parents for children who will find other long-term, hopefully permanent placements. They have no desire to adopt the children they care for, including Andy. Originally, the child welfare agency caseworker asked them to care for Andy for no more than six months. But as the case dragged on and the agency could not secure an acceptable adoptive home, the foster parents decided to continue caring for Andy on a temporary basis. They made it clear to the agency and to Andy that they were not making a long-term commitment to Andy.

The agency is now considering another possible adoptive placement for Andy. The potential adoptive parent is a neighbor of Andy's foster parents, Debbie. Debbie never thought about adopting a child before she met Andy and learned his story. Even though Debbie had an eight-year-old son of her own, she felt that she could care for Andy. In fact, she became deeply committed to pursuing adoption.

Debbie approached the caseworker from the agency and proposed the adoption. The caseworker knew that Debbie had babysat Andy on many occasions, but he was very surprised at her interest in adoption. Many of his colleagues would have immediately ruled Debbie out as a possible adoptive parent. Debbie's son seemed to be healthy and doing well in all other respects, but Debbie was a single parent who worked at a local day care center. Her pay was low, and she was in a financially precarious position. Debbie faced a great deal of stress as a parent. She certainly would not provide the ideal adoptive home.

But the caseworker realized that he would not be able to achieve an optimal adoptive home for Andy. Instead of rejecting Debbie's offer out of hand, the caseworker decided to investigate the situation. He visited Debbie's home. He met her son who was a bit hyperactive but polite. The house was cluttered but acceptable. Debbie's son was doing fairly well in school. At least Debbie made sure that he went to school. Debbie worked a lot of hours, but at least it was at a day care facility that welcomed her son to attend. In fact, her son regularly volunteered to help out with the younger children. Andy could also do this.

In talking with Debbie, the caseworker learned that Debbie had spent a good deal of time with Andy. She seemed to be very committed to him. She felt sorry for him because of his experiences with his mother; more importantly, she simply really liked Andy. They always seemed to enjoy each other.

The caseworker was still on the fence about pursuing an adoption when he left Debbie's house. It seemed like a situation where the family could fall apart with the added stress of another child, a child who would likely experience significant developmental difficulties. But Andy's attorney had accompanied the caseworker on the visit.

She felt strongly that the adoption with Debbie was the only realistic option for Andy. It was probably Andy's last chance to avoid the significant harms of an extended placement in a temporary foster care home.

At the next foster care review court hearing for Andy, the attorney presented extensive evidence on Debbie's home, her relationship with Andy, and her capacity to parent him. She had worked with the caseworker to make this presentation, in the process convincing him of the need to achieve this adoption for Andy. Together they asked the judge to schedule a hearing to terminate the parental rights of Andy's original parents and to approve the adoption by Debbie. Because neither of Andy's parents was present at the hearing and the current foster parents supported the adoption, the judge granted the request. The case was on course to a resolution that would provide Andy with a minimally adequate permanent home. Although the adoptive home would not be optimal in the eyes of many, it would provide Andy with significant benefits. The caseworker's open-mindedness and the attorney's advocacy led to the presentation of a realistic option that the system could actually achieve.

Summation

These cases illustrate the potential benefits of seeking minimally adequate environments for all children. Rather than seeking best or optimal environments and experiencing endless frustration, the lowered goal of minimal adequacy is actually achieved in a timely, efficient manner. With this approach, the public can much more readily secure adequate conditions in basic, essential areas of children's everyday lives. As a result, the public avoids the frustration and failure that inflicts harm on children.

While this approach may provide a transformative, long-term solution for many public systems, it does not provide children with immediate assistance. However, it can guide children and those who care about them in working within public systems that are still officially committed to securing optimal outcomes, but are failing in this effort. Children and their advocates can lower their expectations for public support and work to secure what is realistically available, making sure that this at least provides minimally adequate conditions for development. In the end, this approach leads to strategies in individual cases that are effective within flawed public systems.

Accordingly, this book has consistently pointed to the need for zealous advocates for children. To be effective, advocates need to focus their efforts on realistic goals. This approach requires advocates to possess specific skills and knowledge. First, an advocate must have a thorough knowledge of the law applicable in the specific child's situation. More important, the advocate must know how the particular public system actually functions. This means knowing the realistic options and outcomes, including a detailed knowledge of the services available. With this knowledge, an advocate can fashion a strategy in a particular situation that will be effective in securing minimally adequate conditions for the affected child.

Even more important, the advocate must be able to explain the situation to the affected child. The child's expectations must be realistic. If they are not, the child will be discouraged and frustrated, likely undermining otherwise effective plans and services. Of course, the reality of dysfunctional public systems can discourage children. To combat this effect, the advocate must articulate a vision and strategy of hope for the child. For example, the advocate could explain the realities of the relevant public system and work to align the child's immediate expectations with realistic goals. But the advocate could also work with the child to envision steps that could be taken outside public systems for long-term success. Once they secure minimally adequate conditions through public support, the advocate and child can explore other plans and forms of support that raise the prospect of conditions that exceed those of minimal adequacy.

This is a realistic yet empowering approach that utilizes the dominant strains of public rhetoric to effectively address children's situations. The rhetoric of child well-being is often stated forcefully, but its strength fades as it confronts the challenge of limited resources. The initial strength of this rhetoric could possibly sustain a serious effort to achieve minimally adequate conditions for all children. It will not deliver optimal conditions, but the prospect of securing a minimally adequate floor for healthy development may be achievable.

An important aspect of this minimally adequate condition should be placement of every child within an association that is perceived as closely equivalent to the ideal private family. Such a placement will provide the best hope for each child's condition to eventually rise above the level of minimal adequacy. It will allow the very powerful rhetoric of the autonomous family association to operate on children's situations and everyday lives. In these placements, children will benefit from powerful and sustained public support for the private family. Within current American society, this approach provides the best hope for raising children's conditions significantly above the floor of minimal adequacy in many situations.

An effective advocate for children will pursue this strategy in the resource-poor public systems that currently predominate. The first task for children and families involved in these systems is to secure an effective advocate. This is often the best way to improve children's situation—securing an advocate with realistic expectations for children's everyday lives and a deep commitment to achieve minimally adequate conditions for each child's development. Such an advocate can make a real difference for children and can be the real power broker within broken, dysfunctional, frustrating public systems that serve children and families. Without fundamental reform of these systems, the answer for many children is to mobilize all possible efforts to secure an effective advocate.

Notes

1. See, for example, Carl E. Schneider, "Discretion, Rules and Law: Child Custody and the UMDA's Best Interest Standard," *Michigan Law Review* 89 (1991): 2215; David J. Herring, "Rearranging the Family: Diversity, Pluralism, Social Tolerance and Child Custody Disputes," *Southern California Interdisciplinary Law Journal* 5 (1997): 205.

2. See Robert H. Mnookin, "Child-Custody Adjudication: Judicial Functions in the Face of Interdeterminancy," *Law & Contemporary Problems* 226 (Summer 1975); David J. Herring, *The Public Family: Exploring Its Role in Democratic Society* (Pittsburgh: University of Pittsburgh Press, 2003), 205–9.

3. Herring, *The Public Family*, 74.

4. See, for example, *Miller v. Walker*, 665 A.2d 1252 (Pa. Super. 1995).

5. See Stephanie Coontz, *The Way We Never Were: American Families and the Nostalgia Trap* (New York: Basic Books, 1992), 68–91.

6. See Martha Albertson Fineman, *The Neutered Mother, the Sexual Family, and Other Twentieth Century Tragedies* (New York: Routledge, 1995), 103–12.

7. For a more detailed discussion of the child abuse and neglect situation, see chapter 2.

8. For a more detailed discussion of the child poverty situation, see chapter 3.

9. For a more detailed discussion of the juvenile delinquency situation, see chapter 4.

10. Peter J. Pecora et al., "Improving Family Foster Care: Findings from the Northwest Foster Care Alumni Study," http://www.casey.org/NR/rdonleyres/4E1E7C77-7624-4260-A253-892C5A6CB9E1/300/nw_alumni_study_full_apr2005.pdf (finding that one in four foster children suffer from posttraumatic stress disorder). For a more detailed discussion of the child welfare system, see chapter 2.

11. For a more detailed discussion of the public welfare system, see chapter 3.

12. For a more detailed discussion of the delinquency system, see chapter 4.

13. For a more detailed discussion of the public education situation, see chapter 5.

14. See, for example, Sam Dillon, "Connecticut to Sue U.S. over Cost of School Testing Program," *New York Times*, April 6, 2005, B1; Sam Dillon, "Utah Vote Rejects Parts of Education Law," *New York Times*, April 20, 2005, A14.

15. For a more detailed discussion of the health care coverage situation, see chapter 6.

16. For a more detailed discussion of the situation for unaccompanied alien children, see chapter 7.

17. See generally Christopher Lasch, *Haven in a Heartless World: The Family Besieged* (New York: Basic Books, 1977); Philippe Meyer, *The Child and the State: The Intervention of the State in Family Life*, trans. Judith Ennew and Janet Lloyd (New York: Cambridge University Press, 1983).

18. See, generally, Judith Rich Harris, *The Nurture Assumption* (New York: Free Press, 1998); David J. Herring, "Behavioral Genetics and the Best Interests of the Child Decision Rule," *Michigan Journal of Law Reform* 36 (2002): 1.

19. See Herring, "Behavioral Genetics and the Best Interests"; Mnookin, "Child-Custody Adjudication."

20. See Meyer, *The Child and the State*; Lasch, *Haven in a Heartless World*.

21. See Dorothy Roberts, *Shattered Bonds: The Color of Child Welfare* (New York: Basic Books, 2002); Martin Guggenheim, "The Foster Care Dilemma and What to Do about It: Is the Problem That Too Many Children Are Not Being Adopted Out of Foster Care or That Too Many Children Are Entering Foster Care?" *University of Pennsylvania Constitutional Law* 2 (1999): 141.

22. Guggenheim, "The Foster Care Dilemma"; Roberts, *Shattered Bonds*, 21.

23. See Roberts, *Shattered Bonds*; David J. Herring, "The Adoption and Safe Families Act—Hope and Its Subversion," *Family Law Quarterly* 34 (2000): 329; Pecora et al., "Improving Family Foster Care."

24. See, for example, Peter J. Pecora et al., *The Child Welfare Challenge: Policy, Practice, and Research*, 2d ed. (New York: Aldine de Gruyter, 2000), 262–75, 470–73; David J. Herring, "Foster Care Placement: Reducing the Risk of the Sibling Incest," *Michigan Journal of Law Reform* 37 (2004): 1145, 1171–79.

25. See Fineman, *The Neutered Mother*, 230–36.

26. Fineman, *The Neutered Mother*.

27. See David O. Brink, "Immaturity, Normative Competence, and Juvenile Transfer: How (Not) to Punish Minors for Major Crimes," *Texas Law Review* 82 (2004): 1555, 1559–60; David S. Tanenhaus and Steven A. Drizin, "Criminal Law: 'Owing to the Extreme Youth of the Accused': The Changing Legal Response to Juvenile Homicide," *Journal of Criminal Law & Criminology* 92 (2002): 641, 678–81.

28. See H. G. Bissinger, *Friday Night Lights: A Town, a Team, and a Dream* (Cambridge, MA: Da Capo, 2000); Buzz Bissinger, "Innocents Afield," *New York Times*, December 16, 2004, A43.

29. See John C. Reitz, "Public School Financing in the United States: More on the Dark Side of Intermediate Structures," *Brigham Young University Law Review* (1993): 623, 626–27; Erwin Chemerinsky, "Separate and Unequal: American Public Education Today," *American University Law Review* 52 (2003): 1461, 1473–75.

30. See Paul Krugman, "The Medical Money Pit," *New York Times*, April 15, 2005, A19.

31. See Amnesty International, "United States of America: Unaccompanied Children in Immigration Detention," June 18, 2003, 6–13, http://www.amnestyusa.org/ refugee/pdfs/children_detention.pdf.

32. This case story is based on the author's experiences in representing parents and children in numerous juvenile court child dependency proceedings.

33. See Robert M. Gordon, "Drifting through Byzantium: The Promise and Failure of the Adoption and Safe Families Act of 1997," *Minnesota Law Review* 83 (1999): 637, 681–83; Herring, "The Adoption and Safe Families Act," 342–43.

34. This case story is based on the author's experiences in representing parents and children in numerous juvenile court child dependency proceedings.

Index

106–7, 114; health care and, 164, 173

"Baby Jessica" case, 6
"Baby Richard" case, 6–7
behavior control attempts, 79–81
best interests of the child standard, 9, 216, 223, 228; termination of parental rights, 48, 54; unaccompanied alien children and, 196, 198–99, 203, 205–6. *See also* child well-being metanarrative
block grant programs, 73, 74, 168
bond with parent, 41–42
burden of proof: asylum cases, 198–202; termination of parental rights cases, 5–6

California Supreme Court, 135
CASA. *See* Court Appointed Special Advocates
Catholic Charities of Pittsburgh Refugee Services, 213
Center for Law and Education, 151
charter schools, 126
Chemerinsky, Erwin, 141–42
child abuse/neglect cases, 22, 218, 219–20; case study, 35–42; legal representation of children, 12, 15–16, 38–39
child advocates. *See* advocates
Child Care and Development Block Grant, 76
child care programs, 68, 76–78
child labor laws, 14–15, 18, 23
children: bond with parent, 41–42; communal ownership theory of, 2–3; as valuable resource, 16–17. *See also* children's interests; children's rights rhetoric; child well-being metanarrative

Children and Family Justice Center (CFJC), 62
Children and Youth Advocacy Clinic, 153
children's criminal behavior, 219–21; advocates, 114–15; case study, 93–101, 109–13; Class B felonies, 95, 98–99; dual system design, 102, 111; due process denied, 97, 98, 101–2, 109; increase in violent crime, 106–7; judicial waivers and, 107–8; jury trials denied, 105; juvenile court movement, 102–4; law school programs and clinics, 121–22; loss of legal protections, 94, 110–11; metanarratives and, 104–7, 113–14; minimal adequacy approach, 227–28; parental responsibility laws, 100–101, 111–14; probation, 101; recidivism rates, 111, 117; rehabilitation, 103–4; service organizations, 120–21; status offenses, 112–13; superpredator image of, 106–7, 108, 117; support services, 115–17; transfer to adult court, 94–99, 107–9
Children's Education Law Clinic (Duke Law School), 153
children's interests, 13, 235; adoption cases, 35–40; denied, 5–6, 26–27
children's rights rhetoric, 2, 11–13; adult interest in child well-being, 13–16; growing power of, 16–18
child rescue reaction, 41–43, 47–51, 56–57, 223–24
child savers, 14–15, 21–22
child support requirement, 75–76

About the Author

David J. Herring is professor of law at the University of Pittsburgh School of Law where he initiated the Child Welfare Law Clinic. He is the author of *The Public Family: Exploring Its Role in Democratic Society* (University of Pittsburgh Press, 2003).